THE CIVIL WAR:

The Artists' Record

THE CIVIL WAR:
The Artists' Record

by Hermann Warner Williams, Jr.
Director, The Corcoran Gallery of Art

THE CORCORAN GALLERY OF ART

MUSEUM OF FINE ARTS, BOSTON

Acknowledgments.

THE EXHIBITION recorded in the following pages reflects the contribution in time, knowledge and patience of more than a platoon of collaborators. It represents the results of an effort which started slowly as far back as 1958 and was gradually intensified as the calendar progressed to 1961.

The first raw recruit to join was Larry Wilson, a student at Carleton College who devoted a summer's vacation in 1959 to amassing the beginning of a file of contemporary quotations and a photographic record of the rich material in the Print and Photographic Division of the Congressional Library. Many of the quotations in the catalogue are the fruits of his long hours of delving into original printed source material.

The arrival of Lt. Col. Francis A. Lord on the field of battle improved the morale of the troops. This veteran historian, expert, and the author of the recent book, *They Fought for the Union*, cast a timely and critical eye over the exhibition's outline, suggested improvements and then contributed a raft of pertinent quotations derived from his extensive personal reference library. His knowledge of the literature and source material of this period has been invaluable and his unstinting and always ready co-operation has our sincere appreciation. Mrs. John R. Slidell and Alice Farley Williams have each also spent long and fruitful hours in locating vivid and appropriate quotations and tracing obscure references.

Harold L. Peterson, Staff Historian, The National Park Service, has most generously read the text of the catalogue as well as the quotations, and, in the process, spotted errors and suggested improvements which have greatly benefited the end product.

The preparation of the manuscript in draft form and the assembly of the photographs were capably done by Miss Mercer Preston with assistance from Miss Andrea Kanner and Miss Ruth Hirshman. Miss Carolyn Gates Smith has cheerfully assumed responsibility for overseeing the preparation of the manuscript for the printer in its final stages with her customary efficiency and care. Mrs. Ralph E. Phillips, Curator, has edited the manuscript, smoothing out rough edges and eliminating other defects too numerous to particularize. Mrs. A. Robert Forbes, in her position as Registrar, has attended to the vital and responsible matters of bringing safely together the almost 250 items from all sections of the country as well as from France and Switzerland. The installation of the exhibition in the Corcoran Gallery was designed and executed by Gudmund Vigtel, Assistant to the Director.

We are especially indebted to the staff of the Museum of Fine Arts in Boston for its invaluable assistance: to Perry T. Rathbone, Director, who shared in the selection of the exhibition; to Mrs. Anne B. Freedberg, Assistant in the Department of Prints, and to David B. Little, Registrar, for their help in assembling material and arranging details of transportation at the Boston end; and particularly to Carl Zahn, Designer for the Museum, for the design and production supervision of this catalogue.

For assistance on particular problems and for help in locating material for the exhibition and the catalogue, special thanks are due to many of my colleagues, among them James Foster, Katherine McCook Knox, Roger Cohen, Philip van Doren Stern, Marius B. Peladeau, General and Mrs. John B. Anderson, Harry Shaw Newman, Victor Spark, Rudolph Wunderlich, Abner Raeburn, Mrs. John Nicholas Brown, Alexander Lawrence, Milton Kaplan, and the staff of the *American Heritage*, especially Stephen Sears.

We are particularly indebted to Mr. and Mrs. Lansdell K. Christie for a very substantial gift to the Corcoran Gallery to be used toward the cost of this publication.

And finally we owe our deepest appreciation to the following individuals and institutions for so generously lending to this exhibition their fine examples of the work of the artists of the Civil War: Addison Gallery of American Art, Phillips Academy, Andover; Amherst College; General and Mrs. John B. Anderson; Department of the Army, Office of the Chief of Military History, Washington; Berry-Hill Galleries; Dr. E. Maurice Bloch; The Boatmen's National Bank of St. Louis; Boston Athenaeum; Mrs. William N. Bourne; Mrs. John Nicholas Brown; California Palace of the Legion of Honor, San Francisco; Canajoharie Art Gallery, New York; Winslow Carlton; Carnegie Institute, Pittsburgh; Mrs. Joseph B. Carson; The Century Association; Chicago Historical Society; Cincinnati Art Museum; City Art Museum of St. Louis; The Cleveland Museum of Art; Beverly Mosby Coleman; The Cooper Union Museum, New York; The Corcoran Gallery of Art, Washington; Adelaide Milton de Groot; Detroit Institute of Arts; Duquesne Club; Edward Eberstadt and Sons; Mr. and Mrs. Lawrence A. Fleischman; Fogg Art Museum, Harvard University, Cambridge; Franklin D. Roosevelt Library, Hyde Park; George Walter Vincent Smith Art Museum, Springfield; Stewart E. Gregory; Harvard College Library, Cambridge; Mr. and Mrs. Will Hippen, Jr.; Joslyn Art Museum, Omaha; Kansas State Historical Society, Topeka; Maxim Karolik; Mrs. Henry P. Kendall; Kennedy Galleries, Inc: Mrs. McCook Knox; Kunstmuseum, Basel; The Library of Congress, Washington; The Mariners Museum, Newport News; Maryland Historical Society, Baltimore; Ian McLaughlin; Medical Museum of the Armed Forces Institute of Pathology, Washington; The Metropolitan Museum of Art, New York; N. S. Meyer, Inc.; Museum of Fine Arts, Boston; National Baseball Hall of Fame and Museum, Inc., Cooperstown, New York; The Newark Museum; New Britain Museum of American Art, Connecticut; New Hampshire Historical

Society, Concord; The New York Historical Society, New York; New York State, Division of Military and Naval Affairs, Albany; Mrs. Alexander Nimick; Monseigneur le Comte de Paris; The Pennsylvania Academy of the Fine Arts, Philadelphia; Philbrook Art Center, Tulsa; The Art Museum, Princeton University; Mrs. Harold T. Pulsifer; Santa Barbara Museum of Art; Mr. and Mrs. Nathan Shaye; Shelburne Museum, Vermont; Mrs. O. G. Simplot; Victor D. Spark; State Historical Society of Wisconsin, Madison; The Union League Club, New York; The Union League of Philadelphia; U. S. Naval Academy Museum, Annapolis; University of Georgia Libraries, Athens; The Valentine Museum, Richmond; Virginia Museum of Fine Arts, Richmond; Wadsworth Atheneum, Hartford; James H. Weekes; West Point Museum, New York; Wildenstein and Co., Inc.; Hermann Warner Williams, Jr.; Witte Memorial Museum, San Antonio; Samuel H. Wolcott; Norman B. Woolworth; Yale University Art Gallery, New Haven; Christian A. Zabriskie.

H. W. W., Jr.

The Corcoran Gallery of Art and the Museum of Fine Arts wish to extend their appreciation to the following publishers for permission to quote excerpts from their respective publications: Abelard-Schuman Ltd., New York; M. A. Donohue & Co., Chicago; Georgetown University Press, Washington; F. H. Gilson Company, Boston; Grosset & Dunlap, Inc., New York; D. C. Heath and Company, Boston; Houghton Mifflin Company, Boston; Indiana University Press, Bloomington; Kennedy Galleries, Inc., New York; Alfred A. Knopf, Inc., New York; Little, Brown & Company, Boston; Longmans, Green & Co., Inc., New York; Louisiana State University Press, Baton Rouge; McCowat-Mercer Press, Inc., Jackson, Tennessee; Charles E. Nash & Son, Augusta, Maine; National Gallery of Art, Washington; G. P. Putnam's Sons, New York; Henry Regnery Company, Chicago; Charles Scribner's Sons, New York; The University of North Carolina Press, Chapel Hill; Yale University Press, New Haven.

9

Contents.

Preface.

"THIS IS A SIMPLE STORY of a battle; such a tale as may be told by a soldier who is no writer to a reader who is no soldier."[1]

The Corcoran Gallery of Art, of all the art museums in the country, has its own identification with the Civil War and thus a special reason for its part in the commemoration – not the celebration – of the Centennial of that tragic war. Its first building, designed by James Renwick and nearing completion when war broke out, was requisitioned by the Government and used throughout the period as a storage depot by the Quartermaster-General's Department.[2]

The Corcoran Gallery is happy indeed to share this exhibition with its distinguished sister institution, the Museum of Fine Arts in Boston, the hub of abolitionism in Civil War days.

The story of the Civil War, now a part of the American myth, has been told and retold to an always eager, knowledgeable, and ever growing audience. Its leaders, great, near-great, and only hopefully great, have been examined and all but psychoanalyzed. Their military careers have been closely studied, their errors judiciously probed. We can read more of their personal lives – from their secret neuroses to how they got on with their wives – than we can learn of most of our own contemporaries. Exhaustive studies of the causes leading to the outbreak of war, of the overall strategy of its conduct, of its diplomatic and political history, have been written. The many military campaigns which spread over its full four years have been published, and the histories of its armies, and of the corps, divisions, regiments, companies and batteries which formed those armies, have been zealously compiled. It is doubtful if any other war has been as sedulously studied and as profligately published.

This exhibition then, rather than attempting to retell inadequately the strategic, economic, or military history of the War, which has been so well done in book form, is devoted to but one small segment of the conflict, the study of man embroiled in the horrors of a civil war. Specifically, it is the age-old story of the non-professional combat soldier, who wore the gray or the blue in the War, which is the focus of this exhibition. It has been our endeavor to find telling works of art which

---

1. Ambrose Bierce, "What I Saw of Shiloh", in *Ambrose Bierce's Civil War*, ed. by William McCann, Chicago, 1956, p. 15.

2. Indeed, one of the paintings in the exhibition, *Maryland Heights; the Siege of Harper's Ferry* (no. 72), is by William McLeod, the Gallery's first Director.

we trust will impart to the viewer at least the faint echo of emotions past; to demonstrate, if demonstration were needed, the timelessness of pain, sorrow, the leadenness of exhaustion, the spine-tingling response to an anthem, the sickly sweat of fear, the forced assumption of casualness in the face of imminent death, the bitter loneliness of men without their loves, the atavistic abandonment of civilized instincts in the heat of personal combat. To a lesser extent, the impact of the War on the men and women who stayed at home has also been touched on, for they, too, shared in the suspense and anguish of those troubled years.

Against this background, and to put it to only one specific comparison, the 5,000 illustrations in one publication alone – Miller's *Photographic History of The Civil War*[3] – we come to this work and this exhibition. An exhibition, for better or for worse, has very definite and implacable limitations. Unlike a book, you can't take an exhibition to bed with you – and who would want to? But that is the simple point, an exhibition cannot be a book. While the human eye is practically tireless, the human foot is not. The more hardened and habituated museum-goer, it has been proved, cannot absorb much more than two hundred objects, all the while standing on his increasingly uncomfortable feet. Few people can afford the time to nibble at an exhibition; they must gulp it down at one meal. A book may be read at leisure a chapter at a time; an exhibition must tell its story in one session.

The exhibition is comprised of 236 paintings, watercolors, drawings, prints and a few examples of sculpture. In the selection of works to be exhibited an effort has been made to secure those with the greatest artistic significance within the limitations of availability. Because there are a number of other exhibitions scheduled by museums in various parts of the country, some of the paintings it would have been desirable to include were unavailable. This conflict was a foreseen inevitability. Nevertheless, since the exhibition was necessarily limited in size, the wealth of material available was such that the absence of these works does not materially affect the quality of the exhibition.

It must, however, be stressed that because there were few professional artists living or working in the South during the War, it has been impossible to provide equal pictorial coverage for the North and South.

There are no portraits as such in the exhibition, since it would have been an almost impossible decision to choose which of the hundreds of important leaders to include and which to exclude. Also, it was decided not to include examples of the work of the talented photographers who recorded, so admirably, the static scenes of the War to which their primitive equipment limited them.

It is, perhaps, to be regretted that the present exhibition has intentionally excluded – again for the reason of space – all but a meagre number of examples of the wealth of contemporary lithographs which are little known (aside from those by Currier and Ives, Prang, and Kurz and Allison) and so deserving of study.

With exceptions the scenes depicted show specific events which occurred on

---

3. Francis Trevelyan Miller, *Photographic History of the Civil War*, New York, 1911.

a particular day at a definite location on land or sea. It would be, of course, ideal if the quotations which accompany the illustrations were in the words of an eyewitness to the event depicted. In many cases, however, a vivid or dramatic eyewitness account has not been found, and therefore many quotations have been chosen from eyewitness descriptions of events of a similar nature which perhaps took place hundreds of miles removed, and even in a different year of the War. However, we trust that the quotations, notwithstanding this disparity, capture the essential and typical character of the events shown, for it is generally true that the reactions of men to a given situation have a universal similarity.

233. The Top Sergeant. Unidentified artist, active 1860.

The Artists of the Civil War.

IT IS SMALL WONDER that the Civil War which claimed the attention of the entire nation should also have involved the majority of the artists of the period. The paintings, watercolors, drawings, prints and sculpture which have been selected for this exhibition represent a cross-section of American art covering a span of about five years. This demi-decade, in the second half of the nineteenth century, does not, perhaps, reflect a period of great florescence. Nevertheless, in the overall development of American art it is significant in the study of the history of our national culture.

It was an era of transition. The competition of the photograph as a recording device had already made itself felt. This was especially apparent in the art of portrait painting which was by then already in decline, but this development does not concern us here. Culturally, the shift of interest and influence was swinging from the earlier centers, England and Italy, to which the preceding generations of artists had turned for guidance, to Germany, especially Düsseldorf, and to France. Mass production and distribution, already an American specialty in other fields, were a relatively new phenomena in art and developed to a flourishing state during this period. This was accomplished in three ways. Art in mass-produced form at inexpensive and competitive prices for the first time entered middle class and working class homes through the thousands of gaudy and usually crudely executed lithographs produced in bulk by Currier and Ives and their competitors and imitators, and also through the media of mass-produced plaster sculpture, the famous Rogers groups. To this was added the distribution of original works of art on a fairly large scale through such membership organizations as the American Art Union in New York and its offshoot, the Western Art Union of Cincinnati.

This was also a period of transition from the monopoly of original works of art by the rich private collectors to the rise of that new creation, the public art museum designed for the education of the masses. It is of more than passing interest that two of the first of these new public art museums are the very two which are collaborating on the present exhibition. Another new development which brought art into modest homes was the rise of the illustrated weekly magazine, a form which is still with us today.

These, then, are some of the sociological and technical developments which had their effect on the quality, types and variety of art produced during the years covered in this exhibition.

The unmilitaristic temperament of the American is, perhaps, nowhere more clearly demonstrated than in the fact that in the whole history of American painting there are remarkably few historical painters who specialized in military subject matter. Even John Trumbull whose famous series relating to the Revolutionary War are among our great national treasures was primarily a portrait painter.

In fact the only American painter to make a speciality of military subject matter appears to have been James Walker who, arriving in this country as a child – an immigrant from England – went from New York to New Orleans as a youth and then to Mexico City. He served in the American army in the Mexican War and was present at the capitulation of Mexico City. After the war he established a studio in New York and was commissioned to paint the large Battle of Chapultepec which hangs in the Capitol. He also did a series of smaller subjects relating to the Mexican War which are in the possession of the Department of the Army, and others which are scattered in collections throughout the country. He maintained his interest in military subjects through the Civil War period and painted a number of large historical canvases of some of the more important battles such as the Battle of Gettysburg (No. 136), the Battle of Lookout Mountain (No. 114), and Chickamauga (No. 137). However, his smaller, less pretentious paintings of regiments on review have more spontaneity and appeal to the non-specialist in military lore. His personal familiarity with the military gives his paintings the appearance of authenticity. However, Walker's lead soldier figures have no more personality and character than the toys they so much resemble, and his canvases convey no feeling of mood, nor, indeed, do they display any real mastery of the problems of composition.

Of all the artists who depicted events of the Civil War one in retrospect stands out above the rest. That one is, of course, Winslow Homer. This young man, then in his mid-twenties, having already served an apprenticeship in the lithographic house of Bufford in Boston, was sent by *Harper's Weekly* as a special artist to the front in October of 1861 to report pictorially on the progress of the conflict. He continued working as a special artist only until May of 1862. Subsequently, as a free-lance artist, he appears to have made occasional visits to the scenes of conflict in Virginia up to the siege of Petersburg at the very end of the war. At that time Homer was unknown, no better in the eyes of his contemporaries than any other of the special artists working for the illustrated weeklies. It was only much later that he was to rise to his present position of pre-eminence as one of the great nineteenth-century American painters.

Homer's experience at the front was limited to operations against the Army of Northern Virginia. Some of the sketches which he made at that time were not considered of sufficient timely significance to warrant reproduction. However, Homer was intensely interested in his first-hand experiences and even after the conclusion of the war worked over his accumulation of sketches, developing some of them into paintings which now constitute artistically our most important treasury of Civil War scenes.

In this exhibition we have assembled, with one or two exceptions, all of Homer's oils of Civil War subjects. Some are simple and unpretentious; some, such as *Playing Old Soldier* (No. 30), have more than a trace of earthy humor; all give a fresh and unembellished view of the soldier's life; and some few, such as the *Prisoners from the Front* (No. 172), are profoundly moving documents of human emotion.

Eastman Johnson, one of the key figures in nineteenth-century American painting, although apparently not enlisted as a soldier, nevertheless did follow in the wake of the army for some time. He was on hand for at least three important battles during the course of the Civil War, one of which, Antietam, provided a theme on which he worked for a number of years. This theme became the well-known *The Wounded Drummer Boy* (No. 129). It would seem probable that he made a sketch of this incident at approximately the same time as the battle. However, if so, the sketch has not been located. The first drawing of the subject, owned by the Century Association, is dated 1864. Several versions were painted, and when the last of these was shown at the National Academy in 1892 the catalogue recorded the following: "In one of the battles of the late war a drummer boy was disabled by a shot in the leg. As he lay upon the field he called to his comrades, 'Carry me and I'll drum her through.' They tied up his wound, a big soldier took him upon his shoulders, and he drummed through the fight."[1]

While the painting in its final state is a studio creation, it is nevertheless true that Johnson had observed the incident himself on the field of battle. Although it is not "a slice of life," his academic embellishments stay reasonably close to the spirit of the incident which was repeated on more than one occasion during the course of the War and which, indeed, was so much in the spirit of the time that about a half dozen contemporary songs were composed on this sentimental theme.[2]

Johnson is, however, perhaps at his best in simpler, less pretentious and less heroic endeavors such as the charming genre painting entitled *The Letter Home* (No. 58) and the frankly sentimental *Writing to Father* (No. 209).

Even George Caleb Bingham, whose genre paintings of the river life of the Mississippi have won him an enduring place in the annals of American art, was caught up in the mesh of the Civil War. The single picture he did which directly relates to the War is totally alien to the happy mood which radiates from his other paintings of the jolly flat-boatmen of the Mississippi and of the politicking townsfolk of rural Missouri. This picture, the famous *Order Number Eleven* (No. 194), was painted with great bitterness of feeling which it still imparts to the spectator even today, 100 years later. It is America's loss, certainly, that Bingham, gifted as he was, did not choose to paint canvases of the homely incidents of camp life or of the field, for they would truly have enriched the artistic heritage of the War which has come down to us.

---

1. John I. H. Baur, *Eastman Johnson, 1842-1906*, Brooklyn Museum, New York, 1940, p. 42.
2. Irwin Silber, *Songs of the Civil War*, New York, 1960, pp. 119f.

It is, of course, impossible to discuss all of the artists represented in the exhibition. However, some stand out as of particular interest, either because, though relatively unknown, their work has made a real contribution to our pictorial record of the Civil War or because the examples shown of familiar artists are atypical of their better known works. Such an artist is David Gilmour Blythe who died at the age of fifty in 1865 just as the Civil War was drawing to its close. While Blythe was primarily a genre painter he was also a sculptor, carver, panoramist, illustrator and portrait painter as well as poet. Although he was an uneven painter, which is partially accounted for by the fact that he was addicted to drink, his work possesses a strong individual flavor when he was at his best, often with a satirical bite reminiscent of Honoré Daumier, but in a gentler vein. The paintings in the exhibition by his hand, especially the *Battle of Gettysburg* (No. 117), show him in quite a different and more powerful aspect and are in their freshness among the most significant paintings produced in the United States during these troubled years.

William Morris Hunt, a pupil of Thomas Couture in Paris, friend of Millet and disciple of the Barbizon school, was one of Boston's most influential artists. He is represented in the present exhibition by two works, *The Drummer Boy* (No. 11) and the charming little study of two children playing with toy soldiers (No. 211) which he made as a contribution to one of the Sanitary Commission Fairs held in Boston to raise money to alleviate the suffering of the soldiers in the hospitals and at the front. A distinguished portrait painter and a muralist as well, Hunt's rare genre paintings have a tender and appealing quality which avoids the mawkishness often present in the work of genre painters of this very sentimental epoch.

The Swiss artist Frank Buchser created quite a stir in Washington and nearby Virginia when he visited this country shortly after the end of the War. A dashing character and quite fearless, he had a stormy and romantic temperament. Two American subjects which greatly fascinated him, in part no doubt for their novelty to a European, were the Indian and the Negro, and in practically all of the paintings which he did in the vicinity of Charlottesville the Negro had a major place. The most ambitious of these canvases in the Museum der Stadt, Solothurn, is *The Ballad of Mary Blane* (not in this exhibition), the title taken from a contemporary song. Buchser's fascination with the Negro, which led him to establish a liaison with an attractive mulatto woman, caused him to become a controversial figure in Washington and detracted from the success his American paintings might otherwise have had. *The Volunteer's Return* (No. 218) is typical of his paintings of Negroes, a far from popular subject either in the North or the South at this time. In addition to his Virginia sojourn Buchser also accompanied General Sherman on an inspection trip to the western forts directly after the War. He subsequently painted a number of landscapes in the Great Lakes region which are interesting documents of that area.

Almost totally ignored as a painter, Edwin Forbes emerges from this exhibition as an artist deserving of far greater consideration than he has so far been accorded (Nos. 51, 68, 73, 107, 111). Forbes began to study at the age of eighteen and, in

1859, became a pupil of Arthur Fitzwilliam Tait, a painter of sporting scenes. In 1862 he joined the staff of *Leslie's*, the largest competitor of *Harper's Weekly*, and followed the course of the War until 1865. His deserved reputation as one of the best of the combat artists of the Civil War rests on his published etchings and the drawings in the possession of The Library of Congress which have been widely used from the day of their creation to the present to illustrate incidents in the campaigns of the War, especially in Virginia (15 are included in this exhibition). It is obvious from his work that he had a sensitive and genuine interest in the every-day life of the soldier which he has recorded with penetrating characterization and with a gifted crayon.

Edward Lamson Henry was apparently a somewhat timorous youth, for when the Civil War broke out, although he was well over twenty, he did not attempt to enlist in the army. Instead he worked for a rather brief period in the fall of 1864 as captain's clerk aboard a supply vessel in the service of the Quartermaster General's Department. His lifelong passion for all forms of transportation may be seen in the series of scenes along the Potomac and James Rivers, most of which he sketched from the deck of his vessel. While his paintings of Civil War subjects are relatively few compared to the volume of his total output, *City Point, Virginia, Headquarters of General Grant* (No. 151), which many consider his masterpiece, is, curiously enough, one of this group. Lacking the fire and drama which Meissonier instilled into his paintings of military subjects and which Henry admired and tried to emulate, he substituted for this a wealth of detail which gives his paintings an almost jewel-like quality. One can even recognize a likeness in the almost microscopic figure of General Grant seated before his headquarters.

James Hope was another artist of modest but genuine talent who served as a soldier in the Union forces. Born in Scotland, Hope came to the United States while still in his teens. He lived in West Rutland, Vermont, where in 1844 he took up portraiture as a means of livelihood. Shortly thereafter he removed to Castletown, Vermont, where he taught painting and drawing at the local seminary. When the War broke out he recruited a volunteer company and was commissioned Captain in the Vermont Volunteer Infantry. He was present at eleven engagements. During the War his services were used in part as a topographical engineer which enabled him to make many on-the-spot studies of incidents of the War. After the War some of these studies were developed into a series of large battle paintings which were widely exhibited at that time. James Hope is one of those unpretentious painters whose work enables us to attain an accurate visualization of the War – without editorial comment or false theatricalities. (No. 34)

One of our prolific genre painters, Thomas Waterman Wood, is represented in the exhibition by *The Return of the Battle Flags* (No. 223) which captures him at his best. Wood's genre paintings often have a stiff studio look which detracts considerably from their interest, but in this particular painting there is more genuine feeling than he oftentimes communicates.

As might be expected, the painters of the so-called "Hudson River School," who with single-minded devotion concentrated their efforts on the depiction of the American landscape, were about the only considerable group of painters who were hardly affected by the War. But even here there were exceptions. To Sanford Robinson Gifford, himself a member of the Seventh Regiment, New York State Militia, we owe a small group of delightful combined landscape and figure scenes of the fortifications and camps in the environs of Washington and Baltimore where the Seventh Regiment was stationed (Nos. 20, 49, 55).

Albert Bierstadt is another of the few landscapists who painted Civil War scenes. He returned from his studies in Düsseldorf and Rome in 1857 and shortly thereafter made his first trip through the American West. Famed for his vast canvases of western landscapes, the painting *The Bombardment of Fort Sumter* (No. 119) is unique among his subjects and ranks as one of the most important American landscapes of this period. The scene apparently shows the bombardment of the fortifications of Charleston harbor by the Federal fleet which carried on a protracted naval investment during the last years of the War.

The exhibition also has examples of the work of later American landscapists who hovered on the periphery of the movement as it gradually passed from view. Of these one might mention Peter Moran (No. 98) and his brother Edward (No. 94).

Closely related to the military artist is the marine painter. The great period of marine art in this country had flourished a quarter century earlier when Thomas Birch, Fitzhugh Lane and Robert Salmon were in their prime. Other than Thomas Moran, few of the painters of the Civil War period who depicted naval activities were more than portrait painters of ships. However, there always is an element of romance connected with anything to do with the sea – even the most pedestrian representation has at least the inherent beauty of the vessel itself as a starting point.

Five marine artists are included in the present exhibition. Of two of them, William Torgerson (No. 161) and Edwin Hayes (No. 159), little is known. Undoubtedly one of the best of this period was Xanthus Russell Smith, the son of the landscape painter, Russell Smith. During the War he served in the Union army in the South and painted many naval and land battles, including the *Attack on Fort Fisher* (No. 156). The impressive *U.S.S.* Wabash *Leaving New York for the Seat of War* by Thomas Moran (No. 94), whose chief claim to fame rests on his large paintings of the far West, speaks for itself. Another marine painter of considerable ability, though little known, was Alexander Charles Stuart. Stuart appears to have been born in Scotland and to have served in the Royal Navy before coming to the United States in 1860. He then enlisted in the Union navy in which he remained until 1865. He may have been a member of the crew of the iron-clad gunboat *Monitor* and present during the historic engagement with the Confederate *Merrimac*.[3] It appears that he also saw service in the Gulf Blockading Squadron,

---

3. "Artists of the Civil War", in *The Kennedy [Galleries] Quarterly*, Vol. 2, No. 2 (Part I), New York, 1961, p. 77.

for the watercolor of *The U.S.* Midnight *Hailing the U.S.* Boheo *off Texas* (No. 160) is inscribed as having been done off the coast of Texas.

Conrad Wise Chapman was the major painter to show the course of the War from a Confederate point of view. Chapman, himself the son of a painter, studied in Rome under his father, and soon after the War broke out returned to this country to enlist in the Confederate army. He was enrolled as a private in the 3rd Kentucky Infantry. His first service was in the West where he was wounded at the battle of Shiloh. After his recovery in October 1862 he was transferred to General Wise's brigade in Virginia and was attached to Company B, 59th Virginia Infantry. Early in September of 1863 the brigade was transferred to the fortifications of Charleston, South Carolina. There for the first time, under the patronage of General Beauregard, he was commissioned to do a series of paintings of the fortifications protecting Charleston's harbor. This group of thirty-one views are among the most delightful paintings produced during the course of the War. In their brilliance and sparkle they are reminiscent of Canaletto and Guardi, and, indeed, so far as I know, Chapman never in his subsequent career did anything which equals them. It is unfortunate that it was not possible to include in the exhibition some of these scenes which are prized possessions of the White House of the Confederacy in Richmond. The oils and drawings lent by the Valentine Museum of Richmond, however, show his delightful ability as a colorist and his skill as a draftsman. He, of course, made drawings, sketches and studies for his own pleasure throughout his career in the Confederate army, some examples of which are included in the exhibition. Shown, also, for the first time, are a few examples of his apparently unrecorded series of seven etchings of Confederate camp scenes in the vicinity of Corinth, Mississippi, Diascund Bridge, Virginia, and of the Charleston area from the collection of the Boston Athenaeum.

John Adams Elder also fought in the Confederate army and while *The Scouts' Return* (No. 81) was probably not painted during the War, it undoubtedly is based on the artist's own personal observation. Elder was a portrait, genre, landscape and battle painter who today is comparatively little known. He was born in Fredericksburg, Virginia, in 1833 and studied first under Daniel Huntington and later at Düsseldorf with Emanuel Leutze. After his return from abroad he worked in New York before going back to Fredericksburg shortly before the outbreak of war.

Among this handful of painters depicting scenes from the Confederate's side of the line was a German, Carl G. von Iwonski, whose family was one of the first to settle in New Braunfels, Texas. Subsequently living in other Texan cities, they finally located in San Antonio. Iwonski, primarily a portrait painter, in his somewhat crude but certainly virile canvas, *Terry's Texas Rangers* (No. 24), captures the spirit of these undisciplined Texas cavalrymen who acquitted themselves so bravely during the course of the War.

It is the so-called "special artists" of the illustrated magazines – *Leslie's, Harper's, The Illustrated London News* and *The New York Illustrated News* – that produced the larger part of the corpus of the pictorial records of the War. There appears to have been hardly a facet of the life of the soldier that escaped their crayon. While the artistic quality of their work varies considerably, as some possessed talent in higher degree than others, the over-all standard was remarkably excellent. The quality of the drawings is far superior to that of the wood engravings which were made from them. William Campbell has listed sixteen known special artists and has recorded the fact that they turned out 2,625 drawings.[4] The present exhibition includes only a small sampling of their work, ample enough, however, to illustrate the liveliness of drawing, the inventiveness in choice of subject, the freshness, and the skill in conveying an aura of authenticity which add vastly to the interest of the exhibition. Some of these drawings from the rich resources of the M. and M. Karolik Collection are shown here for the first time.

Supplementing the professional special artists of the illustrated papers and the easel painters, the coverage of the War is given variety by the exertions of the amateur, to whom the epithet "primitive" is customarily applied. Crude by comparison and lacking in the refinements of draftsmanship, perspective and coloring of the professional, these works often have charm, a personal quality and an immediacy of vision. Many of these amateurs were soldiers – as, for example, Voltaire Combe, who was bugler, Company B of the 3rd New York Volunteer Cavalry. His view of a camp, identified through its similarity to another sketch by Samuel J. E. Thayer in the Kennedy Galleries, has a brooding almost oriental flavor (No. 195). John Donaghy (No. 112), David M. Stauffer (Nos. 165, 167, 168, 169), Samuel Bell Palmer (Nos. 12, 64, 103, 178) also were soldier-artists.

The exhibition includes a number of examples of the work of some of the most famous illustrators of the period. One of the most skillful of these was undoubtedly David Claypoole Johnston, a Bostonian who illustrated and issued his own magazine. Apparently a propagandist in his motivation, as is perhaps not to be unexpected from a proper Bostonian of that period, Johnston's drawing (No. 4) has a charm which, in a way, detracts from its propaganda value. Thomas Nast was another of America's great illustrators who is represented in the exhibition by two lively sketches (Nos. 202, 217) which do not indicate the vitriolic qualities typical of his later cartoons when he was engaged in fighting corrupt politicians in New York City. And there is the work of Adalbert John Volck, a Baltimore dentist who possessed extraordinary virtuosity as a draftsman and who is well-deserving of much greater study than he has so far received. Two examples of his witty pen are included (Nos. 179, 199). Although outside the scope of the present exhibition, his pungent attacks, through portrait caricatures, on Northern abolitionists, politicians, publishers and military leaders – for Volck was an ardent Confederate sympathizer – are remarkable satirical drawings. F.O.C. Darley, also a noted graphic artist and book illustrator, makes a convincing picture in his drawing of *Border Ruffians Invading Kansas* (No. 2), although whether or not he had personal knowledge of the event cannot be determined.

---

4. William P. Campbell, *The Civil War – A Centennial Exhibition of Eyewitness Drawings*, National Gallery of Art, Washington, 1961, p. 107.

A fair representation of the printmakers who were active at the time, a number of the rare bronzes of Civil War subjects by John Rogers and some delightful examples of folk sculpture (Nos. 230-236) round out the exhibition.

In view of the wealth of contemporary pictorial documentation which has survived and is reflected in the present exhibition, it is surprising to note that there was, at the time, at least in some quarters, a fear that the War was not being adequately recorded. A prominent member of the New York Historical Society, William J. Hoppin, published his concern in the pages of the *U.S. Army and Navy Journal:*

"So far, the arts of design have very inadequately expressed the heroism, patriotic devotion, the noble charities of the North, or – what, alas! must in numberless cases perish from the remembrance of men without any record – the unimaginable sufferings and the glorious martyrdoms of the loyalists of the South. The pencil and the chisel have done infinitely less than the pen in perpetuating all these things. Indeed, no war which was ever waged has been so thoroughly described in a literary way as will be this gigantic struggle. No war ever enrolled among its soldiers so many men who are skilled in the art of composition. The vast numbers of private letters, diaries, communications to newspapers, official reports, pamphlets, apologies of this or that general, besides the more ponderous and formal histories, will make the literature of this revolution more copious and affluent than that of any war that was ever waged . . . .

"But the pictorial method of preserving memorials of this war has been either neglected or abused. It is true that the illustrated newspapers are full of sketches, purporting to be pictures of important scenes; but the testimony of parties engaged shows that these representations are, when they are not taken from photographs, not always reliable. The desire of producing striking effects sometimes overcomes all other considerations, and the truth is now and then sacrificed to the demand for dramatic action or a pleasing play of light and shadow. Many of these designs are of little value, excepting as studies of costume. Some of them are positively lying and fabulous. If all the terrific hand-to-hand encounters which we have seen for two or three years displayed in the pages of our popular weeklies had actually occurred, the combatants on each side would long ago have mutually annihilated each other, like the famous cats of Irish history.

"The photographers have made by far the most important additions to the pictorial history of the war. They have prosecuted their undertakings under circumstances of great difficulty, and even danger, running the risk of having their dark chambers converted into ambulances, or destroyed by hostile shells. But the caution and deliberation required for successful views of this sort are obviously impracticable in the confusion of a battle, and, therefore, it is not surprising that what we have hitherto obtained in this way has been little besides a representation of that awful 'still life' which the plain shows after the conflict is over.

"We hope that more attention will be paid by the higher artists to subjects of this sort in future. It is well known that Horace Vernet, who has given the most valuable pictures of the French campaign in Algiers and elsewhere, made personal studies of the scenes he painted. We are glad to hear that one of our own distinguished painters has the intention to illustrate the famous battle of Chattanooga by visiting the spot and seeing with his own eyes the remarkable natural features of the scenery, which made that conflict not only one of the boldest, but also the most pictorial in the history of the war.

"But so far, as we have already said, but little has been done in this way. With the exception of Leutze's clear portrait of Burnside, a few excellent groups in plaster by Rogers, and two or three spirited drawings by Darley and Eastman Johnson, scarcely anything has been produced of an enduring character illustrating the war."[5]

This exhibition, had Hoppin lived to see it, would, we hope, have satisfied his qualms. We trust that this worthy gentleman, who showed a concern for posterity and who understood, as few persons have in subsequent years, the importance of an adequate pictorial record of artistic excellence of events of national importance, would be pleased with what has survived to keep the memory of the great trial of this country alive for future generations.

5. *U.S. Army and Navy Journal*, Vol. I, 1863–64, p. 350.

1. George Caleb Bingham, *The County Election*

We read much in the papers about the excited political feeling in Kansas upon the slavery question; and there was the usual supply of inflammatory gas exhaled from the so-called representative men, on both sides, in Congress – all of which was read by the businessmen of the country about as they read of horse races and prize fights, and with about as little idea that such folly could involve the country in war, in the one case or the other.

W. W. Blackford, *War Years with Jeb Stuart*, New York, 1945, p. 11.

1

...and the War Came.

IT WAS INEVITABLE, although there were few who realized it before it came like a thunderclap. To the Maine lobsterman hauling his pots in the chill island-studded coves, and equally to the Scotch-Irish mountaineer in the uplands of the Carolinas, the idea of personal involvement in the controversy over a politician's problem as to whether the new states clamoring for admission to the Union should be free or slave seemed remote. North or South, few believed it would come to war. Slowly, however, men's minds were being prepared. At countless political gatherings the principles of States' Rights were advanced, questions of the hour debated and stern resolutions adopted. The propaganda message of Harriet Beecher Stowe's *Uncle Tom's Cabin* permeated the minds of Northern youth, and, as time passed, the tenor of the printed and spoken word changed from a philosophical and objective tone to one of subjective bitterness and passion.

A foretaste of what was to come was endured by the residents of the border states during the uneasy years before Lincoln's election. Bands of armed Free-State and Pro-Slavery ruffians spread death and destruction over a no-man's land in Kansas and Missouri. Murder, midnight pillage, and the brutal burning and sacking of towns forged and tempered minds and spirits.

The well-to-do young men in Northern and Southern metropolises before the war shared one thing in common: the love of parading in resplendent uniforms. Each large city boasted at least one, and usually more, independent companies, each with its distinctive and usually gaudy uniform. These assembled on gala occasions, marching up the main street behind a band, causing, hopefully, many a young female heart to flutter at the sight of such manly brilliance. Despite their political and social motivations and their lack of readiness for active service, it is none the less true that when war did come it was these units and those of the common militia that first took the field and from which the majority of the volunteer officers were to be drawn.

Slowly, inevitably, the scene was set and the actors prepared for their roles. The conscientious career officers, the graduates of Annapolis and West Point, learned their lines in frontier posts fighting Comanche and Sioux; afloat, from the sea and from the veterans of the old navy. As prologue, "old Osawatomie" appeared before the curtain was raised to make his brief and final dramatic appearance. His attempt to free the slaves intensified the bitterness of the Southern people, and his death inspired a marching song which was a source of strength to the North. Behind the scenes the mechanic at his bench, the shipwright at the

27

ways, the engineer, the inventor, the merchant, the banker, meanwhile were quietly at work building up the resources for the tragedy which was to run for four long years.

It would be a mistake to assume that these resources were all tangible and physical. The North, teeming with factories, railroads, canals and shipping, was vastly superior to the South in those respects. To balance this, the South had cotton, King Cotton, without which the economy of Europe would collapse, or so it was believed. But in North and South lived a breed of men and women of integrity, moral fibre, conviction, firmness, determination, and devotion, upheld both by patriotism and religion without which either antagonist would quickly have succumbed.

Bonfires, cheering crowds, the booming of cannon, the unfurling of state and patriotic flags and the inevitable speeches greeted the telegraphed intelligence of Lincoln's election in the South. The period of suspense and tension was at an end. Unbounded enthusiasm, as for a glorious victory, overran the South, for the news was synonymous with the birth of the Southern Confederacy. The feeling in the North was not so exuberant perhaps, but was fully as unanimous and determined.

6. C. GIROUX, *Cotton Plantation*

Looking out from the side gallery across the wide grassy yard through the trees and wild vines that had been spared when the place was cleared for building, one could see the two long rows of cabins facing each other across a broad sweep of thick Bermuda grass, set with an occasional great tree, grey in the winter with long festoons of moss. Leading from each door was a little, crooked white path, ending at the road down the middle of the grass plot, beaten smooth by the march of the many black feet that journeyed over it in the early dawn, the weary, hot noonday, and the welcome dusk.

Facing the cabins in a grove of trees was the overseer's four-room log house, rough but substantial. Many an occupant for it came and went. Some were too severe on the Negroes; others allowed them to idle away the time, the crop suffering in consequence; some were dishonest and lazy. Altogether it was a difficult position to fill satisfactorily. The men were a coarse, uncultivated class, knowing little more than to read and write; brutified by their employment, they were considered by the South but little better than the Negroes they managed.

Kate Stone, *Brokenburn, The Journal of Kate Stone, 1861-1868*, ed. John Q. Anderson, Baton Rouge, 1955, pp. 4f.

◀ 4. DAVID CLAYPOOLE JOHNSTON, *Early Development of Southern Chivalry*

"It was only yesterday," said George, "as I was busy loading stones into a cart, that young Mas'r Tom stood there, slashing his whip so near the horse that the creature was frightened. I asked him to stop, as pleasant as I could, – he just kept right on. I begged him again, and then he turned on me, and began striking me. I held his hand, and then he screamed and kicked and ran to his father, and told him that I was fighting him. He came in a rage, and said he'd teach me who was my master; and he tied me to a tree, and cut switches for young master, and told him that he might whip me till he was tired; – and he did do it!"

Harriet Beecher Stowe, *Uncle Tom's Cabin*, Boston, 1852, Vol. I, p. 34.

7. A. Berghaus, *John Brown Led to Execution*

He walked out of the jail at 11 o'clock; an eye-witness said: "with a radiant countenance, and the step of a conqueror." His face was even joyous, and it has been remarked that probably his was the lightest heart in Charlestown that day . . . He mounted the wagon beside his jailor, Cap't. Avis, who had been one of the bravest of his captors, who had treated him very kindly, and to whom he was profoundly grateful . . . . He bade adieu to some acquaintances, at the foot of the gallows, and was first to mount the scaffold. His step was still firm, and his bearing calm . . . .

Horace Greeley, *The American Conflict*, Hartford, 1864, Vol. I, p. 298.

8. HENRY CLEENEWERCK, *The First Flag of Independence Raised in the South, Savannah, Georgia, 1860*

9. EDWIN WHITE, *Raising the Flag at Fort Sumter before the Bombardment*

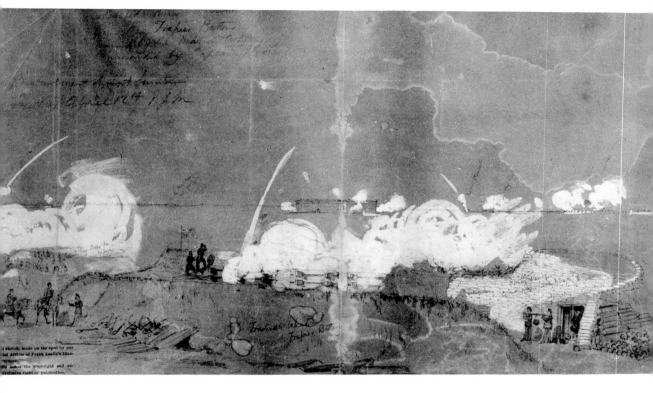

10. WILLIAM WAUD, *The First Gun Fired Against Fort Sumter*

And now, patience! We must wait. Why did that green goose Anderson go into Fort Sumter? . . .

I do not pretend to go to sleep. How can I? If Anderson does not accept terms at four o'clock, the orders are he shall be fired upon.

I count four by St. Michael's chimes, and I begin to hope. At half past four, the heavy booming of a cannon! I sprang out of bed and on my knees, prostrate, I prayed as I never prayed before.

There was a sound of stir all over the house, a pattering of feet in the corridor. All seemed hurrying one way. I put on my double-gown and a shawl and went to the house top. The shells were bursting. In the dark I heard a man say: "Waste of ammunition!" I knew my husband was rowing about in a boat somewhere in that dark bay, and that the shells were roofing it over, bursting toward the Fort. If Anderson was obstinate, Mr. Chesnut was to order the Forts on our side to open fire. Certainly fire had begun. The regular roar of the cannon, there it was! And who could tell what each volley accomplished of death and destruction.

Mary Boykin Chesnut, *A Diary From Dixie*, ed. Ben Ames Williams, Boston, 1949, pp. 35f.

11. WILLIAM MORRIS HUNT, *The Drummer Boy*

~2~

The Call to Arms.

IT WAS a very common misconception, in both North and South, that the war would be quickly over and victory easily obtained. Northerners and Southerners alike felt that the war would be something of a grand military parade and camping-out party. Few were they who, like Grant and Sherman, foresaw what was to happen.

The ladies, North and South, were fully as enthusiastic for the War as the men. The ladies' efforts at the beginning seem to have been especially devoted to the making of handsome colors which were presented to the volunteer units with appropriate ceremonies at which the Colonel of the regiment received them from some fair damsel with assurances that the folds of the flag would never be touched by enemy hands or be carried in retreat. Later, the same ladies were to make bandages, dressings and lint with grim determination, but for the moment, when not making flags, they knitted socks, or made canteen covers and havelocks to protect the necks of the men from the fierce southern sun.

While the ladies were so employed, the elderly gentlemen of means purchased handsome swords or revolvers which they had inscribed and presented to members of their families or close friends. Contributions poured in for the outfitting of the new units being raised, and elaborate uniforms and equipments of the most expensive materials were sometimes provided. This was also the period of the popularity of various patented gadgets. There was a great vogue for such items as armored vests, special haversacks, and rubber drinking tubes with special filters which were advertised to purify the muddiest or slimiest of water and were sold in great quantities, only to be discarded very quickly as soon as the units actually took the field. An agent of the Atwater Armor Company was reported to have ". . . sold over two hundred . . . 'iron clad life preservers' to one regiment in a day. It is said that at least fifty per cent of the regiment first wore away and then swore away this device. The track of the command from Washington to Arlington Heights was marked by these abandoned 'armor plates', the largest quantity being hurled from Long Bridge into the Potomac when the regiment was about to step on 'sacred soil', as an offering to the gods. The balance of the lot, after being rudely perforated with bullets at 'Camp Chase', was ignominiously kicked aside, and the skeletons probably repose there to this day".[1]

---

1. Sheldon B. Thorpe, *The History of the 15th Connecticut Volunteers*, New Haven, 1893, p. 15.

There was a frenzy of excitement in every town as its local unit departed for the front, which was equally as true in the South as it was in the North. As each unit appeared in the streets to march to the train or transport, it was cheered to the echo all along the line of its march. This ceremony was usually repeated at every large city through which the unit passed on its way towards the front, and each parade was usually accompanied by the strains of martial music from the unit's own band, often supplemented by a band of the local community. As the train passed along the countryside, cheering crowds turned out all along its route waving flags and handkerchiefs.

The armies which first concentrated on both sides of Washington were essentially armies of amateur soldiers. They were green to the rudiments of warfare and ignorant of the meaning of discipline. The officers were, by and large, as ignorant as their men. The men, in fact, often elected their own officers except for those who were political appointees. To the independent Yankee and his Southern counterpart it was difficult to accept the principle of subordination. Greenhorns stared about them with a mixture of wonder, envy and gloomy foreboding at the sight of somewhat better trained soldiers touching their hats to officers like regulars. " . . . 'Has it come to this?,' they seemed to be thinking. 'Are free-born Americans to be made slaves of in this fashion?' "[2]

The problems facing the officers attempting to instill discipline into their troops is illustrated by the following anecdote: a Brigadier General on a tour of inspection encountered a gawky lieutenant who had lately been promoted from a sergeancy. "The lieutenant, dressed in trousers and a red shirt, and barefoot, was seated on the head of a barrel, eating an apple and gossiping with a sentry. The general . . . halted in front of him and glared at him. The lieutenant, without rising, and still munching his apple, saluted.

'Who are you?', snarled the general.

The lieutenant gave his name, title, company and regiment.

'What business have you talking to a guard? What are you dressed in that style for? Don't you know any better?'

The lieutenant dismounted from his barrel and tremulously entered upon a defense of his costume and behavior. The general interrupted him. 'What's your business at home?'

'General, I was a carpenter.'

'I should think as much . . . . You may be a good carpenter, but you're a damn poor officer. Be off now, and don't let me catch you talking to a guard again, except when it's your duty to give him instructions.'

And with an expression of disgusted despair, the general stalked away . . .

'I wouldn't have been so mad with that fool lieutenant,' he afterwards explained, 'if he hadn't saluted me with his apple core.' "[3]

There was so much to learn; even the buglers did not know their calls. George

2. John W. De Forest, *A Volunteer's Adventures*, New Haven, 1946, p. 4.
3. *Ibid.*, p. 23f.

S. Fobes, himself a green trooper, thus describes it: "What a lamentable set of blowers they were! I remember how strange it seemed to me they could not do better, being Germans, to whom wind instruments come as naturally as do pretzels and beer. But it mattered little, then, how they rendered the calls: the notes fell upon ignorant ears. With every toot of the bugles, recurring with bewildering frequency, the recruits might be heard calling to each other in vain what *that* meant, while the more careful and conscientious sought their officers for information, probably with as little success."[4]

The first illusions soon faded that the war would be a gay military parade with troops marching with flying colors through pleasant villages without meeting more than comic opera opposition. Incident upon incident slowly brought home the fact that war was far from being a frolic and a romp. The attack on the troops of the 6th Massachusetts, marching through Baltimore on their way to Washington, by a mob of plug-uglies in the streets of that city is one example. These first few soldiers to die were acclaimed as martyrs and heroes and were given funerals with full military honors of a magnificence only accounted for by the fact that the country was not yet hardened to the realization of the full consequences of a fighting war. The entire nation paid tribute to the popular Elmer E. Ellsworth, Colonel of the famous New York Fire Zouaves, who was killed by a blast from a shotgun in Alexandria, Virginia, while taking down a Confederate flag, which, while flying, had been visible from the White House. Ellsworth's funeral was described as follows: ". . . There was the President . . . with Mrs. Lincoln, whose grief could not be concealed . . . the services ended, the procession . . . began to move along Pennsylvania Avenue to the special train in waiting . . . amid notable demonstrations of grief and honor."[5]

But it was the devastating and totally unexpected defeat of the Union forces at the first battle of Bull Run on July 21, 1861, which more than anything else dispelled the optimism in the North and aroused it to a pitch of grim determination.

"It is the most singular field in history; from which the real victors fled, leaving the vanquished in wondering possession! The name will always be full of startling memories to those who recall the gloomy days that followed the battle, and the pale, stern faces that surged about the news offices, as rumor followed rumor, portentous and bewildering. Hardly had the echoes of the contest died away, ere we crowded to the recruiting offices and camps. The merchant, the mechanic, the clerk, the student, gave up home and all in a moment; and of these there were not a few who trembled lest the surgeon's eye should detect some physical disability which they would fain conceal. The air was alive with the roll of drums, and the flag – now dearer than ever before – fluttered in miniature from every window, or floated its full folds from the housetops."[6]

4. George S. Fobes, *Leaves from a Trooper's Diary*, Philadelphia, 1869, p. 11.
5. John W. Forney, in *Philadelphia Press*, May 25, 1861.
6. Fobes, *op. cit.*, pp. 7f.

Gay Street Knoxville Tenn. (1862). (Drawn from Memory)

12. SAMUEL BELL PALMER, *Simultaneous Recruiting for the Confederate and Union Armies, Knoxville, Tennessee, 1861*

On the first day of March 1862 I joined the "Mabry Artillery", and was mustered into the service of the Confederate States at Knoxville, Tenn. We were kept there some time learning the a. b. c. of a soldier's education in an old ten-pin-alley which served us for a barrack. My brother John enlisted at the same time. One Sunday the order came for us to *travel*. I was unwell but was so anxious to commence my soldiering that I overcame my illness, and went with the rest. I had a fine notion about the "romance" of a soldier's life, etc. *I have got bravely over it since.*

Samuel Bell Palmer, *Memories of the War*, manuscript owned by General and Mrs. John B. Anderson, Washington, pp. 1f.

38

13. GEORGE COCHRAN LAMBDIN, *The Consecration, 1861*

The hour was sad I left the maid,
A ling'ring farewell taking;
Her sighs and tears my steps delayed,
I thought her heart was breaking;
In hurried words her name I blessed,
I breath'd the vows that bind me,
And to my heart in anguish pressed
The girl I left behind me.

Anonymous (adapted from Samuel Lover), "The Girl I Left Behind Me." (contemporary song).

16. James F. Queen, *Philadelphia Zouave Corps Passing Independence Hall*

Headquarters, Heavy Curbstone, Light Zouaves, Washington, June 17th, '61

Editors Boston Gazette: – Zouave! Yes, sirs!...I'm full of fight. Although fighting is not my
forte, I do not think I would stand being knocked down. I joined this August body in April,
and we May March daily, for we are getting stronger weekly. I may say in good season,
if we spring upon the enemy he is sure to fall, for our summersaults will be a dose that will
prove the "winter of his discontent." He will have to evacuate. We won't strike light, for the
South has no match for us. When the country called all hands to arms, I thought it a proud
legacy to leave my posterity that I joined a division for the Union. I set my name down,
and there it stands. Nice uniform. Had my hair cut with a knife and fork. Red hair, yellow
jacket, blue shirt, white hat, plantation shoes, pink trowsers, bell buttons on behind, where
I never saw them before. Left the city under encouraging circumstances. Toothache, nail in
my shoe, forgot my rations, something in my eye. Chap in rear file rasping my shins. Got out
of step and hurt my instep....Arrived in Washington all right, nobody being left.
Intentions to sleep in tents, but were intensely disappointed, as we slept out on grass, which,
after all, served as well to all intents and purposes. Placed minute men on watch, who
moved our hands every second, until we thought it really time to strike. Took my turn in
going around. Shot a cow and calf. "Tis meet to be here." Fighting, you see, for the public
weal, placing our lives at stake. Took the hindquarters into headquarters. Pork in various
shapes for rations heretofore . . . . Sergeant Gimlet's drilling is a complete bore, and he
thinks it augers well on the whole . . . . Of course we have our fine times. Had some light
reading sent me by a sexton: "Annual Report of Greenwood Cemetery," "Ghost Stories,"
and his business circular, with price list of coffins, etc. I should like to overtake that
undertaker . . . . Sergeant Gimlet speaks disparagingly of our literary tastes. Says only thing
red in camp is my nose . . . . Yours, jolly and contented, John Bolivar

Boston *Gazette* newspaper clipping in a private collection, Washington.

17. G. GRATO, *The Departure of Union Troops for the Front*

The most intense excitement prevailed throughout the city. Such crowds of people filled the streets as to impede the march of the Regiment; every window had its anxious interested faces; roofs of buildings were crowded with excited men; cheers from the crowds responded to with cheers from the Regiment; the waving of handkerchiefs and flags; and the stirring strains of the Regimental Band – all tended to make it one of the most exciting scenes we had ever witnessed.

At 4 P.M., the train was in motion, and amid deafening cheers and fluttering of handkerchiefs, moved rapidly off. Fainter grew the cheering and soon died away; and the soldiers, excited as they were when they entered the cars, soon quieted down, and it was easy to see there were sober, earnest, thoughtful faces among them. Where are we going? How many of us will return?

Samuel H. Putnam, *The Story of Company A, Twenty-fifth Regiment, Mass. Volunteers*, Worcester, 1886, p. 30.

41

Federal Troops Marching ~~upon~~ into Alexandria on Friday Morning May 24th

Mich 1st & U.S. artillery

18. Unidentified, *Federal Troops Entering Alexandria*

On May 23 Virginia ratified an ordinance of secession, and on the early morning of May 24 the federal soldiers, under the Virginian, General Winfield Scott, crossed the Potomac River and occupied Arlington Heights and the city of Alexandria. "The invasion of Virginia, the pollution of her sacred soil," as it was termed, called forth a vigorous proclamation from her governor and a cry of rage from her press. General Beauregard issued a fierce proclamation, tending to fire the hearts of the Virginians with indignation. "A reckless and unprincipled host," he declared, "has invaded your soil," etc. Virginia needed no such stimulus. The First, Second, and Third Virginia were immediately mustered into service, and my husband was colonel of the Third Virginia Infantry.

Sara Agnes Pryor, *My Day, Reminiscences of a Long Life*, New York, 1909, pp. 162f.

20. SANFORD ROBINSON GIFFORD, *Night Bivouac of the 7th Regiment New York at Arlington Heights, Virginia*

Half a mile farther on the Alexandria Road came orders to halt and stack arms – the Seventh's first bivouac in Virginia. A picturesque bivouac it was. The sleepy dropped on the railway track and slept soundly. The active organized into impromptu forage parties, laid hold on neighboring fence-rails . . . and soon had fires flaming in the air, and raw pork and ham sizzling and frying in better or worse cookery . . . the stacks of arms with canteens, haversacks, and red blankets, pendents; the groups in gay soldiers' costume . . . [made] a memorable picture.

William Swinton, *History of 7th Regiment, National Guard, New York*, New York, 1870, pp. 198f.

21. C. A. HARKER, *Troops Drilling in Camp in View of the Capitol*

20

23. ALFRED WORDSWORTH THOMPSON, *Confederate Camp near Urbana*

While at Urbana our life at headquarters was a delightful one, an oasis in the war-worn desert of our lives. There was nothing to do but await the advance of the great army preparing around Washington, and though constant vigilance was necessary, General Stuart like a good soldier knew how to improve the passing hour in the enjoyment of the charming society the country round afforded. Our horses stood saddled day and night, and Stuart and his staff slept in the open air in the shady yard of the residence of Mr. Cocky, with clothes, boots, spurs and arms on, ready for instant action, but with these precautions we enjoyed the society of the charming girls around us to the utmost. One hour's acquaintance in war times goes further towards good feeling and acquaintanceship than months in the dull, slow period of peace. This no doubt makes a military people like the French call it "Merry War."

W. W. Blackford, *War Years with Jeb Stuart*, New York, 1945, p. 140.

25. ADALBERT JOHN VOLCK, *Troops of the 6th Massachusetts Attacked when Marching through Baltimore*

I immediately took my position upon the right, wheeled into column of sections, and requested them to march in close order. Before we had started, the mob was upon us, with a secession flag, attached to a pole, and told us we could never march through that city. They would kill every "white nigger" of us, before we could reach the other depot. I paid no attention to them, but, after I had wheeled the battalion, gave the order to march.

As soon as the order was given, the brick-bats began to fly into our ranks from the mob. I called a policeman, and requested him to lead the way to the depot. He did so. After we had marched about a hundred yards, we came to a bridge. The rebels had torn up most of the planks. We had to play "Scotch hop" to get over it. As soon as we had crossed the bridge, they commenced to fire upon us from the street and houses. I ordered the men to protect themselves; and then we returned their fire, and laid a great many of them away. I saw four fall on the sidewalk at one time. They followed us up, and we fought our way to the other depot, – about one mile. They kept at us till the cars started. Quite a number of the rascals were shot, after we entered the cars. We went very slow, for we expected the rails were torn up on the road.

John W. Hanson, *Historical Sketch of the Old Sixth Regiment of Massachusetts Volunteers*, Boston, 1866, pp. 40f.

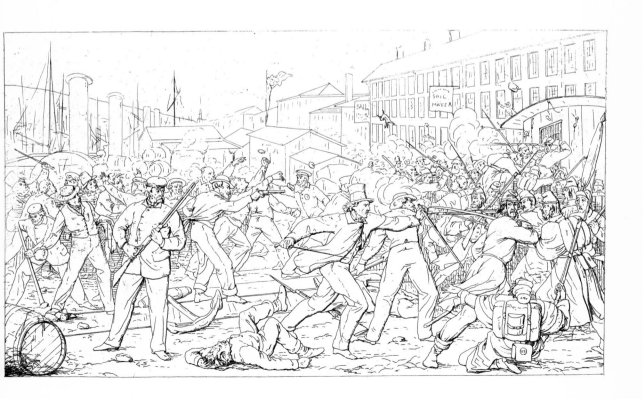

27. Unidentified, *Panic on the Road from Bull Run to Centreville*

But now the most extraordinary spectacle I have ever witnessed took place. I had been gazing at the numerous well-formed lines as they moved forward to the attack, some fifteen or twenty thousand strong in full view, and for some reason had turned my head in another direction for a moment, when some one exclaimed, pointing to the battlefield, "Look! Look!" I looked, and what a change had taken place in an instant. Where those "well dressed," well-defined lines, with clear spaces between had been steadily pressing forward, the whole field was a confused swarm of men, like bees, running away as fast as their legs could carry them, with all order and organization abandoned. In a moment more the whole valley was filled with them as far as the eye could reach. They plunged through Bull Run wherever they came to it regardless of fords or bridges, and there many were drowned. Muskets, cartridge boxes, belts, knapsacks, haversacks and blankets were thrown away in their mad race, that nothing might impede their flight. In the reckless haste the artillery drove over every one who did not get out of their way. Ambulance and wagon drivers cut the traces and dashed off on the mules . . . . Numbers of gay members of Congress had come out from Washington to witness the battle from the adjacent hills, provided with baskets of champagne and lunches. So there was a regular chariot race when the rout began . . . . We found, occasionally, along the road, parasols and dainty shawls lost in their flight by the frail, fair ones who had seats in most of the carriages of this excursion.

W. W. Blackford, *War Years with Jeb Stuart*, New York, 1945, pp. 34f.

28. ALFRED R. WAUD, *The Funeral Procession of General Lander*

The funeral of Brigadier General Lander took place yesterday . . . .

The noble form of the General was attired in full uniform, with sash and sword. The coffin was silver mounted, and a beautiful plate on the lid bore the inscription, "Fred. W. Lander, Brigadier General, died March 2d, 1862, at Camp Chase, Virginia; aged thirty-nine years. Bravest of the Brave."

Soon after the hour of twelve the coffin was closed, and borne for more than a square, immediately in front of the cavalry part of the escort, to a point where stood an ornamented caisson instead of a hearse. The coffin was covered with a splendid American ensign, a wreath of fragrant flowers, and the cap and sword of the deceased.

The members of the deceased General's body guard who accompanied his remains to the city, about thirty in number, were formed on each side of the caisson on which the corpse was borne. . . . the procession . . . proceeded . . . to the railroad station, where the body was placed in a special car and soon left, under escort, for Salem in Massachusetts.

Daily National Intelligencer, Washington, March 7, 1862.

29. WINSLOW HOMER, *Reveille*

On a bright morning, or in the midst of storm and bluster, nothing so fittingly ushers in the day and stirs to activity as the reveille in a military camp . . . The effect is intensified when in a great army stretching out for miles, a single bugle-note gives the signal, and then, as by magic, from every direction break out and roll on in one mass of accelerating sound the roll of drums, the screech of fifes, and the blare of artillery and cavalry bugles.

Francis H. Buffum, *History of the 14th New Hampshire Volunteers*, Boston, 1882, p. 301.

3

Life in Camp.

From Reveille to Taps.

ACCUSTOMING the green amateur soldiers of the Union and Confederate armies to the age-old procedures of army life was not easy or quick. The day for the soldier started with reveille. This call, usually sounded on a bugle or fife and drums, was followed by assembly and roll-call. The sight then presented has daily been re-enacted in military camps for centuries. "The men could be seen emerging from their tents or huts, their toilet in various stages of completion. Here was a man with one boot on, and the other in his hand; here, with his clothes buttoned in skips and blouse in hand, which he was putting on as he went to the line; here was one with a blouse on; there, one with his jacket or overcoat . . . . Here and there was a man just about half awake, having a fist at each eye, and looking as disconsolate and forsaken as men usually do when they get from the bed before the public at short notice."[1]

Following the roll-call, came sick call. Some soldiers feigned illness in an attempt to escape fatigue or guard duty; sometimes they would succeed for a time in deluding the surgeons into believing they were actually sick, but when the doctors were on to their tricks, they really got a taste of medicine. Inveterate boozers also used sick call as an opportunity to secure a stiff drink of commissary whiskey which only the surgeons could prescribe. The prescription for whiskey oftentimes, however, called for a mixture with quinine. The men ". . . with few exceptions, faced this last-named ordeal with the fortitude of regulars. The few who preferred their quinine plain, were granted the indulgence; but the larger few who preferred their whiskey plain, were not so fortunate. It was an axiom with Surgeon Halcomb that quinine and whiskey *mixed* as a dose, was non-cumulative in the system, and therefore perfectly safe, whereas if the two were given separately, the quinine was extremely liable to accumulate, – *in the soldier's pocket*."[2]

Mess call for breakfast, which is described later, followed. Then would come drill – at first, by squads, and later by platoons, companies, battalions and regiments as the soldiers and their officers became increasingly proficient. Meanwhile the fatigue details, which had been designated at assembly, would be carrying out their chores. After the morning's drill, there would be the noon-day mess, then

---

1. John D. Billings, *Hardtack and Coffee*, Boston, 1887, pp. 166f.
2. Sheldon B. Thorpe, *The History of the 15th Connecticut Volunteers*, New Haven, 1893, p. 25.

possibly a little time off, and then more drilling. At the end of the afternoon, there was usually inspection followed by a formal dress parade or review, after which came the evening meal. The final two calls of the day were tattoo, at which time all talking and lights were to be extinguished, and taps, which ended the army day for all branches of the service. Unless an alarm broke out in the night, the soldiers were left to their slumbers, or, as often was the case, to their meditations on home, the length of time in months and days they would serve before the term of their enlistment expired, and their prospects of surviving the vicissitudes of war.

At irregular intervals every soldier would be detailed to guard duty. "The first guard duty is a memorable event to the soldier. Here was my first beat, along this fence. When the keen-looking sabre was belted around the jacket . . . and the clank of the blade in the scabbard startled the recruit as he stepped off with martial tread, he felt then that he was indeed a defender of the flag. His bosom swelled almost enough to fill out the laps in his jacket. He was only puzzled to know what to do with his weapon: how the deuce to carry that scabbard so that it might not trip up his heels, or entangle itself in his legs. But oh, what misery in the long hours of tramp, tramp up and down a prescribed distance, in the hot sun, or in the rain and mud; in the incessant vigilance required to do homage to the officers, who *would* wander by, in blue and golden glory, to seek such salutation. And then at night the rudely broken slumber, the silent and seemingly endless hours, the intense straining through the darkness for the relief, and the informal reception of it when it came . . . He is relieved – that is his happiness – and may rest for four hours. How sudden and sweet is the soldier's first sleep by the guard-house fire, after his maiden watch!"[3]

At the beginning of the war, some troops were quartered in permanent barracks, but as soon as large numbers began to take the field, they, of necessity, were crowded under canvas in temporary camps. At first a great variety of large tents were used, but these were replaced before long by what became known then and since as pup-tents. These were made by buttoning together two rectangular sections of canvas, each section being carried by a soldier and his tent mate. Many are the amusing accounts of the tribulations of sleeping out. "Last night the clouds gathered heavily, and at midnight the rains descended and the floods came. I was awakened by the uproar, and arose in consternation. Found the Corporal already up and outside, securing the ropes and giving the pins an extra drive. The wind roared furiously, swaying and cracking the trees, and rocking our frail tenements to and fro like skiffs upon the sea. The rain was blown about in sheets, penetrated the tent, overflowed the shallow drain, and streamed under the canvas, floating away nearly all the straw of our beds. What remained was water-soaked, so that we could only squat despairingly on our heels until morning, thinking of the home comforts within a bow-shot of us."[4]

3. George S. Fobes, *Leaves From a Trooper's Diary*, Philadelphia, 1869, p. 10.
4. *Ibid.*, p. 9.

42. WINSLOW HOMER, *Pitching Horseshoes*

The Confederates by the middle of the war gave up the use of tents to a great extent. During the winter months it was often the habit of the men of both armies to build crude log huts. Sometimes the roofs were fashioned of the pup-tents, but often sloping roofs were made, using any available boards or even thatching. Occasionally these were made more comfortable by the inclusion of a fireplace built of mud, a barrel with the heads knocked out, serving as chimney. These frequently caught fire, much to the enjoyment of dwellers in other huts.

When the volunteers first took the field, there was a great variety in their uniforms. At one extreme were the fancy but impractical dress uniforms which some of the old independent companies still affected, which included, for example, bearskin busbys like those worn in the British Brigade of Guards to this day. There was one regiment of Highlanders (the 79th New York) completely outfitted in plaid trews, bonnets and broad swords. The number of units, Confederate and Federal, affecting the fez and the zouave uniform with red baggy pants was quite large. Early in the war, there were Union troops in gray and Confederate troops in blue, but the majority of the Southern troops, when uniformed at all, wore a rough yellowish-gray uniform. Charles Coffin thus describes the uniforms of a group of Confederate soldiers at Fort Donelson in Tennessee: "There were all sorts of uniforms, brown-colored predominating, as if they were in the snuff business and had been rolled in tobacco-dust. There was sheep gray, iron gray, blue gray, dirty gray, with bed blankets, quilts, buffalo-robes, pieces of carpeting of all colors and figures, for blankets. Each had his pack on his shoulder. Judging by their garments, one would have thought that the last scrapings, the odds and ends of humanity and of dry goods, had been brought together."[5]

Of course, the majority of Union soldiers wore the regulation blue coat and lighter blue pants. Some of the early issue uniforms were shoddy to the extreme, for example: "The black overcoats issued to the nine months men were the masterpiece of efforts in that direction – the flimsy fabric almost like tissue, the dyeing of the wretchedest. We have known trousers and dress-coats to be completely spoiled by the inky liquid which exuded from the overcoats in a rainstorm. So easily did the coloring infusion leave on a suggestion of moisture, that it was a camp jest that the coats were made for steeping. And a certain nondescript liquid called indifferently tea or coffee as the cook might fancy, was commonly known as overcoat tea – one boiled coat producing a barrel of tea. Besides, the very looks of these garments shamed the men. The more comfortably you clothe soldiers, the more neat and becoming their uniform, the better they will do duty. Make their dress a laughing-stock, if you would have them lose self-respect, like a parti-colored convict. But as it is now, the uniform is a source of pardonable pride; furloughed men and discharged men, even, being glad to wear it in the streets."[6]

Soldiers, in general, have a proclivity to improve on civilian vocabulary, and the soldier in the Civil War was no exception. As a result, while many of the

5. Charles Carleton Coffin, *The Boys of '61*, Boston, 1886, p. 83.
6. *U.S. Army and Navy Journal*, Vol. I, 1863–64, p. 180.

colloquialisms which came into vogue have failed to survive, such as that which follows, we, nevertheless, owe to them several picturesque words which still enliven our vocabulary. "An Army correspondent gives a new word which has lately been coined and which is synonymous with 'gobble' and with 'skedaddle', and is used for any other word and for want of any other word. He says, 'A corps staff officer dismounted near me a moment ago. I inquired where he had been riding. He informed me that he had been sent out on a general *scyugle*, that he had *scyugled* along the front, where the Johnnies *scyugled* a bullet through his clothes; . . . that after he had *scyugled* his dinner he proposed to *scyugle* a nap — and closed by asking how I *scyugled*".[7]

While "scyugled" met well deserved oblivion, other words of Civil War origin which still to some minor degree are used today include "gunboat" (a clumsy looking shoe), underground (derived from the abolitionists' underground railroads), goober peas (peanuts), shoddy, sideburns (derived from General Burnside's hirsute adornments), "pup-tents", "hooker" (a female of uncertain virtue), ironclad (as an ironclad agreement), and bushwhacker.

Despite Victorian morality, the soldier of the Civil War was addicted to profanity. "It is wonderful how profane an army is. Officers who are members of the church, officers who once would not even play a game of cards, have learned to rip out oaths when the drill goes badly, or when the discipline 'gets out of kilter'. You perhaps remember that Corporal Trim's comrades 'swore terribly in Flanders'. The habit results partly from ennui and vacuity of mind. 'He knew not what to say, and so he swore', is Byron's explanation. Furthermore, we are all irritable through hardship, and passionate through habits of domination coupled with imperfect obedience."[8]

In general, the soldier of the Civil War was of a religious bent, but on occasion he found that those sent to guide and comfort him in these matters were no better than they should be, as is illustrated by the following: ". . . In easy range of the rebel guns [near Fredericksburg], we were mustered for pay. At four o'clock P.M. it was proposed by a congress of chaplains, to hold divine service in the brigade, preparatory to the general slaughter anticipated during the next forty-eight hours. Everything was quiet over the river, and not a sign betrayed to the innocent twelve hundred dollar shepherds, the gathering storm, as they collected in the center of a hollow square, and fervently pleaded the cause of the Lord and the country. They were eloquent in their appeals to our patriotism, and pictured in glowing colors the halo of glory that would enfold the martyred dead, and the armfuls of shoulder straps that would find resting places upon the blue coats of the surviving heroes. Counseling all to stand firm, to shrink not from the terrible ordeal through which we were called to pass, to be brave and heroic, and God being our shield we would have nothing to fear, – when came a slight puff of smoke, followed by another, and yet another, in quick succession,

7. *Ibid.*, p. 694.
8. John W. De Forest, *A Volunteer's Adventures*, New Haven, 1946, p. 42.

30. WINSLOW HOMER, *Playing Old Soldier*

A surgeon of a New-York regiment in Gen. Davidson's brigade was much puzzled during the Winter of 1861, to account for so many of the men having coated tongues. It was almost a distemper in the regiment. After much diligent inquiry he discovered that among the privates was a druggist who furnished for a trifle his comrades with a white mixture, which they applied to their tongues whenever desirous of getting off from duty. The discovery was not made, however, until after nearly the whole regiment had deceived him at one time and another.

U. S. Army and Navy Journal, Vol. I, 1863–64, p. 314.

just across the river, and then a rushing sound like trains of cars and terrific explosions all around us of 'whole blacksmith shops.' The explosion of shells, the neighing of horses, and the sharp commands were almost drowned by the shouts and laughter of the men, as the brave chaplains, hatless and bookless, with coat-tails streaming in the wind, went madly to the rear over stone-walls, through hedges and ditches, followed by, 'Come back and earn your twelve hundred dollars! Stand firm! Be brave and heroic and put your trust in the Lord!' The scare was soon over, but no persuasions could induce the chaplains to come back and speak in meeting, so it was never known what the Lord had done for them."[9]

In general, however, soldiers found Sabbath in camp a considerable ordeal. "The idleness of the Sabbath was a great evil, as there was nothing to read, and card-playing and cock-fighting were the chief amusements. This was also our wash-day and the ration of soap issued for six men was only enough to wash one shirt; hence this was given by lot to one of the mess, and the others were content with the virtue of water alone. While our regiment was often commended for its ability in building fortifications, no one ventured to compliment its cleanliness."[10]

Eagerly anticipated was the arrival of the paymaster who put in his appearance at uncertain, widely spaced, and irregular intervals. Then after the command was mustered, the men would be paid off by companies. Some of the family men sent part of their pay home to help support their wives and children, but many, in soldier fashion, would go through the accumulation of several months in a few hours, aided by the sutler, and the fortunes of games of chance.

The amateur soldier of the Civil War was slow and reluctant to relinquish his personal independence to the impersonal and inflexible way of life set up by Army regulations. "The recruit in his baggy contract suit, practicing 'eyes right,' is an object of both pity and ridicule. He has lost his identity, and all his claims to equality with even a fife-major are ignored. He finds it harder to hold his temper than to hold his little fingers on the seams of his trousers; hence, the first day's drill usually ends with solemn promises to 'lick seven or eight corporals and a lieutenant, when the war is over' – and a night in the guard tent for calling the drill-sergeant offensively arbitrary, and needlessly particular in rehearsing such d – d nonsensical gyrations.

"A 'private' is anything but *private*. There is nothing in or about him that is respected as exclusive. The day that he is enlisted sees his whole person exposed to the critical eye of the surgeon – his lungs sounded, bowels manipulated, limbs bent, joints cracked, teeth examined, eyes tested, while he undergoes the closest scrutiny, in search of cutaneous eruptions and varicose veins.

"After a few short months the lice claim close acquaintance, and the wood-ticks explore the second and third cuticle.

"In camp, his tent is ransacked. His knapsack opened every Sunday morning to the view of some inspector. His gun, equipments, and all there is on or about

9. A. R. Small, *The 16th Maine Regiment in the War of the Rebellion*, Portland, 1886, pp. 101f.
10. William G. Stevenson, *Thirteen Months in the Rebel Army*, New York, 1862, p. 43.

this private, is made conspicuously public. Although the United States Army Regulations guarantee him the exclusive privilege of keeping his opinion of officers and measures as his private property, he is tortured into expression, and then is published throughout the army as 'prejudicial to good order and military discipline,' and he gets into the guard house.

"There was no aristocracy among the privates. They were thoroughly democratic."[11] But once adjusted to the loss of personal freedom to make decisions, he became a fine soldier.

11. Small, *op. cit.*, pp. 20f.

31. CONRAD WISE CHAPMAN, *Third Kentucky Confederate Infantry at Mess before Corinth, Mississippi, May 11, 1862*

Having had nothing to eat since early morning, and having ridden eighteen miles, and stood in the ranks several hours, my appetite was keen, and I gladly accepted Giraud Wright's invitation to "dine" with him. My host provided the "dinner" by dipping a tin cup into a black camp kettle and procuring one iron spoon. He then invited me to a seat on a rock beside him and we took turns at the soup with the spoon, each also having a piece of hard-tack for his separate use. Alas! my dinner, so eagerly expected, was soon ended, for one or two spoonfuls of the greasy stuff that came out of the camp kettle completely turned my stomach, and I told my friend and host I was not hungry and would not take any more. Inwardly, I said, "Well, I *may* get used to standing up and being shot at, but this kind of food will kill me in a week!"

Randolph H. McKim, *A Soldier's Recollections*, New York, 1911, pp. 27f.

33. WILLIAM McILVAINE, JR., *Battalion Drill on the Pamunkey River*

I commensed writing yesterday, but was obliged to stop to attend drill, a very common incident in soldier life. The first thing in the morning is drill, then drill, then drill again. Then drill, drill, a little more drill . . . . Between drills, we drill, and sometimes stop to eat a little, and have a roll-call.

O. O. Norton, *Army Letters of O. O. Norton, 83rd Penn. Infantry*, Chicago, 1903, pp. 28f.

35. JAMES WALKER, *The 12th New York State Militia on Parade*

The summer weeks wore on. By and by the effect of discipline became apparent. The candidates for glory, having had their rotund garments skilfully tailored, and their faces bronzed by sunshine and storm, began to look like soldiers. The companies march like squads of automatons. The buglers wind their horns more musically, and every call is obeyed promptly and without question. The drills and parades are splendid sights, crowding these fields and fences with spectators.

George S. Fobes, *Leaves From a Trooper's Diary*, Philadelphia, 1869, p. 13.

36. JOHN J. PORTER, *Presentation of the Charger "Coquette" to Colonel Mosby by the Men of His Command, December, 1864*

Near Bloomfield, the train wreckers met the four-man detail with the captured money. In line they waited until it could be counted and they could be given their proportionate shares – $173,000 divided into eighty-four parts, affording each about $2,100. Mosby would have none of it. Seeing that their insistence would not sway him, his men made up a purse and bought him "Croquette" [sic. "Coquette"], a thoroughbred he had spied in a pasture at Oatland, later his favorite horse.

Virgil Carrington Jones, *Ranger Mosby*, Chapel Hill, 1944, p. 219.

37. WINSLOW HOMER, *Home Sweet Home*

Christmas came warm and serene, a surprise even to the citizens of that latitude. Many private boxes reached the camp in season, and these, with a special issue of fresh beef and vegetables, made the occasion an enjoyable one. The night was clear and the moon at its full. It was no hour for strife or bitterness. Where but a few days before the hot muzzles of a hundred and more cannon on each side had hurled death across the narrow valley, now stood various military bands playing the old time tunes of the Union to the listening thousands of soldiers. As the night wore along, the musical selections on both sides shaded off to "The Girl I Left Behind Me," and finally as if by a common impulse, the strains of "Home, Sweet Home" broke out right, left and centre from friend and foe, till the air was tremulous with melody.

Sheldon B. Thorpe, *History of the 15th Connecticut Volunteers*, New Haven, 1893, p. 41.

40. WINSLOW HOMER, *In Front of Yorktown*

41. JAMES F. QUEEN, *The Night in the Apple Orchard*

Three days and nights of solid sleep! It was better than kingdoms and the glory thereof. Except when I was on duty, or eating, I did little but lie folded in slumber. The hard ground was miraculously softened, and fitted my weary limbs like down. No one can imagine the luxury of rest to the utterly weary; it is like the first draught of water to one who has pined with thirst; it must be proven to be comprehended.

John W. De Forest, *A Volunteer's Adventures*, New Haven, 1946, p. 99.

Passing the Time.

ONE NEVER HEARS about boredom in the face of the enemy. However, during the long intervals unbroken by skirmishing and marching, time hung heavy on officers and enlisted men's hands alike. To pass the hours after the daily routine of camp life much ingenuity was called into play. The one thing uncharacteristic of the American soldier in the Civil War was idleness, especially in the Union armies. There was a compulsion to keep busy at something; "bunk fatigue" is a twentieth century development. In static situations the officers could put on elaborate balls or minstrel shows, but the enlisted men were pretty much left to their own devices. There was no U. S. O. With so many skilled men eager to keep themselves busy, whenever an opportunity came such as the celebration of a holiday, soldiers went to work with great gusto to fabricate elaborate decorations for their camps. "On the day preceding Christmas . . . we decorated the camp . . . with hundreds of cedar and fir trees; every street was adorned with them . . . including the flag pole."[12]

Cards, especially cribbage and euchre, were a stand-by. The men worked off their animal spirits in horse play – tossing some unfortunate comrade in a blanket or drawing blood in a snowball mock battle; in tests of strength, foot races, wrestling, boxing, leapfrog, broad jumping, free-for-all scuffles; and in practical jokes of every description. On occasion more exotic spectator sports were followed, such as cockfights or cockroach races. Cricket, football and baseball were especially popular group sports.

Music was a great favorite, usually choral, sometimes with the accompaniment of a banjo, a violin or a bone player. Comic songs and Negro melodies were most frequently sung. Occasionally there were band concerts. Francis H. Buffum thus describes a spontaneous concert which occurred in the fall of 1864 in the Shenandoah Valley: ". . . from around a conspicuous fire on a hillside, there came the clear notes of a favorite soloist. From every regiment in the vicinity the song was reinforced by the leading vocalists. Like a contagion the melody spread; and, at every campfire gathering strength . . . till the entire army-corps was drawn into the chorus."[13]

Officers and men found that liquor was one of the blessings of the soldier's life – one which the sutlers, when permitted, were only too happy to encourage. And, as in every war, the companionship of the opposite sex, if only of brief duration, was sought and found by the boys and men in uniform, many of whom had never been more than a few miles from home before.

Whittling was a popular civilian pastime, and was, of course, carried on by the soldiers. Many were the briarwood pipes carved by hand with a penknife from the roots dug out of the ground. Soldiers and sailors alike also made objects out of bone – crosses, earrings, tie-pulls, and so forth.

---

12. Fred C. Floyd, *History of the Fortieth (Mozart) Regiment*, Boston, 1909, p. 112.
13. Francis H. Buffum, *History of 14th New Hampshire Volunteers*, Boston, 1882, p. 312.

43. CONRAD WISE CHAPMAN, *Playing Cards in Camp near Corinth, Mississippi*

Some of the more intellectually inclined regiments, during winter quarters, organized courses and lectures on a variety of subjects: languages, literature, philosophy and history. Reading anything that could be obtained was perhaps the most common manner of passing the time. One bored soldier was indeed so desperate that, having nothing else to read and finding his camp trunk lined with old newspapers, he dumped out its contents, held it up to the light and, turning it as he read, avidly scanned top, bottom and sides. This is borne out by John D. Billings, the author of *Hardtack and Coffee:* "... There was no novel so dull, trashy, or sensational as not to find someone so bored with nothing to do that he would wade through it. I, certainly, never read so many such before or since. The mind was hungry for something, and took husks when it could get nothing better."[14]

The soldiers were particularly eager to read the newspapers. "Whether in swamp, morass, or on a mountain-top, the men ... yearned to know what was going on at home. They wanted to know what the people thought of them, how they were describing the situation of the armies, what they told of their battles...."[15]

But in spite of every such expedient, time hung heavy on the hands of the volunteer during the long months of inactivity when the armies were in winter quarters. Boredom, and too much opportunity to indulge in self-pity was conducive to a severe loss in morale especially among those who were introverted and thus possessed less resilience of spirit.

14. Billings, *op. cit.*, p. 65.
15. Francis T. Miller, *Photographic History of The Civil War*, New York, 1911, Vol. VIII, p. 33.

44. ALFRED R. WAUD, *A Snowball Battle near Dalton, Georgia, March 22, 1864*

The Seventeenth New York made a large snow fort near their parade-ground, and in the afternoon one-half of the regiment was ordered to defend it against the other half. A lively snow-ball fight then took place. The fort was taken, recaptured, and retaken again several times, and black eyes and bloody noses witnessed the sanguinary nature of the conflict. The battle was fought under the regimental officers, and the movements were directed by the notes of the bugle. The rule of battle was, that any man who was too hard pressed could lie down, when he must not be struck; but he was counted as a dead man, and the "hospital cadets," as the band was called, would come up with stretchers and ambulance and carry him to the rear. Half a dozen soldiers surprised a captain near the parapet, and attempted to take him prisoner. A party of his men, seeing the movement, also took hold of the unlucky officer to prevent his being carried off, and it was for several minutes doubtful if he would survive the pull. Finally, being a strong man, he succeeded in keeping his limbs whole, and his party pulled him away from the enemy.

John L. Parker, *History of the Twenty-Second Massachusetts Infantry*, Boston, 1887, p. 63.

Opposite: 47. EDWIN FORBES, *The Arrival of Newspapers in Camp*

But then we have remedial influences even in camp, and we hail them with no little delight. Daily the news-boys make their appearance, calling out: "Washington Chronicle and New York papers!" They enjoy an extensive patronage. With these sheets many moments are pleasantly spent, as their columns are eagerly perused.

Willard Glazier, *Three Years in the Federal Cavalry*, New York, 1870, p. 32.

46. WINSLOW HOMER, *The Briarwood Pipe*

Now the pipes, of course. Pass the Killy-kanick; or Billy Bow-legs, is it? How the smoke circles around the pole, filling the top of the old Sibley tent. Here is a comrade writing a letter home; another reading a paper, smoking the while; another is doing a bit of mending; and others are having a game – Old Sledge, may be – with the same old greasy cards that have done duty for so many months. Old Comrade, tell me, is not this real comfort?

Samuel H. Putnam, *The Story of Company A, Twenty-Fifth Regiment, Mass. Volunteers*, Worcester, 1886, p. 221.

47

48. EDWIN FORBES, *Ball of the 2nd Corps on Washington's Birthday, 1864, in Camp near Brandy Station, Virginia*

In the 12th Regiment they had some large tents put together and floored, which served as a dancing hall . . . . The ladies (wives of the officers) danced with much vigor until a late hour . . . . I fear that the presence of the wives in camp had a bad influence on their husbands' martial spirit . . . .

T. L. Livermore, *Days and Events*, Boston, 1920, pp. 319; 322.

49. SANFORD ROBINSON GIFFORD, *Preaching to the Troops*

Washington is all one stirring drama; but the "thing to see," among the daily sights, is the evening parade and vespers of the Rhode Island Regiment. A lawn of green meadow, lying in the lap of a curved ridge, beyond the grove, forms the parade; and this as the spectator looks down upon it from the terrace above, is the foreground of a landscape in itself absolutely delicious. But the regiment, with its Kossuth hats and glittering arms, and with the quiet tone of its uniforms, completes the picture with wonderful effect. The poetic part of it is prayer. The grounding of arms, the sudden stillness of the drums, the stepping forward of the Chaplain, and the distinct and well-chosen words of the invocation and blessing, left scarce a dry eye among the spectators; and how salutary and elevating must be such influences to the soldiers themselves, needs but little skill for the divining. I can scarcely imagine a righteous battle better prepared for, than by the closing hymn that was sung after the prayer, accompanied with the music of the military band. The voices of the men swelled up like the trained tumult of an advancing host, through an atmosphere that was all aglow with the red and gold of a magnificent sunset, and the smoke of the camp fires among the trees seemed to pause and tremble with the reverberation . . . .

Augustus Woodbury, *A Narrative of the Campaign of the First Rhode Island Regiment*, Providence, 1862, pp. 38f.

Coffee, Salt Horse, and Hardtack.

AS MIGHT BE EXPECTED, food was of unceasing importance to the soldier. In some cases, of course, the individual soldier "never had it so good"; but under field conditions, both in the armies of the North and of the South, hardships, which it is difficult for us living one hundred years later to understand or appreciate, were common. The staples of the army ration were made up largely of salt or fresh beef, flour or bread, which usually came in the form of hardtack or crackers, and coffee.

50. Unidentified, *The Commissary Department of the 6th Massachusetts*

What was hardtack? It was a plain flour-and-water biscuit . . . . Although these biscuits were furnished to organizations by weight, they were dealt out to the men by number, nine constituting a ration . . . While hardtack was nutritious, yet a hungry man could eat his ten in a short time and still be hungry. When they were poor and fit objects for the soldiers' wrath, it was due to one of three conditions: First, they may have been so hard that they could not be bitten; it then required a very strong blow of the fist to break them. The cause of this hardness it would be difficult for one not an expert to determine. This variety certainly well deserved their name. They could not be *soaked* soft, but after a time took on the elasticity of gutta-percha.

The second condition was when they were mouldy or wet, as sometimes happened, and should not have been given to the soldiers. I think this condition was often due to their having been boxed up too soon after baking. It certainly was frequently due to exposure to the weather. It was no uncommon sight to see thousands of boxes of hard bread piled up at some railway station or other place used as a base of supplies, where they were only imperfectly sheltered from the weather, and too often not sheltered at all.

The third condition was when from storage they had become infested with maggots and weevils. These weevils were, in my experience, more abundant than the maggots. They were a little, slim, brown bug an eighth of an inch in length, and were great *bores* on a small scale, having the ability to completely riddle the hardtack. I believe they never interfered with the hardest variety.

John D. Billings, *Hardtack and Coffee*, Boston, 1887, pp. 113f.

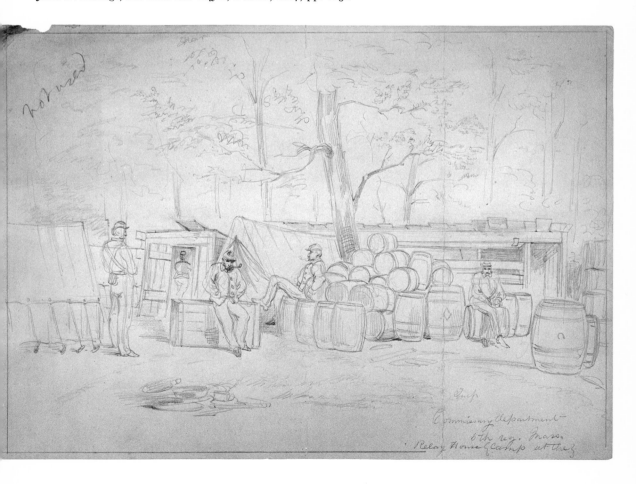

Sometimes there were, in addition, pork and bacon, and sugar and salt. Almost never was there enough. "We are getting our regular rations now, boiled beef and pones of wheaten bread. You may also by good management continue to purchase extras at a neighbouring farmhouse, but provisions are very scarce and it is not often the people have anything to sell."[16]

The preparation of food in settled situations was oftentimes done in company messes by soldiers assigned as cooks. However, in most instances in the field, the preparation of food, such as it was, was an individual chore. So little attention was paid to cleanliness that it is a wonder the armies on both sides did not exterminate themselves without recourse to ammunition. Every soldier on the march had a bag containing his rations slung over his shoulder. This was called a haversack – "an odorous haversack, which often stinks with its mixture of bacon, pork, salt-junk, sugar, coffee, tea, desiccated vegetables, rice, bits of yesterdays' dinners, and old scraps husbanded with miserly care against a day of want sure to come. Oh, the perfume of that haversack!"[17] In addition, each soldier and officer also carried with him a tin cup, a tin plate and a knife and fork. With these in hand, he would prepare such food as was available over a camp fire.

Of all the staples of army diet, hardtack was perhaps the most common, and certainly has been the most mentioned in contemporary soldier accounts. One Union soldier thus describes his calculation for taking rations for a three day march as follows: "four hard-tack for breakfast (with coffee), six hard-tack for dinner (with salt horse), four hard-tack for supper (with coffee again) – forty-two hard-tack, all told, for three days. . . ."[18] Green and inexperienced soldiers found hardtack hard to take, but veterans, while never developing a fondness for it, accepted the inevitable as part of life and made merry over its shortcomings: "We thank thee, Oh Quartermaster Brown, for the bountiful supply of hard-tack thou hast seen fit to bestow upon us, but for God's sake, sprinkle in a little soft bread with it, or there won't be a tooth left in the Twenty-fifth Regiment."[19]

A more varied diet was obtained when the soldiers were permitted to forage on the enemies' territory. Then they could live on such delicacies as roast pig, turkey, geese, chickens and mutton, and such luxuries as hoecakes, peanuts and sweet potatoes. Some soldiers had an instinctive ability to forage: "These fellows would make a bee-line for anything in the way of eatables, from any bivouac, in the darkest night that ever 'blew.' People in the South had a way of burying sweet potatoes in the ground for winter use. These chaps would go direct to these places in the dark, as though they had buried the potatoes there themselves. So with water. I have seen a fellow start as soon as we had come to a halt, take a tin cup and a few

16. John Dooley, *John Dooley – Confederate Soldier, His War Journal*, ed. Joseph T. Durkin, Washington, 1945, p. 56.

17. Small, *op. cit.*, p. 20.

18. Samuel H. Putnam, *The Story of Company A, 25th Regiment Mass. Volunteers*, Worcester, 1886, p. 247.

19. *Ibid.*, p. 55.

canteens, and strike right out into the blackest night, and in twenty or thirty minutes return with plenty of water. He took no thought about it, made no inquiry, but went straight for it, and always was successful. I did not understand it – I do not now; it was, and is to-day to me a mystery. These men were invaluable to a company – they might be called company bummers."[20]

The most accomplished foragers were, of course, the cavalry, since they had a means available for getting much further afield than the infantry or other arms. Occasionally the process of foraging could have its excitement. In one instance some dozen Union foragers, returning with their horses loaded with live chickens, turkeys and pigs dangling from their saddles, were suddenly confronted by a body of Rebel cavalry. "They formed in line, fired a volley, and started upon a charge. The galloping of the horses, accompanied by the flapping of wings, the cackling of hens, gobbling of turkeys, the squealing of pigs, stampeded the horses of the enemy, and gave the bummers an easy victory."[21]

20. *Ibid.*, pp. 211f.
21. Coffin, *op. cit.*, pp. 398f.

51. EDWIN FORBES, *Drummer Boy Cooling His Coffee*

52. JASPER GREEN, *The Return of a Foraging Party to Phillipi*

There was no arm of the service that presented such favorable opportunities for foraging as did the cavalry, and none, I may add, which took so great an advantage of its opportunity. In the first place, being the eyes and the ears of the army, and usually going in advance, cavalrymen skimmed the cream off the country when a general movement was making. Then when it was settled down in camp they were the outposts and never let anything in the line of poultry, bee-hives, milk-houses, and apple-jack, not to enumerate other delicacies which outlying farm-houses afforded, escape the most rigid inspection. Again, they were frequently engaged in raids through the country, from the nature of which they were compelled to live in large measure off southern products, seized as they went along; but infantry and artillery must needs confine *their* quests for special rations to the homesteads near the line of march. The cavalry not only could and did search these when they led the advance, but also made requisitions on all houses in sight of the thoroughfares travelled, even when they were two or three miles away, so that, in all probability, they ate a smaller quantity of government rations, man for man, than did any other branch of the land-service; but they did not therefore always fare sumptuously, for now and then the cavalry too were in a strait for rations.

John D. Billings, *Hardtack and Coffee*, Boston, 1887, pp. 241f.

54. WINSLOW HOMER, *The Last Goose at Yorktown*

"Why," said the old fellow, "I had the finest lot ov chickens, turkeys, pigs, an' sheep as ever you seen, but dam' my buttons ef you fellers ain't gone an' tuk everything except this ole muel an' an ole goose. There was two ov them geese, an' they tried one uv 'em; but ef a hull rigimint didn't break their teeth out after tearin' away at that ole goose, well, I don't know what loosin' teeth is. Why, Gin'ral, ef I hadn't brought the muel away they'd a eatin him." . . .

The general looked at him with contempt. "Pray what regiment did all this damage?"

"The 13th Iowy," said the man.

"They weren't my men, thir," said General Smith. "Ith's a damned lie; they never were on your farm. I know my boys too well. If it had been the 13th Iowa they'd have taken everything on the place, and wouldn't have left a goose or a mule or anything else. No, thir, my boys don't do things in that way. If you don't keep your eye on that mule they'll get him away from you before sundown."

David D. Porter, *Incidents and Anecdotes of the Civil War*, New York, 1886, pp. 185f.

55. SANFORD ROBINSON GIFFORD, *The Evening Meal of the 7th Regiment New York near Frederick, Maryland, 1863*

How nicely rails work in for fires – just the right size and so dry! And then the fact is, soldiers are always hungry, and it is part of a soldier's duty to bring in to his squad round the bivouac fire something in the way of rations, and nothing comes amiss that can be eaten or drank, or in any way used for the comfort of the squad. One brought a chunk of salt pork – good; another, onions – good again; another cabbages; another, an old iron kettle. Corporal Jaalam Gates brought a back-load of sweet potatoes. It seems the Corporal had found a lot of potatoes, and no way to "tote" them along. He quickly took off his drawers, tied up the legs, filled them with the coveted potatoes, and brought them on his back to our bivouac amid the shouts of the boys as he made his appearance.

Samuel H. Putnam, *The Story of Company A, Twenty-Fifth Regiment, Mass. Volunteers*, Worcester, 1886, pp. 67f.

56. Unidentified, *"Robbers' Row" — Sutlers' Shacks at Hilton Head*

Each regiment was supplied with one of these traders, who pitched his...tent near camp, and displayed his wares in a manner most enticing to the needs of the soldier. The sutler was of necessity both a dry-goods dealer and a grocer, and kept, besides, such other articles as were likely to be called for in the service. He made his chief reliance, however, a stock of goods that answered the demands of the stomach . . . [especially] canned goods . . . [including] meats, fruits, and vegetables . . .

John D. Billings, *Hardtack and Coffee*, Boston, 1887, pp. 224f.

"Robbers Row"
"Sutlers Row" Hilton Head, S.C.

57. George Cochran Lambdin, *Winter Quarters in Virginia – Army of the Potomac, 1864*

Walnut Hills Mar. 26th/62

My Friend

I am happy to inform you that on the 25th, at 7 o'clock, after a little more than an hours illness, Lucy gave birth to a beautiful daughter.

In the midst of her trouble, she received your last letter, which, at intervals, she read. It is difficult to say which gave her most pleasure, the darling daughter at her side, or the letter in her hand, suffice it to say between both she was very happy. She is very smart, and the child is a little pet creature, weighing eight pounds, with large black eyes, and hair as black as a coal, a very strong voice, important for a good singer. An hour after these were her words, "Were it not for the little thing at my side, I should hardly know any thing had happened," this will give you some idear [sic] of her suffering. She wishes me to say she is glad you have received your boots. She feels anxious that you should have the pistol, but knows not how to send it, What shall we do? We are *both delighted* that you have received your appointment, particularly as it is less dangerous. Edgar says tell my Dear Father I will try to be a good boy . . . Lucy will write as soon as able.

From your Friend
H. A. Parker

P.S. Again Lucy says "Tell him not to worry about your horse one will be provided. She also says, come home as soon as you can."

Letter in private collection, Washington, D. C.

Antidote to Loneliness.

A MAN'S NEED for companionship of the opposite sex was probably the greatest cause of dissatisfaction with the soldier's life. This was especially true, of course, during the long periods of inactivity when thousands of men were confined to winter camps and a monotonous and primitive existence.

The easiest and most practical antidote to dispel somewhat the feeling of loneliness which attacked all men separated from their families was found through correspondence. "Men squatted, *à la Turque*, upon divans of turf or earth, or even muddy logs, about camp-fires under the cold stars . . . and wrote home . . . Clumsy fingers, which hadn't uncorked an ink bottle since the owner's last one was shied out of the schoolhouse window years before, wrestled with exasperating pen, delusive ink, and intractable paper. Crouching in tent or stockade-bunk, in barracks or about the crackling rail fires, our matter-of-fact volunteers whipped their distracted thoughts into letter composition."[22]

But under field conditions, even the simple operation of writing a letter was not always easily accomplished: "I wish you could understand how difficult I find it to write even one letter. . . This half-sheet of foolscap was begged from a brother captain who begged the whole sheet from the adjutant general of our brigade. The ink was loaned me by another officer, and I hope somebody else will give me an envelope. The pen, thank Providence, is mine, and I still possess one postage stamp."[23]

The arrival by adjutant's orderly or courier of a mail-bag full of answering letters from home was eagerly awaited. "These messages are the best reminders we have of our home-life, especially when they are brim-full, as is usually the case, with patriotic sparkling, and with affections purest libations. These letters have a double influence; while they keep the memories of home more or less bright within us, and at times so bright that as we read we can almost see our mothers, wives, and sisters in their tender Christian solicitude for us, they also stimulate us to greater improvements in the epistolary art."[24]

Best of all medicines for the improvement of morale was the arrival in camp of anything wearing petticoats. The sight of a woman was in itself a great boost to morale, even though the lady might be the wife of an officer and the enlisted men could only hope to hear her voice and see her from a distance. Many wives were more than willing to share the discomforts of life in camp, and indeed a good many visited the front during periods of quiet. Here, in general, the Confederates had the advantage, as the front was closer to home. However, in many cases men had to restrain their wives from joining them at the front for a variety of reasons, the

---

22. Buffum, *op. cit.*, pp. 167ff.
23. De Forest, *op. cit.*, p. 169.
24. *Ibid.*, pp. 32ff.

58. EASTMAN JOHNSON, *The Letter Home*

It was long past noon before these repairs were even partially made; and, having got the
bodies of my boys into something like order, the next task was to minister to their minds,
by writing letters to the anxious souls at home; answering questions, reading papers, taking
possession of money and valuables; for the eighth commandment was reduced to a very
fragmentary condition, both by the blacks and whites, who ornamented our hospital with
their presence. Pocket books, purses, miniatures, and watches, were sealed up, labelled, and
handed over to the matron, till such times as the owners thereof were ready to depart home-
ward or campward again. The letters dictated to me, and revised by me, that afternoon,
would have made an excellent chapter for some future history of the war; for, like that which
Thackeray's "Ensign Spooney" wrote his mother just before Waterloo, they were "full of
affection, pluck, and bad spelling," nearly all giving lively accounts of the battle, and ending
with a somewhat sudden plunge from patriotism to provender, desiring "Marm,"
"Mary Ann," or "Aunt Peters," to send along some pies, pickles, sweet stuff, and apples,
"to yourn in haste," Joe, Sam, or Ned, as the case might be.

Louisa M. Alcott, *Hospital Sketches*, Boston, 1863, p. 43.

59. EASTMAN JOHNSON, *News from the Front*

Dec. 25 . . . Applications for furloughs have been so frequent of late, that Sergeant-major
Maxfield sent up his application, based upon Deuteronomy, twentieth chapter, seventh verse:
"And what man is there that hath betrothed a wife, and hath not taken her? Let him go
and return unto his house, lest he die in battle and another man take her." If it is approved,
he says he shall ask for an extension, referring to Deuteronomy twenty-fourth chapter, fifth
verse: "When a man hath taken a new wife, he shall not go out to war, neither shall he be
charged with any business; but he shall be free at home one year, and shall cheer up his wife
which he hath taken." Much to his surprise, he obtained his leave, while the applications
of two officers were disapproved.

A. R. Small, *The Sixteenth Maine Regiment*, Portland, 1886, p. 159.

most usual of which was that they were without funds to maintain them should they arrive. "I detail these hardships to deter you from rushing on here to join me. Please understand that I am totally without money, living from hand to mouth in a wild, beggarly way, and not even able to pay the postage on this letter."[25]

The officers fairly frequently, and the men more rarely, were permitted to go on leave or furlough to visit their homes. These furloughs were eagerly sought after but not often obtained. The lucky recipient, of course, on arriving home, enjoyed his reunion with family and friends and the pleasures of civilian life to the full. Some, however, did not easily re-adjust to the soft life which they had formerly known. "I found it very odd to be once more in a fine house furnished with elegant bedsteads, sofas, pier glasses and other such luxuries. Observe that it was my first night inside of walls in over six months. I could not sleep; the broad mattress and clean sheets were torments; the indoor air was an oppression. I tossed about till near morning, when I dressed in desperation, stole down to the parlor, and there caught a nap on a sofa."[26]

The monotony and tensions of a soldier's life were such that they must occasionally find release. Men out of sheer boredom would take exaggerated chances such as standing up briefly in full view of the enemy in an exposed position and inviting a shot. One of the best safety-valves was laughter. The soldier who could suggest or do anything laughable was considered a great benefactor to his comrades, for by this the boredom of camp life or the tension of fighting was broken. "A good joke, which runs through the command like a bubbling brook along the flowering meadows, is worth more to us than a corps of nurses with cart-loads of medicine."[27]

Yet we find a good many instances recorded of men without any detectable symptoms of organic disease, who lost the will to live and died, as their comrades put it, of nostalgia.

25. *Ibid.*, p. 164.
26. *Ibid.*, p. 43.
27. William Glazier, *Three Years in The Federal Cavalry*, New York, 1870, p. 162.

60. FRANÇOIS FERDINAND D'ORLÉANS, Prince de Joinville, *Ladies at a Picnic
near the Front*

Nor should the delightful society of several of the officers' wives, who after a time joined
the regiment, be omitted among the civilizing agencies that acted on the character and
conduct of the men. Their very presence exerted an influence for good, and cheered the
atmosphere with social sunshine. A woman in camp, like "a babe in a house," is "a well-
spring of pleasure."

John W. Hanson, *Historical Sketch of the Old Sixth Regiment of Massachusetts Volunteers*,
Boston, 1866, pp. 153f.

61. WINSLOW HOMER, *Defiance: Inviting a Shot before Petersburg, Virginia, 1864*

It was almost certain death to show one's head above the works, and yet a sort of dare-devil
fellow, belonging to one of the guns, mounted the works, and catching his red cap from his
head, swung it defiantly at the enemy. Just then a bullet struck him squarely in the fore-
head, and he toppled over, from all appearances, dead. The stretcher-bearers lifted his body
and bore it to the rear, where they left it, with many others, either dead or wounded.

Soon the field surgeon, passing that way, began to examine the bodies, and chanced to
see this one . . . .

Upon close examination he found that the skull was not broken, and proceeded to cut the
ball out. A large musket ball was taken from beneath the skin, and was found to have been
flattened out as thinly as a copper cent.

The man was not dead, only stunned to insensibility, and in time revived. Two weeks
later that fellow was again at his post. After this he often said that the bullet had never
been made which would crack his skull, and as he never was shot again, we will have
to believe him.

Theodore Gerrish and John S. Hutchinson, *The Blue and The Gray*, Bangor, 1884, pp. 220f.

Walking the Straight and Narrow.

THE FIRST READING of the articles of war came as a great surprise to the majority of citizen soldiers of the two amateur armies. Most of these articles ended "shall suffer death, or such other punishment as by a court-martial shall be inflicted." When the officers read the articles of war to the assembled companies, as was required, after intoning "shall suffer death" they often dropped their voices so that the soldiers, even those standing nearest to the reader, could scarcely hear what followed. The death penalty was sandwiched all through the articles of war, and, at the close of the reading, the average recruit felt condemned, remembering nothing but "shall suffer death" and expecting to hear the Captain order out a detail to execute the sentence on the spot. However, the death penalty was actually carried out only, with rare exceptions, upon spies or men who had deserted to the enemy and had been recaptured.

The offenses against military order and discipline were infinite; however, the most common one was drunkenness. The regulations against the use of spirits naturally led to many ruses for obtaining it. At the commencement of the war the troops encamped around Washington had a constant supply of liquor notwithstanding the efforts to keep it from them. There were hardly any lengths to which the men would not go to get liquor. It appears that several hundred barrels of commissary whisky was sent to Acquia Creek. The brigade commissary of one of Burnside's divisions was sent there repeatedly for a supply, but every barrel furnished him would disappear from the cars before reaching its destination. "At length, despairing of obtaining any of the stuff by order, he proceeded personally to Acquia Creek for a supply. He obtained one barrel, and, standing it up in the car, seated himself upon the top, confident that no one could get that away from him. What was his dismay, on springing down on the platform at Falmouth, to find the barrel coming with him, empty. Some ingenious soldiers had bored a hole up through the bottom of the car, when the train had halted at Potomac Creek or Burk's Station, tapped his barrel, and drained it to the dregs."[28]

Some of the punishments then inflicted for infractions of regulations were cruel and degrading according to our present standards. For relatively minor offenses enlisted men were forced to stand on a barrel for a half day, or even a full day at a time. Prisoners were also forced to march through the company areas wearing on their backs large placards labeled with such legends as these: "Coward", "I skulked", "Thief", "Deserter." Drumming out of camp, a picturesque form of punishment, was administered for cowardice and, occasionally, for desertion. When this occurred, the guilty one was stripped of his equipments and uniform and marched through the camp with a guard on either side and four soldiers with fixed bayonets following behind, while a fife and drum corps brought up the rear droning out the Rogue's March. "The barrel shirt punishment is generally inflicted

---

28. *U.S. Army and Navy Journal*, Vol. I, 1863–64, p. 314.

upon such as have been guilty of some petty or shameful misdemeanors and have been sentenced by a court martial to this ignominious and ludicrous mode of expiation. The barrel shirt is simply a flour barrel minus both head and bottom, with two holes made in the staves. The culprit is clothed with this staving garment, thrusts his arms through the holes, gets his chin over the rim, and has to walk up and down a given space under guard for as many hours during the day as are appointed by his sentence. He finds it quite embarrassing and his legs are at a loss how to proceed. I have never seen any one hung up by the thumbs, which punishment, they say, is very frequent in the Yankee army. I have seen, however, what may be thought a novel punishment for an offense by no means unusual. Some of the men being caught in the act of straggling from their regiments were brought back and made to march in a circle, like horses working a threshing machine, at the same time having billets of wood tied to their ankles in order to impede their progress. But this novelty I have seen but once."[29] Men were also required to pace up and down carrying a knapsack loaded with stones or bricks, or to carry a heavy log on their shoulders for long periods. Another punishment was to force a man to mount a sharp edged wooden "horse" and to sit astride the top rail which oftentimes stood ten feet above the ground. Bucking and gagging was common. This punishment forced a man into a squatting position, whereupon a bayonet was placed in the culprit's mouth, a stick beneath his knees, and he was bound in this position with his hands behind his back.

Whereas flogging was dropped as a form of punishment before the Civil War by the Federal Government, it was permitted in the Confederate army: "This evening (March 9, 1863) our Brigade is ordered out to witness a horrible sight. One of the 24th Va. Infantry being tried by court martial for cowardice at the battle of Sharpsburg is condemned to be whipped publicly and then dishonorably dismissed from the service . . . .

"We are all drawn up in line and the poor man is tied to a pole about fifty yards in front of us. His hands are stretched above his head and his shirt stripped to the waist. The executioner being likewise a criminal who is to earn his release from punishment by inflicting this disgrace on his fellow man.

"The word being given, the executioner began his disgusting work, the wretched man wincing and his flesh shrinking neath every blow which one after another were delivered in quick succession until 39 were rec'd. by the culprit. In truth it is a horrid sight, and the executioner was so overcome by his feelings that as soon as his work was done his eyes filled with tears and he wept – wept! This horrible event transpired without the loss of blood to anyone, and the wretched creature (or happy individual, had he truly a craven heart) pockets his dishonorable discharge and leaves for parts unknown."[30] Some of the severe forms of punishment inflicted lasting physical injuries to the men from which some never fully recovered.

---

29. Dooley, *op. cit.*, pp. 73f.

30. *Ibid.*, p. 83.

63. WINSLOW HOMER, *Punishment for Intoxication*

The stringent regulations against the use of ardent spirits leads to many ruses for obtaining
it. When the troops were encamped near Washington at the commencement of the war, they
were found to have liquor constantly, notwithstanding the strenuous efforts made to keep it
from them. After several weeks they were detected smuggling it into camp in their gun
barrels.

U.S. Army and Navy Journal, Vol. I, 1863–64, p. 314.

Human nature being what it is, the degree with which discipline was enforced varied from unit to unit according to the personality of the officers in command. Some were undoubted martinets and overly strict; others were altogether too easygoing. The good officer knew when he had to see an infraction of discipline and when he could have the happy faculty of not seeing too much. Discipline was maintained and much amusement furnished to Company H of the 15th Connecticut by the following incident: "Adjutant Brown looked for all the world that night . . . , as if he had just stepped out of a band box. He read one document after another, and finally one which reduced Orderly-Sergeant . . . Burritt to the ranks. There was an exchange of glances sidewise in Co. H, as if to say 'I told you so.' Then Adjutant Brown drew forth another order from headquarters 15th Connecticut Volunteers which promoted Private Burritt to be Orderly-Sergeant of Co. H in consideration of distinguished services. Burritt was a private for just exactly three minutes."[31]

While the amateur armies did not take readily to the limitations on their personal liberties imposed by army regulations, once they realized the necessity, the problem of discipline was not great in either army. Most of the troublemakers were found not among the volunteers but among the conscripts, the riff-raff of the slum areas of the cities.

31. Sheldon B. Thorpe, *The History of the 15th Connecticut Volunteers*, New Haven, 1893, p. 243.

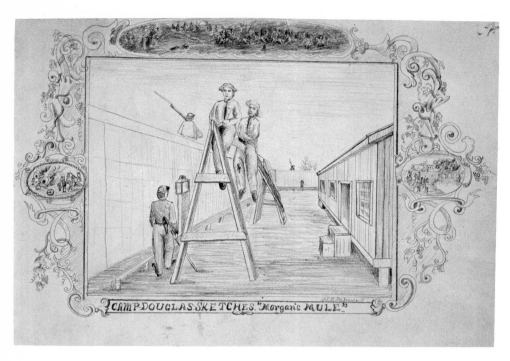

64. SAMUEL BELL PALMER, *Riding Morgan's Mule*

65. JAMES WALKER, *A Drop Too Much*

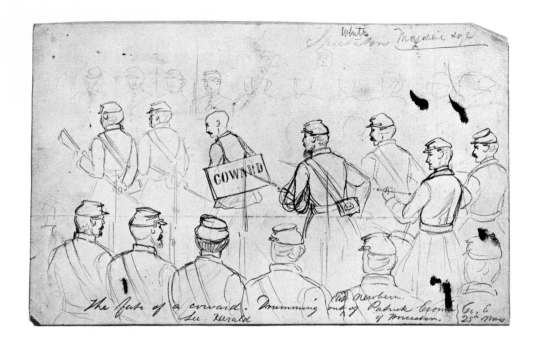

The Fate of a coward. Drumming out of Newbern. Patrick Cron of Worcester. Co. E 25th Mas
See Herald

66. Unidentified, *The Fate of a Coward: Drumming out of Camp at New Bern*

Drumming out of camp was a punishment administered for cowardice. Whenever a man's courage gave out in the face of the enemy, at the earliest opportunity after the battle, he was stripped of his equipments and uniform, marched through the camp with a guard on either side and four soldiers following behind him at "charge bayonets," while a fife and drum corps brought up the rear, droning out the "Rogue's March." He was sure of being hooted and jeered at throughout the whole camp. There were no restraints put upon the language of his recent associates, and their vocabularies were worked up to their full capacity in reviling him. After he had been thoroughly shown off to the entire command, he was marched outside the lines and set free. This whole performance may seem at first thought a very light punishment for so grave an offence, and an easy escape from the service for such men. But it was considered a most disgraceful punishment. No man liked to be called a *coward*, much less to be turned out of the army in that disreputable way, and the facts recorded on his regimental roll side by side with the honorable record of his fellows. He was liable to the death penalty if found in camp afterwards. Many more men deserved this punishment than ever received it. There were very few soldiers put out of the service by this method.

John D. Billings, *Hardtack and Coffee*, Boston, 1887, p. 155f.

67. Unidentified, *Military Execution of James Griffin, alias John Thomas Barnett, a Private of the 11th Pennsylvania Cavalry, for Desertion and Highway Robbery at Portsmouth, Virginia, September 17, 1863*

The next morning I had my first sight of a military execution. I wish it could have been my last. The entire brigade was ordered out to witness it. As the command stood waiting, in three sides of a hollow square, with an open grave in the centre of the fourth side, a deep, solemn, oppressive stillness weighed down upon all hearts. This stillness was broken by a low, soft, plaintive strain of music which came floating on the sultry air across the plain, from beyond the rise of ground in the direction of the camp he had left. It was the sound of a funeral dirge from muffled drums with the subdued notes of an accompanying band. A funeral dirge for a living man! . . . A cart drawn by a pair of white horses bore the con- demned soldier seated on this coffin, accompanied by the kindly priest, while a military

88

escort marched on each side with arms reversed as though the man were already dead. The firing party, the guard and the music completed the gloomy procession. It was nearly half a mile away and it seemed a long, long while in coming.

Low and soft as the breathing of an Æolian harp, mournful and oppressive as a midnight funeral knell, the approaching music rose and fell in swelling and dying cadences, while listening ears ached in sympathy . . . . It was hard to bear.

The fettered deserter was helped from the cart . . . . The priest knelt with him in prayer; then bade him good-bye and retired . . . . the firing party took position in front of him a dozen paces distant as he knelt on his coffin with bandaged eyes and pinioned arms. Twelve men were of the firing party. Eleven of the rifles were loaded with bullets and one with a blank cartridge. No one knew which rifle lacked its bullet, so that every soldier might think it possible that it was his . . . .

The dirge had died away. A stillness, even more painful than its wailing notes, had succeeded. This was broken by the low, clear spoken words of command: "Ready! Aim! Fire!" There was a sharp explosion. The condemned man fell forward on his coffin. The surgeons were quickly at his side. Five bullets had pierced his chest. Yet the pulse still beat and there was a low, moaning respiration. Soldier hands were not steady in aiming at a comrade's heart. The second party came forward; the orders were repeated; eight more bullets entered his chest and head. The deserter was dead!

The entire brigade was marched in column by the open grave . . . . The band struck up a lively air, as always in going from a soldier's grave, and the command returned to the camp again. None who witnessed that sight could ever forget it.

Alfred S. Roe, *The Twenty-Fourth Regiment Massachusetts Volunteers*, Worcester, 1907, pp. 431f.

MILITARY EXECUTION

Of James Griffin, alias John Thomas Barnett, a Private of the 11th Pa. Cavalry, for Desertion and Highway Robbery,
At Portsmouth, Wa, Sept. 17th, 1863.

68. EDWIN FORBES, *Mess Boy Sleeping*

These boys are pretty tough specimens. They each have only one garment of a kind. When that gets dirty, they will take it off and wash it and either wait until it dries, or wear it and let it dry on them . . . . At this season (October), my mess boy sleeps on the bare ground with anything or nothing over him as it happens. He is now only fourteen.

M. W. Tyler, *Recollections of the Civil War*, New York, 1912, pp. 47f.

Hurry up and Wait.

TO THE CITIZEN SOLDIER, used to ordering his time efficiently as a civilian in accord with the principle that "time is money", the wastage in the use of man-power in the army was annoying. Ready enough to put up cheerfully with discomfort when necessitated by military exigencies, he found it hard to stand around doing nothing, especially if it meant going hungry without adequate reason.

Soldiers' diaries repeatedly have accounts of their being ordered to be ready to march the following morning – of breaking camp, of striking their tents, of sending extra equipment off to be stored and passing the night in the open, perhaps in rain, in preparation for the anticipated movement – and then having the orders postponed repeatedly. "... The men became sour, weary and discouraged; there seemed to be no established plan of action; we would go into camp, and have orders to arrange and police our company streets and parade ground, as we would probably remain for weeks. We would all forget our weariness, and work with a will, and then when everything was in 'apple-pie' order, it would be 'strike tents,' and then march half-a-dozen miles, and go through the same experience again. Thus days and weeks passed away."[32]

The movement of large bodies of infantry, artillery, cavalry, and their wagon trains of supplies has always been difficult to plan and more so to execute without a hitch. With few roads, and those often in almost impassable condition due to mud, bottlenecks were frequent, especially when rivers had to be forded, or when an army had to pass through a gap in the mountains. As a result delays were a common occurrence. "There I waited until late in the evening for our Regimental train to come up, *but it didn't come.* I wish some of the wiseacres at home who sit in their cozy offices and write censorial articles about the inefficiency of Generals in failing to follow up their victories and in annihilating this and t'other army could have stood where I did on that memorable day and watched the slow process of this immense train of wagons which was almost steadily passing here all day and at nightfall scarce one half had crossed the little stream. They [the armchair strategists] might then understand what it is to move a large army over rough, muddy, and rocky roads, having but one road for troops, baggage, ordnance, ammunition, Quartermaster's stores and Commissaries."[33]

Even in a battle there was a great deal of waiting. Regiments were often brought up on the double only to be held in reserve within earshot of the battle. At other times a regiment might actually be on the line of battle and still not be committed. Then the soldier might pass a day, exposed to the broiling sun and possibly under enemy artillery fire with no chance to retaliate, waiting as patiently as possible for a change in the situation.

By the time a soldier could call himself a veteran, he was habituated to waiting.

---

32. Theodore Gerrish, *Reminiscences of the Civil War*, Portland, 1882, p. 123.
33. Dooley, *op. cit.*, p. 11.

The trooper assigned to the mounted escort of a general was used to standing to horse for long hours waiting for the general to mount to go on a reconnaissance, or participate in a review. He was accustomed to falling in in marching order with his knapsack loaded, and waiting for the orders to march. He was used to getting ready to do anything in the military calendar and then to wait resignedly – without particular interest whether whatever was scheduled took place or not. When he reached that state of mind he was a veteran.

69. WINSLOW HOMER, *Escort for a General*

Dec. 5 This was a day of annoyance and surprise, through the vacillating policy of some "superior." First came an order saying, "Colonel, you will have your regiment ready to move at a moment's notice." Soon after came an orderly with the welcome intelligence that the command to move was cancelled, and he rode away. Scarcely had the echo of his horse's hoofs ceased, when out of the woods, like a jack-in-the-box, sprang orderly number three who, with the air of a corps commander, placed in the hand of Colonel Farnham an order to hold the regiment in readiness to move at an hour's notice. Heavens! had there been a time since August, 1862, when we were not "in readiness to move"? The three orders were duly entered, quietly folded, and with a piece of red tape around either end laid gently away; and the men continued to put the camp into shape.

A. R. Small, *The Sixteenth Maine Regiment*, Portland, 1886, pp. 157f.

70. CONRAD WISE CHAPMAN, *Camp of the 59th Virginia Infantry, Wise's Brigade*

. . . Nothing happens in camp capable of being joked upon, but some camp wag must have his say. To strangers the jokes may appear ludicrous, as oftentimes they are in fact. But to us who have so often heard them, they have ceased to be funny unless something ridiculous accompanies the jest; as for instance if the one jested upon takes the matter seriously and shews temper or resents it in any manner.

Frequently the citizens have to pass by, and any kind of linen shirt will bring down a cry upon them of "come out of that *biled* (boiled) shirt; we know you're in thar;" . . . . If anyone with long and exquisitely greased and twisted moustache rides by, he is told to take them mice out of his mouth; 'taint no use saying they ain't thar – see their tails a waggin'. Again, some good old farmer with very large hat is urged to "come from under that hat; he can't fool them – see his legs a dangling." Another time a courier dashing by at *fool* speed is suddenly halted by the urgent cries of several breathless wags, and when he draws up to enquire the cause of his detention is provokingly told that his horse's caudal appendage is loose (or unscrewed), and if he is not very careful it will soon *drop out*. This is the most provoking joke of all and may be practiced only upon the uninitiated.

John Dooley, *John Dooley – Confederate Soldier, His War Journal*, ed. Joseph T. Durkin, Washington, 1945, pp. 60f.

71. WINSLOW HOMER, *In Front of Yorktown, 1862*

The heat is tremendous. Flies are thicker than in Egypt, and mosquitoes thicker than in Guilford. But it is astonishing how healthy and contented our bronzed veterans are. They build themselves hovels of rails and boards, bake under them like potatoes in hot ashes, and grumble at nothing but the lack of tobacco. A soldier is not a hero in fighting alone, his patience under hardship, privation and sickness is equally heroic; sometimes I feel disposed to put him on a level with the martyrs.

John W. De Forest, *A Volunteer's Adventures*, New Haven, 1946, p. 151.

94

73. EDWIN FORBES, *A Lull in the Fight – Battle of the Wilderness*

May, 1864, initiated a campaign of corduroy roads, bridges, and earth-works, and until
September there was a smell of new earth about us, suggestive of planting time at home.
We digged, we tramped; we tramped, chopped wood, and digged. It was shovel and shoot,
shoot, shovel, and dig. We dug before reveille, and fought before noon; marched a short
distance, and if it weren't good shooting, piled up the ground. Often the rebels objected;
then we would have a fight, and appropriate their works – if we were the smartest. After
supper, and half a ration of good(?) government whiskey, and further stimulated by a whole-
some respect for somebody in gray in front of us, we turned to the fresh air new earth, and
the morning light showed the herculean labor of a few hours. Zigzag lines and parallels
crossed the ground in every direction. Oftentimes the gray of the morning would find the
gray of the rebellion but a few yards in front of us, looking over works a foot higher than
ours. Sometimes the presence of the enemy would be announced by the whistling through
the fog of a bullet uncomfortably near one's head, or the dull thud of a bullet, as it put out
the life of some mother's boy. But we had no time for mourning. "Portable breast-works on
the tramp" they called us. We alternately shouldered spades and muskets, and saw visions
of Richmond and peace in the future.

A. R. Small, *The Sixteenth Maine Regiment*, Portland, 1886, pp. 175f.

74. ALBERT BIERSTADT, *Attack on a Union Picket Post*

In a day or so after I arrived in Loudoun, we began operations on the outposts of Fairfax.
The weak points were generally selected for attack. Up to that time the pickets had passed a
quiet life in their camps or dozing on the picket posts, but now they were kept under arms
and awake all night by a foe who generally assailed them where he was least expected. At
first they accounted for our attacks on the theory that the farmers and cripples they saw
in the daytime ploughing their fields and taking care of their flocks collected in bands at
night, raided their camps, and dispersed at daybreak. But when they went around at night
searching the homes for these invisible foes, they generally found the farmers in bed, and
when they returned to camp, they often found that we had paid them a visit
in their absence.

John S. Mosby, *Memoirs of Colonel John S. Mosby*, ed. Charles W. Russell,
Bloomington, 1959, p. 151.

On Picket, Scouting and Skirmishing.

GIVEN A CHOICE of evils, picketing was generally considered by the soldiers to be a pleasant detail. For one thing, those on picket duty were relieved of all other camp requirements such as fatigue duty, drills, and parades. Men were assigned to picket duty for a limited period, on the completion of which they were relieved by another detail. Like most other army duties, being on picket tended to become very monotonous, although one never knew when excitement would flare up. General Orders to the contrary, the advanced pickets of both sides were soon on familiar terms with those of the enemy. They exchanged hardtack and pork for corn bread and tobacco. During comparatively quiet periods, and especially in the first years of the war when both armies went into winter quarters, it was an understood arrangement that there should be no firing on the picket line when officers were not around. When officers of either army were present, or when a movement was in progress, this suspension of hostilities did not apply. In most cases the picket posts were near enough for voices raised a little above the volume of ordinary conversation to be heard by the opposing side. It is even on record that on occasion Union and Confederate picket lines exchanged positions, which provided some degree of comfort. One such case can be cited: "One morning when we galloped down to the block house from our reserve, we surprised the Johnnies. They had been a little late in getting breakfast, and their horses had their nosebags on. We were just as much surprised as they were, and we stood six to six. Carbines and revolvers were pointed, but no one fired.

" 'Give us time to put on our bridles and we'll vacate,' said the sergeant of the rebel picket. 'All right; go ahead,' our sergeant replied. The Johnnies bridled their horses, mounted and rode down the mountain. 'We kept a good fire for you-all,' the rebel sergeant remarked as they left. 'And you'll find it burning when you come back tonight,' was the Yankee sergeant's reassuring reply."[34]

However pleasant picket duty may have been in good weather, in inclement weather it was certainly rigorous. For, whatever the weather, the picket must be on his post and attentive to any movement on his front, because he was the eyes of the army disposed at some distance to his rear. "O the interminable length of those 'wee sma' hours,' when Birney and I stood to horse just inside the thickets, cold, weary, half starved, and half asleep, awaiting the tardy dawn! We expected every moment to hear the sound of hostile hoofs. It seemed as if daylight would never come. Nor was it the least part of our misery to see our poor brute companions gnawing the bushes around them in the extremity of their hunger."[35]

Pickets, when an advance of the enemy was in progress, were not expected to maintain their positions at all costs. It was their duty to fire on the approaching

---

34. Stanton P. Allen, *Down in Dixie*, Boston, 1888, pp. 165f.
35. Fobes, *op. cit.*, pp. 71ff.

skirmishers, thus delaying them and warning the larger bodies of troops in reserve, and then to retreat and rejoin the main body. This did not, however, apply in trench warfare, which came as a late development in the war. The pickets before Petersburg and Vicksburg did not retreat, but fired their muskets to give notice of any advance by the enemy and stuck to their posts.

While pickets were assigned to definite locations from which they could not stray, scouts, given the hazardous duty of obtaining information as to the location, strength and intentions of the enemy, roamed between the lines and even behind the lines. The scouts of both armies were picked men, the most alert and daring soldiers that could be found. Sometimes, when penetrating enemy lines, they put on the uniform of their antagonist, and, thus, if captured, were liable to be shot as spies – and many were executed. The armies of both sides owed much to their scouts. Through their quick discernment, self-reliance, and ability to carry out rapidly plans made on the spur of the moment to suit the circumstances as they presented themselves, vital information was afforded the commanding officers at the headquarters.

Maintaining contact with the enemy was also accomplished by skirmishers. Even during periods of comparative inactivity, a patrol or raiding party was occasionally sent out to "feel" the enemy, to drive back opposing pickets on their reserves, or to accomplish a minor mission.

Many of these minor actions were just as bitterly fought as were the titanic struggles at Gettysburg or Chickamauga. Because the number of men involved was few and the results of little significance in the overall conduct of the war, scant attention has been paid to them. Yet, most of the time of the fighting man was consumed in these skirmishes and forays. Through them, fully as much as in the great battles, the soldiers learned the art of war – to take advantage of cover, to conserve ammunition, and to develop skill in personal combat. Here the parade ground soldier became a veteran fighter: "Every hollow in the ground had a soldier in it; every tree had a soldier behind it. We covered ourselves as best we could, which as skirmishers we had a right to do; and obeying the order of our Captain, 'Don't waste your powder, boys,' we fired carefully, and took great pains that we fired lying down, and rolled over on our backs to load."[36]

36. Putnam, *op. cit.*, p. 72.

76. CONRAD WISE CHAPMAN, *Quarter Guard of the Confederate Forces at Diascund Bridge, Virginia, March 10, 1863*

That night I stood picket on the Potomac with a detail of the Third Arkansas Regiment. I remember how sorry I felt for the poor fellows, because they had enlisted for the war, and we for only twelve months. Before nightfall I took in every object and commenced my weary vigils. I had to stand all night. I could hear the rumblings of the Federal artillery and wagons, and hear the low shuffling sound made by troops on the march. The snow came pelting down as large as goose eggs. About midnight the snow ceased to fall, and became quiet. Now and then the snow would fall off the bushes and make a terrible noise. While I was peering through the darkness, my eyes suddenly fell upon the outlines of a man. The more I looked the more I was convinced that it was a Yankee picket. I could see his hat and coat — yes, see his gun. I was sure that it was a Yankee picket. What was I to do? The relief was several hundred yards in the rear. The more I looked the more sure I was. At last a cold sweat broke out all over my body. Turkey bumps rose. I summoned all the nerves and bravery that I could command, and said: "Halt! who goes there?" There being no response, I became resolute. I did not wish to fire and arouse the camp, but I marched right up to it and stuck my bayonet through and through it. It was a stump.

Sam R. Watkins, *"Co. Aytch," Mawry Grays, First Tennessee Regiment*, Jackson, 1952, pp. 59f.

77. WINSLOW HOMER, *Relief of the Outer Picket*

We went on picket in our turn. The line ran along the top of Water Mountain for some distance, and we occasionally exchanged compliments with Mosby's men. The first night we were on picket, a little down to the south of the mountain, I went on duty at nine o'clock. The post was across a creek and near an old stone mill. It rained, sleeted and snowed during the night, and the creek filled up so that the "relief" could not cross over to my post when the time came to change the pickets. As a result I remained on post till daylight. It was one of the longest nights I ever put in during my army service.

Stanton P. Allen, *Down in Dixie, Life in a Cavalry Regiment in the War Days*, Boston, 1888, p. 164.

79. EDWIN FORBES, *Pickets Trading between the Lines*

July 3 – This Sabbath was quiet, only an occasional shot on the skirmish line, and the booming of a sixty-four-pounder away up on the right of the line. The First Corps and the rebel troops in its front suspended hostilities as if by mutual consent. Guns were stacked, and many of the men lay around on the works, talking with the enemy just across the way. Occasionally a Yankee and a rebel would meet between the lines and exchange coffee and tobacco, and offer an *Enquirer* for a *Herald*. The Johnnies were careful to cut out the "news," and the Yanks, equally cautious, passed over a mutilated paper.

A. R. Small, *Sixteenth Maine Regiment*, Portland, 1886, pp. 193f.

◀ 80. WINSLOW HOMER, *Two Federal Scouts*

The sergeant turned his eyes without turning his head and discerned an ambuscade of men in grey or butternut uniforms lying still under the shelter of leaves and long grasses. Rising in his stirrups, he coolly surveyed the road in front of him, and then a country crossroad which fell in from the right. "Nothing here," he said aloud. "We'll ride back and report."

The party went off at a walk until they were some twenty rods away from the ambuscade, when they put spurs to their horses and made a burst for the head of the advancing Eighth New Hampshire. A Rebel whom we captured three hours later said to us, "If that sergeant hadn't been so cool, he would have caught his death. I had a bead drawn on him; . . . ."

John W. De Forest, *A Volunteer's Adventures*, New Haven, 1946, p. 57.

81. JOHN ADAMS ELDER, *The Scouts' Return*

I wish it to be understood that a scout is not a spy who goes in disguise, but a soldier in arms and uniform who reconnoitres either inside or outside an enemy's line. Such a life is full of adventure, excitement, and romance.

John S. Mosby, *Mosby's War Reminiscences and Stuart's Cavalry Campaigns*, New York, 1887, p. 218.

83. WINSLOW HOMER, *The Sharpshooter*

A sentinel was doing duty on the Confederate works, and the Union sharpshooters were attempting to pick him off.

From the top of a large pine tree was seen a puff of smoke, and the sentinel fell dead. The distance was so great that no danger had been apprehended, nor could the report of the rifle be heard. When the Federal line had been driven back, the distance from where the sentinel fell, to the top of the tree, was taken, and proved to be nineteen hundred and sixty yards; or, one mile, two hundred yards.

Theodore Gerrish and John S. Hutchinson, *The Blue and The Gray*, Bangor, 1884, pp. 221f.

84. WINSLOW HOMER, *Feeling the Enemy*

Skirmishing is not nearly so trying as charging or line fighting. In the first place, you generally have cover; in the second, if you are shot at you can also shoot. Now to fire at a person who is firing at you is somehow wonderfully consolatory and sustaining; more than that, it is exciting and produces in you the so-called joy of battle. I was presently shouting with enthusiasm, cheering my men with jokes and laughter, jumping over fallen trees instead of crawling under them, and running about regardless of exposure. Then the close whistle of bullets, or their loud *whack* as they buried themselves in the stumps near me, would drive me temporarily to shelter.

John W. De Forest, *A Volunteer's Adventures*, New Haven, 1946, pp. 111f.

85. ALFRED R. WAUD, *Reconnaissance of the Enemy Position in Front of Fairfax Court House, October 18, 1861*

While some distance away, heavy firing was heard; and word was passed along the line, that a conflict was imminent . . . . It was evident that the main body of the Johnnies were in hiding, as only one or two scouts were in sight. The troops were hurried up, every officer who had a glass anxiously surveyed the situation, and a general plan of attack was discussed.

Francis H. Buffum, *History of the 14th New Hampshire Volunteers*, Boston, 1882, p. 78.

Reconnaissance in force by Genl Gorman before Yorktown.
Rebel Battery only three hundred yards distant behind the woods

86. WINSLOW HOMER, *Reconnaissance in Force by General Gorman before Yorktown, 1862*

Volunteers, Draftees and Replacements.

IN THE FIRST FLUSH of enthusiasm for the War there was no shortage of volunteers who flocked to the colors North and South. Stirred by the purest of patriotic motives on both sides, they had but two intentions: first, to enlist in some company or regiment, and second, to move at once to the immediate front of the enemy where they could fight it out and settle the conflict without delay. This first wave called to the colors the cream of the young men of the South and the North. In the border states recruiting for both Union and Confederate armies went on simultaneously. "When a train carrying a Union company to General William Nelson's camp took on board a company of Confederates on their way to Camp Brone, a 'treaty' was made by the opposing officers according to which the men were placed in separate cars."[37]

Before very long it became necessary to organize war meetings to stir lagging enthusiasm and to encourage enlistment. At these rallies the veterans of the War of 1812 or of the Mexican War were trotted out and worked for all they were worth. Musicians and orators blew and spoke themselves red in the face. The old stand-bys, "Columbia, the Gem of the Ocean," "Battle Cry of Freedom," "Dixie" or "Maryland, My Maryland" were sung by choruses to stimulate the audience further. The patriotic maiden lady who waved a flag or a handkerchief almost constantly and who "would go in a minute if she were a man" was a stock participant. So was the man who was willing to make up one out of fifty – or any other safe number – and enlist when he understood all too well that no such number could be obtained. And there also was usually one wealthy gentleman present who would agree to put his name down on the enlistment roll provided that Mr. A or Mr. B would also put down their names. Nevertheless, despite a certain holding back on the part of some, new regiments were filled up, and the process was somewhat speeded up by the establishment of town, city, state, and federal bounties.

Along with the physically, morally, and mentally sound, it was inevitable, despite the order that none but able-bodied men would be received, that many individuals in unfit physical condition were recruited as well as others who were essentially timid. A. R. Small describes the latter group in these words: "They put on uniforms, hung a sword or bayonet on one side, a pistol on the other; and hung tales of heroism on the other sides, and on various places were pinned artificial records of campaigns. They sang patriotic songs, appeared on parade, and thought how they would figure in history."[38] Some such, of course, got to the theatre of war but most were discharged before they left their native state.

There came a time, however, in both the North and South, when voluntary enlistments could not be counted upon to maintain the army at its proper and in-

---

37. James G. Randall, *Civil War and Reconstruction*, Boston, 1937, p. 278.
38. Small, *op. cit.*, p. 13.

The meeting at the Court House on Saturday night was — a fizzle. It is true the Court House bell — valued at $2,000 — was cracked in calling the assemblage together, the Court Room was filled by a highly respectable audience of ladies and gentlemen, the Madison Brass Band poured forth stirring music, three speeches were delivered, which were frequently applauded, but . . . the object of the meeting — the promotion of volunteering — was almost totally ignored . . . .

Rev. Mr. Barns made a lengthy speech, combining the excellencies of a funeral oration, and a Fourth of July address, in which he urged the young men to volunteer, for the following weighty reasons: "It is sweet to die for one's Country," an astonishing large proportion of those who have gone into the army from this County have had the high privilege of thus dying; there is still room for more . . . .

Capt. Williams, Post Commandant, made the speech of the evening. He has seen service, has a game leg, and made a game speech. He spoke rapidly, his face beaming with enthusiasm, which was communicated to the audience. His speech was full of snap, of fire, of the drum and fife, a speech such as we might expect from a true soldier. Under its cheering influence the cloud was lifted from the sombre faces of the audience. They became satisfied that they were not attending a funeral . . . .

We truly believe that had the meeting been properly organized, and all the speeches been of the character of Captain Williams', many young men in the audience would have emulated the character of their brave fellows in the army . . . .

Madison, Indiana newspaper clipping in a private collection.

creasing strength. It was necessary to raise it by draft. This was greeted with glee by the veterans in the field, for it is only human for a volunteer to look back to his home town and hope that some of his soft-living contemporaries would join and participate in life in the field. Their viewpoint was expressed in these words: " 'There's A——, he was always urging others to go, and declaring that he himself would make one of the next quota.'. . . 'I want to see him out here with a government suit on.'. . . 'Yes, and there's B——, who has lots of money. If he's drafted, he'll send a substitute.' "[39]

The act permitting the drafted man to find and pay for a substitute was a source of much abuse and even of immorality. It brought forth two new and despicable characters, the professional deserter and the substitute broker, a man "who establishes an office and offers to furnish substitutes . . . . He pays bounties and gathers men in gangs for sale, and when the committees of any town are hard pressed to fill up their quotas they send to the substitute broker and buy his wares at exorbitant rates . . . . The result has been that men in all parts of the United States have been compelled to see their sons bought and sold by these infamous brokers."[40]

The payment of extraordinarily high bounties of $700 or more to each enlistee produced another class of opportunists, men who attempted, and too often succeeded, in enlisting to secure the bounty and then deserting at the earliest opportunity and re-enlisting again under another name, receiving an additional bounty. These were the notorious bounty-jumpers. As a class they had no more intention of fighting than they had of committing suicide.

The draft, on the whole, was well received as an obvious necessity by both the South and the North. However, conscription was a blow to Southern morale. A South Carolinian writer said: "The Conscript Act will do away with all the patriotism we have. Whenever men are forced to fight they take no personal interest in it . . . . My private opinion is that our Confederacy is gone up, or will go soon . . . . A more oppressive ban was never enacted in the most uncivilized country or by the worst of despots."[41] In the North it resulted in one serious instance of resistance: the New York draft riot of July 13-16, 1863. The violence of the riot in New York was due principally to the large proportion of unassimilated foreigners in that city, especially the Irish, who feared Negro labor competition.

For a number of years, until the abandonment of the exchange of prisoners of war between the North and South, released prisoners of war would return home on flag-of-truce vessels and rejoin their regiments. Since there were always men on leave, convalescents and stragglers who did not know how to find their units, the Provost Marshal's duty was to collect these strays and send them to distribution camps. One such military depot, as they were officially called, located at Alexan-

39. Billings, *op. cit.*, p. 69.
40. *Congressional Globe*, 38th Congress, 2nd Session, p. 1075.
41. J. W. Reid, *History of the Fourth Regiment of South Carolina Volunteers*, Greenville, 1892, p. 76.

dria, Virginia, and known familiarly as "Camp Misery," "...was a sort of pen, into which all who could limp, all deserters and stragglers, were driven promiscuously."[42] From time to time detachments of these sad individuals were returned under guard to regiments in the field. In this way, with an occasional lot of raw recruits, the regiments were kept more or less up to strength. But as the war wore on, there were many so-called regiments which had started with a thousand men or more and which had shrunk to two or three hundred – the equivalent of only two or three companies.

42. George W. Adams, *Doctors in Blue*, New York, 1952, pp. 189f.

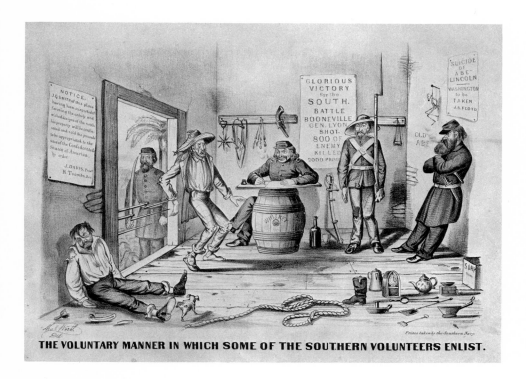

THE VOLUNTARY MANNER IN WHICH SOME OF THE SOUTHERN VOLUNTEERS ENLIST.

89. THOMAS WORTH, *The Voluntary Manner in which Some of the Southern Volunteers Enlist*

A private letter to us from a cavalry officer on duty in Southwestern Tennessee says: —
I have been out with my regiment scouting for three weeks in the region lying between the Tennessee and Mississippi Rivers, northeast of Memphis. For the first few days, we were after a guerrilla company, who were engaged in hunting up, or hunting down, conscripts with dogs. Brutal and horrible as it may seem, it is nevertheless strictly true, and you may rely on it, that at this very hour, hundreds of the people of West Tennessee, Mississippi and Alabama, are being hunted down with bloodhounds. I could not realize it until by the most positive evidence I find it true. We were once almost within hearing of the baying of the hounds, and sent out a scouting party who came very near catching some of the devils. If they had been caught, they would have received short shrift.

U.S. Army and Navy Journal, Vol. I, 1863–64, p. 329.

90. JOHANNES ADAM SIMON OERTEL, *Convalescents from Fortress Monroe Returning to Duty*

The change which has come over our men since their two little battles is very curious. Not so very long since they were like the nine-months' fellows; they nearly all wanted to go home. Now it is difficult to get even a broken-down man to accept his discharge. They rarely grumble about the restraint in which they are kept, they stay contentedly within the narrow limits of the regimental camp; one would think that they were afraid to leave it. This is an odd state of mind for six hundred healthy fellows, some of them wild heretofore in life and reckless in character.

John W. De Forest, *A Volunteer's Adventures*, New Haven, 1946, p. 79.

91. ALFRED R. WAUD, *Exchanged Prisoners of War Rejoining the 31st New York*

In the centre of the arch, surrounded by a wreath of evergreen, were the words, "Welcome Brothers" . . . . One who did not understand the situation would have thought that an insane asylum had been turned loose. We hugged each other, laughed, cried, prayed, rolled over in the dirt, and expressed our joy, each in his own way.

John G. B. Adams, *Reminiscences of the Nineteenth Massachusetts Regiment*, Boston, 1899, p. 180.

92. EDWARD LAMSON HENRY, *Regiment Entraining for the Front*

Before starting, the engine gives two preliminary snorts, which, with a yell from the official of "all aboard," warns the passengers to hold on; for they are closely followed by a tremendous jerk, which sets the cars in motion.

Every passenger is allowed to use his own discretion about breaking his arm, neck, or leg, without interference by the railway officials.

People are continually jumping on and off whilst the train is in motion, and larking from one car to the other. There is no sort of fence or other obstacle to prevent "humans" or cattle from getting on the line . . . . This piece of railroad was in a most dangerous state, and enjoys the reputation of being the very worst of all the bad railroads in the South. It was completely worn out, and could not be repaired. Accidents are of almost daily occurrence, and a nasty one had happened the day before.

After we had proceeded five miles, our engine ran off the track, which caused a stoppage of three hours. All male passengers had to get out to push along the cars.

James Arthur Lyon Fremantle, *The Fremantle Diary*, ed. Walter Lord, Boston, 1954, pp. 50; 100f.

4

Army on the Move.

==

By the Cars.

THE UNITED STATES at the outbreak of the Civil War was, by and large, a country of small towns, villages, and relatively isolated farms, notwithstanding the older cities along the Eastern seaboard and the relatively new, burgeoning metropolises, such as Chicago, Cincinnati, and St. Louis. To many of the volunteers who had never before been more than twenty miles away from their rural homes, it was a novel experience to take the cars to the camp of assembly. For many it was their first ride in a railroad train; to some, no doubt, the opportunity which the war offered of getting away from the humdrum daily routine of chores was almost in itself a sufficient inducement to don a uniform. The perusal of diaries of the period shows that many of our Americans were discerning and critical observers of the new regions through which they passed. Their diaries abound with penetrating observations as to the relative richness of the soil, the abundance, quality and nature of the crops which they observed from the train windows. The soldiers also showed a keen interest in the local peculiarities and customs of the unfamiliar territories through which they were passing. Comparisons, both adverse and favorable, were apparently made with a reasonable degree of detachment.

While the railroad at the time of the Civil War was by no means a new invention, the War provided the first testing grounds on a large scale of its potentialities as a tool in the strategy of war. There is no question that the increased mobility rail communication afforded the field commanders was one of the decisive factors of the War. Not only were the cars used to deploy large bodies of men from one theatre to another rapidly, quietly and secretly, thus enabling a commander to secure a surprise preponderance of strength, but also, the railroad was, of course, used to carry essential commodities close to the front. Through its use to concentrate quickly large quantities of ammunition, food, and other military necessities wherever they were desired, an attack could be staged, executed and sustained with slight if any diminution of power, despite the fact that the main base of supplies might lie at a considerable distance to the rear. So important did the railways become to the successful prosecution of the War that the United States Military Railroad, as a separate entity, was established to operate its own independent system. The ingenuity with which railways were built and the speed with which they were constructed was truly amazing. High, seemingly flimsy, wooden trestle bridges were built which one shudders to see, but which successfully upheld the passage of heavily laden trains. Railroad artillery and armored trains, which many of us are inclined to assume came at a much later date in the development of American military technology, were constructed and successfully employed.

Naturally the value of the railway to the North and to the South occasioned earnest efforts on both sides to destroy the rail communications of the opponent. Many battles were fought to secure control of railroad centers and to prevent the enemy from making use of those facilities.

At the start of the War the country was criss-crossed with many lines of independent railroads, each of which had its own gauge of track. As a result, a long trip in the same railroad car was practically an impossibility, for at each terminal it was almost always necessary to leave one train, cross the city to another depot and board the next independent line.

At that early date the safety devices which we accept as normal were practically non-existent. As a result, accidents were common. And because the rolling stock was built almost exclusively of wood, when a derailment or collision occurred, the injuries were apt to be catastrophic. M. W. Tyler gives a rather prosaic account of one such accident: ". . . At midnight we were loaded on freight cars, and started on our way southward, with most of the men asleep on the floor of the cars. A few miles out . . . our train crashed into a passenger train mostly filled with soldiers returning . . . from hospitals . . . . We rescued out of the wreckage the mangled remains of more than thirty victims of the collision."[1]

Travel by the cars, while undoubtedly exciting, was certainly far from being comfortable. Most of the troops, when close to the front, were packed into baggage or freight cars, which on the previous trip may have carried horses or cattle; sometimes the trains were so crowded that troops rode on the roofs; even the wounded were at times transported from a battleground on flat cars with no cover over their heads or protection from the wind. In the summer, the heat was, of course, terrific, and dust swirled through the cars. In winter, since usually there was no heat, troops suffered severely from the cold and exposure.

---

1. M. W. Tyler, *Recollections of the Civil War*, New York, 1912, p. 34.

93. ALFRED WORDSWORTH THOMPSON, *Confederate Troops Leaving Martinsburg for Harper's Ferry*

Once at the front, troops were no longer transported in passenger coaches but ". . . were unceremoniously hustled into a train of baggage cars. 'Are we cattle, to be used in this way? Do they think because we are so far from home, they can use us like hogs?' The mood and the comment seem ineffably silly to a veteran soldier . . . . A clean box car was a luxury."

Francis H. Buffum, *History of the 14th New Hampshire Volunteers*, Boston, 1882, p. 61.

By River and Ocean.

IT WAS BUT NATURAL, with the large mercantile fleet at the disposal of the Federal Government by purchase or charter, that movement of troops by sea would be widely used. The Confederates, on the other hand, because they possessed few ocean-going vessels and lacked control of the sea lanes, did not possess that advantage although, of course, they did use to a considerable extent the inland waterways, canals, and particularly the tributaries of the Mississippi for the movement of troops.

Some of the flotillas assembled at New York and at Norfolk in connection with large scale expeditions, such as that which sailed to split the Confederacy in two by seizing the control of the Mississippi, were of tremendous size. The motley array of vessels included river boats, coastal schooners hitherto used for lumber and ice, yachts, merchant vessels of all types hastily converted for use as transports, supply ships and war ships, in varying degrees of seaworthiness, including even ferry boats with one gun fore and aft. Into these vessels were crammed the regiments for the attacking expeditionary force together with cavalry and artillery horses, the supplies of food, ammunition and all the varied paraphernalia of war. As many of these vessels were old, leaky, and far from clean, conditions below decks, where the enlisted personnel were largely confined, were far from pleasant. The officers fared somewhat better, as usually they occupied the cabins above decks. Sometimes many days would elapse before a flotilla would actually depart, and frequently the voyages were of such long duration that supplies, even of drinking water, ran low, and the men were put on reduced rations. If it so happened, and it usually did, that the vessels encountered stormy weather, words are inadequate to describe the conditions which prevailed when hundreds of sea-sick landlubbers were confined in airless quarters in the holds.

Some of the vessels used as transports were also so overloaded with troops and cargo as to be dangerously unseaworthy. Indeed, there were several instances of transports foundering in heavy weather with a loss of many lives.

While most voyages ended with the debarkation of the troops at a dock in peaceful confusion, some terminated with an amphibious landing in the face of enemy fire. In such cases the troops were disembarked from the transports into surf boats, which were rowed or towed to the beaches where the troops landed through the surf ready to go into action. Amphibious landings have always been hazardous undertakings. In the unsuccessful attack of General Butler's forces at Cape Hatteras in August of 1861, "The landing of the men from the transports was attempted before daybreak on the morning of the 28th, but owing to the extremely heavy surf and rapid and dangerous currents, which nearly always prevail at this exposed point of the coast, but 345 [out of 860] men in all succeeded in reaching the shore . . . . Many of the boats were swamped or waterlogged . . . ."[2]

2. Matthew J. Graham, *The Ninth Regiment New York Volunteers*, New York, 1900, pp. 79ff.

94. EDWARD MORAN, *The U.S.S.* Wabash *Leaving New York for the Seat of War*

On the morning of January 13th the men crowded in the close, illy ventilated hold, were in woeful plight, the tiers of berths having spaces between the boards of their bottoms, permitting the passage of substances solid or liquid of small size readily, and the occupants of these berths with rare exceptions in the throes of sea sickness, and without ordinary appliances for its relief. The contents of hundreds of disordered stomachs cast in every direction, and dripping through the berths upon the occupants of the berths below, and gathering in foul and filthy and fetid pools, creeping from side to side with every roll of the ship poisoned the close and stifling atmosphere with odors indescribable; in which the men lay half paralyzed by the severity of their illness and created a condition that cannot be fully expressed. Early the next morning, a detail was made from the few who had escaped sea sickness, the men brought to the upper deck in the better air, and the hold thoroughly cleansed. Even amid their discomfort, the gaiety of youth was not wholly overcome, the usual grim jokes were passed on each sufferer as he leaned in misery over the vessel's side, and he in turn joined in the merriment when his tormentors were called to occupy his place.

Joseph T. Woodward, *Historic Record and Complete Biographic Roster, 21st Maine Volunteers,* Augusta, 1907, p. 18.

96. ALFRED R. WAUD, *Amphibious Landing of General Butler's Forces at Cape Hatteras, August, 1861*

Before noon the signal was made for the assaulting column of sailors and marines to land. From thirty-five . . . ships of the fleet boats shoved off, making, with their flags flying as they pulled toward the beach in line abreast, a most spirited scene . . . [After landing] the entire force sprang forward . . . [but was repulsed] with a loss of some three hundred in killed and wounded . . . .

Thomas O. Selfridge, *Memoirs*, New York, 1924, pp. 128ff.

97. E. T. COTTER, *U.S.S.* Sabine *Rescuing Marines from the Foundering*
   Steamer Governor

" . . . On Friday morning, about ten o'clock, the wind began to freshen, and by twelve or one
blew so violently that they were obliged to keep her head directly to the wind, and thereby
leave the squadron, which apparently stood its course. Throughout the afternoon the gale
continued to increase, though the Governor stood it well until about four o'clock." The
vessel was much damaged by sea and wind, and was in danger of going down. "At day-break
preparations were made for sending boats to our relief, although the sea was running high;
and it being exceedingly dangerous for a boat to approach the guards of the steamer, in
consequence the boats laid off, and the men were obliged to jump into the sea, and thence
hauled into the boats. All hands were thus providentially rescued from the wreck, with the
exception, I am pained to say, of one corporal and six privates, who were drowned or killed
by the crush or contact of the vessels . . . ."

Report by Major John G. Reynolds as quoted in Richard S. Collum, *History of the United
States Marine Corps*, Philadelphia, 1890, p. 122.

By Horse and Mule.

NOTWITHSTANDING the use of railroads, canal boats, river steamers and sea-going vessels to transport men and supplies, both armies relied on the horse and his country cousin, the mule, to provide the motive power of the armies in the field. Many thousands of horses were used by the cavalry, many more by the artillery, and mules pulled thousands of wagon loads of food, ammunition and other supplies. The loss in animals by exhaustion from overwork, inadequate care and fodder was huge, and to this must be added the loss in battle.

In the South, the cavalry and artillery attracted the cream of the volunteers entering the army. This no doubt was due in part to a distaste for marching on foot, and to the glamour associated with the dashing appearance of a troop of cavalry or a battery of horse artillery on the march. Nevertheless, the mounted services from the enlisted man's point of view had their drawbacks, for at the end of a long exhausting march, it was necessary first to take care of one's charger before one could feed himself. Not only did he have to be fed, but he had also to be groomed, watered, and the equipment cleaned and maintained. The one real advantage the mounted soldier possessed over the infantryman was that, being mounted, he could range farther in search of food when foraging was permitted. However, it must be remembered that the horse was susceptible to injury, and a sprained tendon or a thrown shoe might force the rider to dismount and march leading his lame horse.

That the mounted soldier was no more comfortable than his fellow-sufferer in the infantry is borne out in many journals: "Night was fast approaching, and the rain – the relentless rain – still fell. It was long after night-fall when the last shelter was up. But our miseries were only intensified by the night. There was nothing to eat that was not soaked and sodden; no lights, no wood that would kindle. There was also but little food and less of other comfort for the horses, who pawed impatiently, often neighing piteously, all through the cold, drenching night, immersed half-way to their knees in water.

"There was nothing to do but squat upon our saddles, shivering and dozing while the water and mud ran in streams under us and over our feet."[3]

Another cause of discomfort to the cavalryman was the need to support from a single leather belt around his waist all the armament which he was required to wear with the exception of his carbine, which was attached to a sling passing over the shoulder. "A large . . . proportion, of our cavalry soldiers especially, are disabled by diseases directly or indirectly traceable to the physical discomforts and fatigues to which they are subjected through imperfections in their accoutrements, which have been patiently accepted as without remedy. The weakest part of the body and the part where pressure can least be borne, is across the small of the

3. George S. Fobes, *Leaves from a Trooper's Diary*, Philadelphia, 1869, pp. 23f.

back and over the abdomen. Yet it is precisely here that the cavalry soldier is compelled to bear the entire weight of his arms, ammunition and accoutrements. If he seeks to remedy the evil by removing the sabre that drags so heavily at his side and hang it on his saddle, his horse lying down may ruin it . . . . The regulation boot is too small, too, to suffer him to adopt the California style of wearing his 'Colt' in its leg, and it will not do to part with the cumbersome cartridge-box to strap it to his saddle, lest in the hurry of dismounting to fight on foot, he leave it behind him. So, according to rule, he is compelled to bear the weight of his entire armor on a single belt which spans his waist, and at which his sabre, flying about with the motion of his horse, trotting or galloping, tugs with successive jerks that threaten to disembowel him. Then the belt must be snug fitting to support the ten or twelve pound-weight of accoutrements, and thus the evils of tight-lacing are added to the other discomforts to which he is subjected. Rupture, hemorrhoids, weak back, and diarrhoea, the diseases current among the cavalry, are in a large degree attributable to this cause."[4]

While most of the cavalry in the service of the Confederate and Union armies was equipped with sabre, carbine, and revolver, there was one spectacularly different regiment in the Union army. This unique regiment, the 6th Pennsylvania Cavalry, which was organized in Philadelphia by Colonel Richard H. Rush, was equipped with a lance from December 1861 until May 1863 when this weapon was discarded for the carbine, it being considered unsuited to the wooded country of Virginia through which the command operated.

While the Union trooper was often not properly equipped, his counterpart in the Confederate cavalry was even less well off.

"Our cavalry in Virginia entered service miserably armed and equipped . . . . The majority were armed with double-barreled shot-guns, and crooked, old-fashioned, condemned sabres, generally without temper, and incapable of receiving or retaining an edge or a point.

"Their saddles and bridles were private property, such as are commonly used in the country, sufficing for ordinary wear, but unfit for the hard riding and exposure of service. As these wore out, the government was at length able to furnish a scant supply, but of a character almost worthless. The leather of the bridles and sword belts could generally be torn like paper. The buckles bent like tin. The saddles invariably and constantly galled the horses' backs. After a short use the trees spread, the nails came out, and no conceivable number of blankets under one of them could prevent its torturing any horse it was put upon.

"The consequence of this, and the emaciated condition of the horses (who have never received any long forage regularly, and last winter were, in addition, reduced to half rations of corn – six pounds) is, that from one-half to two-thirds of every company has at all times been unfit to take the field. Sick and disabled horses dismount many more men than the inevitable human maladies of a camp.

---

4. *U.S. Army and Navy Journal*, Vol. I, 1863–64, p. 229.

99. WINSLOW HOMER, *Rush's Lancers, the 6th Pennsylvania Cavalry, Embarking at Alexandria*

In our service, both regular and volunteer, as at present organized, we have nothing but cavalry; or rather, as that is the genuine term for mounted troops, we should say we have no distinctions of corps in that arm. During the Mexican war, and since 1838, indeed, we had dragoons, at least in name, and at one time a regiment of mounted riflemen. Soon after the war broke out they were all merged into the single cavalry corps. But of *lancers*, we have in the regular service made not a single experiment, and *but* a single one, that of Colonel Rush's regiment, among the volunteers. The fate of that is well known; the steeds are not dust, but "the lances are rust," turned in to the "quartermaster," and unlikely to see the light again. The regiment, losing its old designation, is now the 6th Pennsylvania cavalry. And yet in the European services the lancers have been a favorite corps, and the lance a useful weapon. The philosophy of it in charging *au fond* upon infantry in line or square is evident. The bayonets of the infantry, added to the length of the horses' neck, keep the trooper at such a distance that he cannot use his sabre; while the lancer, with a weapon from eleven to sixteen feet long, overcomes the distance, and impales the footman in spite of his bayonet.

U. S. Army and Navy Journal, Vol. I, 1863–64, p. 185.

98. PETER MORAN, *Federal Cavalry Camp at Dawn*

Three hundred horses were received . . . . A strong wind had been blowing all the day before and at night about two inches of heavy snow fell . . . . The horses stood tied to the picket line, their feet in snow and liquid mud and their backs braced against the storm but ate their rations of oats with keen appetites.

Newel Cheney, *History of the 9th N. Y. Cavalry*, Poland Center, 1901, pp. 80f.

100. WINSLOW HOMER, *The Return of Sheridan's Troopers*

After a cavalry raid, it was often almost impossible to distinguish one uniform from another. As a trooper on Sheridan's Trevillian raid said: "Toward the close [of the raid] men and horses went into bivouac in one common coating and blending of yellow tint. The clouds of impalpable dust rose up as we marched, and on the last day . . . the slowly rising dust which enveloped us rose above the tree-tops and clearly exposed our progress to the enemy, who shelled the column from this indication of our position. . . . The remaining hours [of the raid] were anxious ones. We walked our men in, and were hungry!"

N. D. Preston, *History of the 10th New York Cavalry*, New York, 1892, pp. 209f.

Many a hale man has been confined to camps for weeks, whose horse, otherwise fit for duty, wanted a shoe or the nails to put it on."[5]

The Confederacy was, however, not alone in lacking proper equipment as the following description of the wagon train of General Fremont's army at the beginning of the War clearly shows:

"General Sigel was the first to receive orders to march his division . . . and he was very prompt to obey . . . . Sigel scoured the country and gathered up every thing with wheels. His train was the most motley collection of vehicles it has ever been my lot to witness. There were old wagons that made the journey from Tennessee to Missouri thirty years before, farm wagons and carts of every description, family carriages, spring wagons, stage-coaches, drays, and hay-carts. In fact, everything that could carry a load was taken along. Even pack-saddles were not neglected. Horses, mules, jacks, oxen, and sometimes cows, formed the motive power. To stand by the roadside and witness the passage of General Sigel's train, was equal to a visit to Barnum's Museum, and proved an unfailing source of mirth."[6]

While the horse provided mobility to the artillery and the cavalry, the mule – the good old army mule – was the prime mover of the immense trains of wagons used by the Commissary and Quartermaster Corps. Humorous by its very appearance, the mule was an unfailing source of amusement and of exasperation. For, as is well known, the mule has a mind of its own. With variations the following theme was repeated many times during the course of the War. A chaplain noticed "Three men were up to their middle in the brook, pulling and lifting at some large object, which . . . turned out to be the dead body of a mule . . . . [The men] began to belabor the carcass with clubs and whips; and after some minutes of this process, as if brought to life by this cruel abuse, up springs the deceased mule, and trots off to his tying-post as lively as ever."[7]

Whereas the mule was not often the object of devoted affection on the part of his caretakers, the same does not apply to the horse. The charger of the cavalry service and the individual mounts of the officers were frequently much beloved by their owners. Understandably so, for not only did they carry them fearlessly and safely through many actions but, through their animal instincts and perceptions, frequently avoided catastrophies, the menace of which the rider was unconscious.

5. *U. S. Army and Navy Journal*, Vol. I, 1863–64, p. 197.

6. Thomas W. Knox, *Camp Fire and Cotton-Field; Southern Adventure in Time of War*, New York, 1865, p. 98.

7. Dunn Browne, *Mr. Dunn Browne's Experiences in the Army*, Boston, 1866, pp. 121ff.

102. EDWIN FORBES, *General Kilpatrick's Raid on Richmond*

After making general havoc of railroad stock and Rebel stores, we . . . reached our old camp at midnight, having marched upward of eighty miles in thirty hours.

In consequence of the jaded condition of our horses it was necessary to make frequent halts . . . when a halt was ordered, some men would dismount, and, sinking to the ground through exhaustion, would quickly fall asleep. With the utmost difficulty they were aroused by their comrades when the column advanced. Calling them by their names, though we did it with mouth to ear, and with all our might, made no impression upon them. In many instances we were compelled to take hold of them, roll them over, tumble them about, and pound them, before we could make them realize that the proper time for rest and sleep had not yet come.

Others slept in their saddles, either leaning forward on the pommel of the saddle, or on the roll of coat and blanket, or sitting quite erect, with an occasional bow forward or to the left, like the swaying of a flag on a signal station, or like the careerings of a drunken man. The horse of such a sleeping man will seldom leave his place in the column, though this will sometimes occur, and the man awakes at last to find himself alone with his horse which is grazing along some unknown field or woods . . . . Sometimes a fast-walking horse in one of the rear companies will bear his sleeping lord quickly along, forcing his way through the ranks ahead of him, until the poor fellow is awakened, and finds himself just passing by the colonel and his staff at the head of the column!

William Glazier, *Three Years in the Federal Cavalry*, New York, 1870, pp. 74f.

103

104. EDWIN FORBES, *Heavy Artillery Marching in the Rain in Pursuit of Lee after Gettysburg*

Next morning we were up at sunrise, and, after a hasty breakfast we commenced our march again. We found very soon that taking artillery up a rough mountain road was no joke. The horses balked on the first ascent. Then we cannoneers had to dismount and assist them by rolling at the wheels, one of us carrying a big rock to "scotch" with. At one place we had to unlimber the piece and pull it up by hand. At 12 o'clock we reached the summit of the mountain.

Samuel Bell Palmer, *Memories of the War*, manuscript owned by General and Mrs. John B. Anderson, Washington, pp. 12f.

106. Edwin Forbes, *Supply Wagons and Troops Crossing Pontoon Bridges*

The construction of a ponton [sic] bridge was commenced, but, owing to the swiftness of the current and unavoidable delays, it was not until Wednesday evening that it was sufficiently advanced to permit the passage of troops.

The ponton [sic] bridge, on Wednesday and Thursday, was in continual use, and stood the test of the heaviest burdens. It was thrown across the river about three hundred yards above the piers of the railroad bridge destroyed by the rebels. It was about thirty feet in width, one-third of a mile in length, and consisted of planks placed upon a number of small boats stationed with their bows to the current. A few temporary disarrangements of the planks occurred, but beyond this and the drowning of several horses the passage of the troops was effected in entire safety. The loss of property was confined to the upsetting of one army wagon loaded with grain, the occupant making his escape after a chilling bath.

Daily National Intelligencer, Washington, March 5, 1862.

107. EDWIN FORBES, *Two Negro Camp Followers*

You will have little difficulty in deciding where a regiment begins or ends. It begins with a field officer and ends with a mule. Originally it ended with several army wagons; but now that portion of regimental headquarters baggage which has not gone to the wagon-train is to be found stowed about the mule, that is led along by a contraband. Yes, the head, ears, and feet which you see are the only visible externals of a mule. He is "clothed upon" with the various materials necessary to prepare a "square meal" for the colonel and other head-quarters officers. His trappings would, seemingly, fit out a small family in household goods of a kind. There is a mess-kettle, a fry-pan, mess-pans, tent-poles, a fly (canvas), a valise, a knapsack and haversack, a hamper on each side, a musket, and other matter which goes to make the burden at least twice the size of the animal. Four mules were regarded as having the carrying capacity of one army wagon. At the end of the brigade you will see two or three of these mules burdened with the belongings of brigade headquarters.

John D. Billings, *Hardtack and Coffee*, Boston, 1887, pp. 340f.

By Shanks' Mare.

DESPITE THE FACT that, for almost the first time in modern warfare, the Civil War saw the advent of the railroad as a means of moving troops to the front and from one section of the front to another, nevertheless, when close to the enemy, the soldier was still called upon to use his own two feet almost exclusively. In the literature of the War some of the most moving passages in the memoirs of participants are those devoted to their experiences on the march. The soldier oftentimes was practically a packmule. By actual weight he on occasion carried as much as ten days' rations, which amounted to about 26 pounds, his personal arms, equipments and 60 rounds of ammunition which totaled some 28 pounds – or a total of 54 pounds.[8] Much has been written about the superiority of the Union soldiers' personal equipment and uniforms – but that was not always the case, and not infrequently Union soldiers, as well as Confederate, marched through storms of sleet and snow without overcoats, without shoes, without hats, and many without so much as a flannel blouse or a blanket.[9] The veteran travelled light, discarding all non-essentials until "his entire outfit is reduced to nearly 'the little end of nothing, whittled to a point!' "[10]

Even worse than the snow was the experience of marching long distances through mud. The pictures in the exhibition cannot adequately delineate the qualities of Southern mud, but Charles Coffin made a noble effort when he wrote, "There was thick mud, thin mud, sticky mud, slushy mud, slimy mud, deceptive mud, impassable mud, . . ."[11] Then, too, we must not forget the dust. The movement of thousands of feet throws up such dense and prodigious clouds that to quote another soldier ". . . one who has not witnessed the phenomenon will find it difficult to imagine it in all its vastness and nuisance. The officers dodge from side to side of the road to escape the pulverous suffocation; and the men, bound to their fours, choke desperately along in the midst of it. The faces become grimed out of all human semblance; the eyelashes are loaded, the hair discolored, and uniform turns to the color of the earth. It frequently happens that you cannot see the length of your regiment, and it has occurred to me that I have been unable to see the length of my own company of perhaps twenty files."[12] The same author describes vividly the effect of marching with complete equipment in extremely hot weather: "I have seen the sweat standing on the woolly fibres of their flannel sacks [coats] like dew."[13]

---

8. A. R. Small, *The Sixteenth Maine Regiment*, Portland, 1886, p. 96.

9. *Ibid.*, p. 38.

10. Willard Glazier, *Three Years in the Federal Cavalry*, New York, 1870, p. 170.

11. Charles C. Coffin, *The Boys of '61*, Boston, 1886, p. 52.

12. John W. De Forest, *A Volunteer's Adventures*, New Haven, 1946, p. 96.

13. *Ibid.*, p. 94.

It was a vastly different proposition, psychologically and even physically, to march victoriously in pursuit of a defeated antagonist than to march as a part of a defeated army struggling in desperation to keep ahead of a pursuing enemy and capture. "Could these blackened, bearded, tattered, begrimed veterans who swooped down upon the slop barrels of the cook houses 'like a wolf on the fold,' greedily clutching the contents in their hands and cups and ravenously devouring scraps of 'soft bread' and fresh beef; could these blackened and in many cases wounded men, shoeless, hatless, blanketless, be the army of the Union? Could these officers with dusty and battered equipments, scarcely a badge of rank discernible, weary and footsore, be their commanders? Where was all the pomp and panoply of war? But so it was."[14]

Prodigious feats of marching were accomplished by both Union and Confederate soldiers. One soldier's laconic entry in his diary thus records one of the most killing marches of the War – under date of Friday, June 26, William W. Heath wrote, "I march to Dranes Vill [sic, Dranesville] to day 35 miles in 24 howars [sic]."[15] All soldiers seemed to agree that a forced march is the most terrible physical trial to which the human frame can be subjected. Many a soldier has recorded his feeling that he would rather take a chance for survival in another battle than have to endure another such march. "It was an interesting sight to see a column break up when the order came to halt, whether for rest or other reason. It would melt in a moment, dividing to the right and left, and scattering to the sides of the road, where the men would sit down or lie down, lying back on their knapsacks if they had them, or stretching at full length on the ground. If the latter was wet or muddy, cannoneers sat on their carriages and limber-chests, while infantrymen would perhaps sit astride their muskets, if the halt was a short one. When the halt was expected to continue for some considerable time the troops of a corps or division were massed, that is, brought together in some large open tract of territory, when the muskets would be stacked, the equipments laid off, and each man rush for the 'top rail' of the nearest fence, until not a rail remained. The coffee would soon begin to simmer, the pork to sputter in the flames, and, when the march was resumed, the men would start off refreshed with rest and rations."[16]

But perhaps the worst thing about marching, from the enlisted man's point of view, was the fact that he almost never knew why he was marching – all he knew was that he was ordered to set out on the road and oftentimes would march all day, halt, and then that same night or the following morning would march back almost to the place from which he had originally started. "An order to fall in may come at any moment. Such orders generally arrive at night in the awkwardest moment possible. Then we march like fury for hours; and then nothing comes of it; we

---

14. Sheldon B. Thorpe, *The History of the 15th Connecticut Volunteers*, New Haven, 1893, p. 21.

15. Unpublished manuscript diary, William W. Heath, *Diary of William W. Heath*, Newbury, Vermont, January 1 to December 21, 1863, in the collection of Marius B. Peladeau, Washington, D. C.

16. John D. Billings, *Hardtack and Coffee*, Boston, 1887, p. 348.

108. DAVID GILMOUR BLYTHE, *General Abner Doubleday Watching His Troops Cross the Potomac*

Then, this very crossing of a stream often furnished an interesting scene in the march of the column. A river broad and deep would be spanned by a pontoon bridge, but the common creeks of the South were crossed by fording. Once in a while (in warm weather) the men would take off most of their clothing and carry it with their equipments across on their heads. It was no uncommon experience for them to ford streams waist-deep, even in cool weather. If the bottom was a treacherous one, and the current rapid, a line of cavalry-men was placed across the river just below the column to pick up such men as should lose their footing. Many were the mishaps of such a crossing, and, unless the enemy was at hand, the first thing to be done after reaching shore was to strip and wring out such clothing as needed it. With those who had slipped and fallen this meant *all they had on* and what was in their knapsack besides, but with most it included only trousers, drawers, and socks.

John D. Billings, *Hardtack and Coffee*, Boston, 1887, p. 344.

march back again. Of course, the general understands it all, and perhaps Omniscience does, but nobody else. Well, this is soldiering of course, to do as we are ordered, and ask no explanations."[17]

There was naturally a great deal of grumbling at these inexplicable marches, but it is a tribute to the military qualities of the soldiers of both armies that, grumbling notwithstanding, the marches were made again and again.

---

17. De Forest, *op. cit.*, pp. 166f.

109. WINSLOW HOMER, *Infantry Column on the March*

For the next ten miles it was a fight against nature. Every effort was made to cheer the men onward and beguile them from a sense of their miseries. The staggering drummers were forced to beat the march for the staggering regiments. Some of the field officers dismounted and walked at the head of their commands. At one halt, Lieutenant Colonel Van Petten ran foot races in his big boots with a private, to make the soldiers laugh at the unusual buffoonery. Staff officers rode up and down the line, giving orders to yell and setting the example of uproar. The company officers carried the rifles of tottering men, and hastened from straggler to straggler, cheering, ordering, and threatening, but, I think, never striking; for no one could find it in his heart to maltreat poor fellows who were almost at the last gasp with pain and fatigue. We reeled, crawled, and almost rolled toward Alexandria. As night fell, the pace increased, and the whooping became continuous, and we seemed like a column of maniacs. But in the last two miles, in the pitchy darkness between eight and nine of the evening, a silence of despair descended upon us, and then the regiments melted like frost in sunshine. I could not see who fell out of my company, and I did not care. My whole official sentiment of honor was concentrated, under the flame of intense physical suffering, into the one little idea of getting myself to Alexandria with the colors, no matter who else dropped by the way. The few men remaining in the organization reeled on speechlessly. If they passed a dying artillery horse, they no longer shouted, with savage defiance, "Fresh horses! . . ."

John W. De Forest, *A Volunteer's Adventures*, New Haven, 1946, p. 101.

110. EDWIN FORBES, *Washing Day — Column on the March, May 15, 1864*

111. EDWIN FORBES, *Marching in the Rain after Gettysburg*

112. JOHN DONAGHY, *Troops Marching, New Kent Court House*

It is growing warmer. The column has now got straightened out, and for the last hour has moved forward quite rapidly. The road is evidently clear of all obstructions, but the heat and speed begin to tell on the men. Look at the ground which that brigade has just vacated after its brief halt for rest. It is strewn with blankets, overcoats, dress-coats, pantaloons, shirts — in fact, a little of everything from the outfit of the common soldier. As the Second Corps advanced into the Wilderness on the morning of May 4, 1864, I saw an area of an acre or more almost literally covered with the articles above named, many of them probably extras, but some of them the sole garment of their kind, left by the owners, who felt compelled, from the increasing weight of their load, to lighten it to the extent of parting with the blankets which they would need that very night for shelter. This lightening of the load began before the columns had been on the road an hour. A soldier who had been through the mill would not wait for a general halt to occur before parting with a portion of his load, if it oppressed him; but a recruit would hang to his until he bent over at an angle of 45° from a vertical, with his eyes staring, his lower jaw hanging, and his face dripping with moisture. If you were to follow the column after, say, the first two miles, you would find various articles scattered along at intervals by the roadside, where a soldier quietly stepped out of the ranks, sat down, unslung his knapsack or his blanket-roll, took out what he had decided to throw away, again equipped himself, and, thus relieved, hastened on to overtake the regiment. It did not take an army long to get into light marching order after it was once fairly on the road.

John D. Billings, *Hardtack and Coffee*, Boston, 1887, pp. 342f.

113. JAMES R. HAMILTON, *General Grover's Forces Marching to the Attack near Port Hudson*

At last an unpleasant moment, not unlike that in which you take your seat in a dentist's chair, came to the author of this history. When the colonel said, "Captain, take out your company and relieve Company G," I felt that heavy heart within me which man is almost always conscious of as he deliberately approaches the confines of visible death. With a smile of simulated gayety I turned to my men and shouted, "Fall in!" Five minutes thereafter, the ice of suspense broken, the blood heated with advancing and fighting, that gayety became real.

John W. De Forest, *A Volunteer's Adventures*, New Haven, 1946, p. 111.

114. JAMES WALKER, *Battle of Lookout Mountain*

. . . morning was clean and frosty . . . the guns of Bridges' Battery gave the signal, and the men in blue dashed forward in line of battle by brigades, skirmishers in front, followed by reserves in mass . . . . From the great ridge the enemy poured down redhot flames of death and destruction . . . . It was at least a fifth of a mile from [our stopping place] . . . to the crest bristling with cannon . . . . The regiments in Blue fight their way upward and the 'Johnnies' turn their backs . . . leaving batteries on batteries behind . . . .

J. H. Haynie, *The Nineteenth Illinois*, Chicago, 1912, pp. 258ff.

Heat of Battle.

The Artillery.

SERVICE IN THE ARTILLERY developed a team spirit which was not required for campaigning in the infantry to the same degree. In the artillery every man had his own special duties to perform which were essential if the battery was to be effective. If one man failed to do his job accurately, not only did this adversely affect the fire on the enemy, but he could also imperil the lives of his comrades. Many are the stories of the cannoneer whose job it was to thumb the vent, sticking to his duty and suffering severe burns when the leather thumb-stall which protected his finger was burned to a crisp by the heat of the barrel. If he had relaxed the pressure of his thumb for a moment, a premature explosion could have occurred and killed or maimed the men loading the cannon at the muzzle end. The cannoneers oftentimes gave pet names to the dogs of war and, when a good shot was made, affectionately patted their brazen lips.

Nothing was perhaps more feared than the effect of artillery fire. Yet, as troops became accustomed to it, they developed the callousness which the day to day living in danger usually produces. "These evening fusillades rarely did any damage. So harmless were they considered that President Lincoln and other officials frequently came down to the trenches to be a witness of them. But, harmless as they usually were to our side, they yet often enlisted our warm personal interest. The guns of my own company were several times a mark for their particular attentions by daylight. At such times we would watch the shells closely as they mounted the sky. If they veered to the right or left from a vertical in their ascent, we cared nothing for them as we then knew they would go one side of us. If they rose perpendicularly, and at the same time increased in size, our interest intensified. If they soon began to descend we lost interest, for that told us they would fall short; but if they continued climbing until much nearer the zenith, and we could hear the creaking whistle of the fuse as the shell slowly revolved through the air, *business of a very pressing nature suddenly called us into the bomb-proofs;* and it was not transacted until an explosion was heard, or a heavy jar told us that the bomb had expended its violence in the ground."[1]

Early in the War artillery was rarely placed behind earthworks but fired from a position usually within easy visibility of the enemy. As a result many guns and many horses were lost. As the War developed, however, the artillery, whenever possible, sought the shelter of earthworks which were of a very elaborate nature, especially during sieges. The same protection when afforded to infantry, also served to diminish casualties materially. "For an hour we had the heaviest cannonading we had ever experienced, and yet the Regiment, being behind the earthworks, had only five men wounded, and, singular as it may seem, all these by a single shot. These men were grouped together, and the shot struck right in the midst of them; one man had his foot taken off, another had a leg broken, a third was hit in the head, a fourth had both legs mangled, and the fifth received a slight contusion on his side. The ball could not be found. The men were taken to the hospital and in amputating the leg of one of them . . . the ball was actually discovered in his thigh, and proved to be a three pound shell."[2]

The artillery of the Civil War was almost exclusively muzzle-loading, but there were considerable technical developments in ordnance during the course of the War. Both sides used rifled guns as well as the standard smooth bore cannon. Contact fuses for artillery shells were developed, and time fuses were improved. One interesting curiosity was the revival of rockets which had not been used to any extent since the War of 1812. General McClellan had one battery of rocket guns which was captured by the Confederates and then used against the Union forces. However, this was the only such battery in either army.

---

1. John D. Billings, *Hardtack and Coffee*, Boston, 1887, p. 60.

2. Samuel H. Putnam, *The Story of Company A, Twenty-Fifth Regiment, Massachusetts Volunteers*, Worcester, 1886, pp. 302f.

117. DAVID GILMOUR BLYTHE, *Battle of Gettysburg*

Men cover the ground in fragments, and are buried in detail beneath the iron hail . . . .
Caissons explode, and wheels and boxes strew the ground in every direction. Horses by the
score are blown down by the terrible hurricane, and lie shrieking in agony . . . . [We open fire]
and men go down by scores but others fill the gaps . . . . They go down like jack-straws —
they lie in windrows.

A. R. Small, *The Sixteenth Maine Regiment*, Portland, 1886, pp. 122ff.

115. ALFRED R. WAUD, *Artillery Battery Firing on Advancing Confederate Infantry at White Oak Swamp Bridge*

Nine men, including the gunner, are necessary for the service of a field piece. When, from necessity, the detachment consists of less than nine, the higher members are struck out, and additional duties are imposed upon those remaining. The gunner is at the end of the trail handspike . . . [and] gives all the executive commands in action. He is answerable that all the numbers perform their duties correctly. He communicates the orders which he receives for the kind of ammunition to be fired . . . he sees that each fuze is properly prepared . . . he gives the command LOAD . . . [he sights the gun] . . . and gives the command — FIRE.

Instruction for Field Artillery, Washington, 1861, pp. 107f.

119. ALBERT BIERSTADT, *The Bombardment of Fort Sumter*

I went yesterday evening to Fort Sumter . . . . The Federals use a powerful calcium light at Battery Gregg, with which they illuminate Sumter to such a degree that it is impossible for steamers to go up to the wharf at night, as they used to go; and we had to land in row boats. They were shelling very rapidly, and it became most exciting when we neared the fort, especially when we came into the glare of the calcium light, and they could see us . . . . The bomb-proofs are lofty and spacious, and well ventilated. The last bombardment has not injured them in the slightest degree; indeed, they are, if anything, really stronger than before, from the amount of *debris* knocked down upon them. Major Elliot, the commandant, was kind enough to take me . . . on to the parapet, to show me the effects of the bombard-ment — a courtesy, by the by, which, considering the lively way in which shells were flying about us, was indicative of very genuine politeness. We had not been half a minute in the area when one of the lookouts got his jaw broken with a bit of shell; and we had hardly got back, when another poor fellow was brought out, with two-thirds of his head knocked off. Under the circumstances, we did not stay long; still, I had time enough to take a good look around and see all I wished. The place is undoubtedly very much injured; indeed, it is hardly possible to do the walls any further damage. The sea front is almost entirely knocked into the area, and you can now walk up from the area to the top of the walls that once faced the sea.

U.S. Army and Navy Journal, Vol. I, 1863–64, p. 346.

121. FRANK VIZETELLY, *Attack on Fort Fisher*

A correspondent on Morris Island writes: — "As there is no manual laid down for the three-hundred-pounder Parrott I subjoin that in use. The piece is on its carriage and 'from battery.' Implements, no two in the same place and no one in its proper place. The instructor gives the command 'load her up!' At this command the gunner says, 'some of you fellers bring a shell,' and 'John bring a cartridge.' Some of the 'fellers' take a small handbarrow and

bring a shell. Gunner says, 'Stock in that powder.' 'Now boys, hold on till I get out a fuse.' 'Stick it in.' All hands by hard heaving get the shell to the embrasure. Gunner says, 'Swab her out.' She is swabbed out. 'Now, heave and haul, and in it goes.' It goes in accordingly. 'Now, ram it down.' It is rammed down. 'Now, run her in.' She is run in. 'Screw down the recoil bands.' They are screwed down. Gunner aims. 'Slew her round a little!' 'All right!' 'Where's that primer?' 'Now, git out of the way everybody.' All go to windward, and No. 3 steps round a corner, so as not to be hit if the gun bursts. Gunner says, 'Blaze away!' She blazes away. Remark of the gunner on returning to the gun: 'How are you Sumter?' Repeat.''

U.S. Army and Navy Journal, Vol. 1, 1863–64, p. 231.

122. Unidentified, *The Fight for the Colors*

. . . the Federals shouted out, "Boys we have got old Scott's colors." A gallant son of the Emerald Isle was our color bearer; he had won the position by valor at Murfreesboro, and those who saw him can never forget his looks and words as he whirled his horse around and waving his flag over his head, cried out at the top of his voice, "It's a d— lie, Scott's colors will never go down." Of course that drew upon him the fire of all the Federals near by. All of us were retreating as rapidly as possible, and all of a sudden the point of the color-staff struck a tree and broke, down the flag went to the ground, but in less time than it takes to tell it the old bearer had sprung from his horse and was tying it around his body; four or five Federals rushed up to him, ordering him to surrender, but he vaulted into his saddle and with a scornful look upon his face said, "Now, d—n ye, when you get it ye'll get me," and with bullets whistling around him he galloped off.

Howell Carter, *A Cavalryman's Reminiscences of the Civil War*, New Orleans, n.d., p. 62.

The Cavalry.

THE CAVALRY was one of the three major combat arms. At first the Confederate cavalry was vastly superior to that of the Union, but as the War progressed the trend was reversed. The initial superiority of the Confederates was due, among other factors, to their having a larger quantity of horses suitable for mounts as well as more experienced horsemen. The volunteers of the Union cavalry, in most cases, had never before bestrode a horse, and were totally unfamiliar with weapons, let alone the intricacies of mounted drill and the complicated manoeuvres of a mounted regiment. This applied not only to the troopers, but to most of their officers as well. It is no wonder that untrained horses, green men and inexperienced officers had their hands full in trying to master in a few weeks the techniques which in our regular cavalry required three years for a raw recruit to master. Such sights as that which an officer of the 10th New York Cavalry describes with chagrin and frankness must not have been uncommon: "My company had been mustered into the service only about six weeks before and had received horses less than a month prior to this march . . . .

"[We started out]. Such a rattling, jingling, jerking, scrabbling, cursing, I never before heard. Green horses – some of them had never been ridden – turned round and round, backed against each other, jumped up or stood up like trained circus horses. Some of the boys had a pile in front, on their saddles, and one in the rear, so high and heavy it took two men to saddle one horse and two men to help the fellow into his place . . . . [The general] went like greased lightning . . . . In less than ten minutes Tenth New York Cavalrymen might have been seen on every hill for two miles rearward . . . . Blankets slipped from under saddles and hung by one corner; saddles slid back until they were on the rumps of the horses; others turned and were on the under side of the animals; horses running and kicking; tin pans, mess-kettles, patent sheet-iron camp stoves . . . flying through the air . . . .[I ordered the men to close up] but they couldn't . . . . Their eyes stuck out like maniacs. We went only a few miles, but the boys didn't all get up till noon."[3]

The cavalry fought in a variety of ways. There were cavalry charges in which the sabre alone was used. "The First Michigan struck the rebels on their left flank, about in the middle and actually went clean through them, cutting them in two parts. The sabre was all they used. Many a rebel was knocked over, horse and all, by being struck with the horses of the First, and many more were killed and wounded by the sabre."[4] Again, the weapon used in a charge might be the revolver, but not the carbine, except in the Confederate service where considerable reliance was placed on the double-barrelled shot gun as well as the carbine, often a cut-down infantry musket. It was also quite common for the cavalry to fight dis-

---

3. N. D. Preston, *History of the Tenth Regiment of Cavalry, New York State Volunteers*, New York, 1892, pp. 54ff.
4. Samuel Harris, *Personal Reminiscences of Samuel Harris*, Chicago, 1897, pp. 34ff.

123. EDWIN FORBES, *A Cavalry Charge*

With that he drew his sword, shouted the command, *"Draw Sabre! Charge! Follow me!"* and plunged away down the slope with his little brigade at his heels.

It was gallantly done. The red sunset glanced like blood upon our twelve hundred blades as we swept like an avalanche upon the foe.

The rebels opened upon us with artillery, and stood their ground until we had come to close quarters with their skirmishers. Then their first line gave way, bearing back the second, the whole mass scampering off in confusion up the ridge. Their guns were hastily limbered and drawn off. In fifteen minutes from the start, not an armed foe was in sight. A dozen or so were killed, and over a hundred captured. Our casualties amounted to a few wounded.

George S. Fobes, *Leaves from a Trooper's Diary*, Philadelphia, 1869, p. 57.

mounted, and in such cases one out of each four men had to serve as horse holders for those on the line.

While the Union commanders were slow to appreciate the value of the cavalry and during the first years misused it by splitting it up into small bodies where it was employed for escorts, couriers and headquarters guards, the Confederates from the start used it effectively. As the War developed the Federal cavalry frequently used their horses to get them to the scene of battle, where they dismounted and fought on foot, and, armed as the best units were with the famous Spencer repeating carbines, they were effective against much larger opposing forces armed with single shot weapons. The Confederate cavalry deteriorated as the Federal cavalry came into its own. "Our . . . [Confederate] government permitted the cavalry branch of our army to melt gradually out of existence by the policy it adopted toward us. The men were required to own their horses, and when a cavalryman lost his horse, in battle or otherwise, he was put in what, in soldier parlance, was called Company 'Q'. This was a quasi organization of dismounted men, who followed the cavalry like a nightmare . . . . We had cavalry in our Virginia army, from Georgia, North and South Carolina, and Alabama, . . . when one of them lost his horse, he either went into Company 'Q', or to his far-off Southern home for another . . . . At that time, there were thousands of good horses in Virginia, in the hands of speculators, skulkers, and citizens generally, which should have been purchased or confiscated, and turned over to the cavalry; but this most important branch of the service was absolutely neglected, and went to pieces for the want of horses, at the very time Sheridan was organizing a corps of the finest mounted infantry in the world."[5]

There was nothing in the War more stirring to the emotions than the spectacle of a regiment or brigade of cavalry charging, and nothing more trying to the nerves of an infantryman than the sight of a column of cavalry galloping directly towards him. Even on the march a column of cavalry was a glad sight – with insight and accuracy it was caught by Walt Whitman:

> *A line in long array where they wind betwixt green islands,*
> *They take a serpentine course, their arms flash in the sun – hark to the*
>   *musical clank,*
> *Behold the brown-faced men, each group, each person a picture, the*
>   *negligent rest on the saddles,*
> *Behold the silvery river, in it the*
>   *splashing horses loitering stop to drink,*
> *Some emerge on the opposite bank, others are just entering the ford –*
>   *while,*
> *Scarlet and blue and snowy white,*
> *The guidon flags flutter gayly in the wind.*[6]

5. John N. Opie, *A Rebel Cavalryman*, Chicago, 1899, p. 158.
6. Walt Whitman, "Cavalry Crossing a Ford," in *Complete Poems and Prose*, Philadelphia, 1881, p. 235.

The experiences of a trooper were basically the same as those of any fighting man. Of course, there were exceptional circumstances such as that experienced by General Hindman of the Confederate army at Shiloh, which almost outdoes anything recounted by Baron Münchausen: "Just before the retreat, occurred one of the most remarkable incidents of the battle; few more wonderful are on record. General Hindman, than whom no more fearless, dashing, or brave man is found in the Rebel service, was leading his men in a fearful struggle for the possession of a favorable position, when a shell from the Federal batteries, striking his horse in the breast and passing into his body, exploded. The horse was blown to fragments, and the rider, with his saddle, lifted some ten feet in the air. His staff did not doubt that their general was killed, and some one cried out, 'General Hindman is blown to pieces.' Scarcely was the cry uttered, when Hindman sprang to his feet and shouted, 'Shut up there, I am worth two dead men yet. Get me another horse.' "[7]

There was always considerable good-natured professional rivalry and banter between the infantry and the cavalry. "An hour's trot on the Nolensville pike brought us up to the rear divisions of McCook, plodding merrily along in the rain and mud, joking betimes, and filing aside to allow our cavalcade to pass – not without remark, of course, for your 'dough-boy' seldom loses an opportunity to gibe at his mounted comrade. Said one tired fellow, as he splashed along:

" 'Here comes these jockey-soldiers, ridin' over us; soft thing they have of it!'

"His remark was greeted with many approving comments.

" 'Bah!' growled an old sergeant, who had evidently seen both arms of the service, 'it's not so soft as it seems, Charley. A fellow's got enough to do to take care of himself in a campaign like this, without havin' a horse to look to. Besides, when the fightin's over there's no rest for the trooper; he's got to go it always. Tell ye boys,' continued the veteran, elevating his voice, 'let them be cavalry that wants to be, I'd rather march this way and fight this way.' "[8]

---

7. William G. Stevenson, *Thirteen Months in The Rebel Army*, New York, 1862, p. 167.
8. George S. Fobes, *Leaves from a Trooper's Diary*, Philadelphia, 1869, p. 35.

124. ADALBERT JOHN VOLCK, *General Stuart's Raid on the White House, Virginia*

Bright and early on the morning of the 28th of June the cavalry was on the march to the "White House", fifteen or sixteen miles distant. . . . Not being able to take it, the next best thing was to make them destroy the vast depot of supplies at the place; and to this end Stuart dismounted some of his men and marched them about in sight of their lines to make them think we had infantry, and then he made Pelham fire quantities of ammunition at long range into the place, changing the position of the guns from time to time to make them think we had a great number. The ruse succeeded and soon after night-fall great columns of smoke and a bright illumination announced that they were setting fire to the great town of canvas and board houses that had sprung up at the place since its occupation by the Northern army . . . .

Escorted only by Col. W. H. F. Lee's regiment, General Stuart and staff went in to take possession. The destruction had been great, but yet vast quantities of things remained which had either been overlooked in the hurry of the evacuation or had failed to burn. It was a curious thing to see the evidences of the luxury in which the Federal army indulged . . . . Their sutler's shops were on the most elaborate scale — quantities of barrels of sugar, lemons by the millions, cases of wine, beer and other liquors of every description, confectionery, canned meats, and fruits and vegetables, and great quantities of ice, all still in excellent condition.

W. W. Blackford, *War Years with Jeb Stuart*, New York, 1945, pp. 74f.

125. EDWIN FORBES, *Cavalry Fight near Aldie, Virginia*

We struck the Confederate cavalry . . . and skirmished for a long time . . . . I gave the command, "Draw saber . . . . Charge!" As we neared the woods the battery fired one round . . . . I met Hawes who was wounded . . . the blood issuing between the buttons on his jacket. I ordered two men to . . . take him to the rear. Getting the men into column again, I went back to Lieutenant Boyd . . . [and ordered another charge]. He raised his saber and said, "Come on, boys!" and was shot through the heart, and fell to the ground, striking against my horse as he went down. I then charged with what was left up to the knoll.

N. D. Preston, *History of the Tenth Regiment of New York Cavalry*, New York, 1892, p. 95.

127. VICTOR NEHLIG, *The Fight at Sangster's Station*

The order to charge, followed by its instant execution, had such an overwhelming and paralyzing effect upon the enemy that for the space of a few seconds those nearest to us seemed utterly to lose the power of motion. Many throwing down their arms, raising their hands, and pleading for mercy and surrender, they doubtless thinking they had unaware run into the main part of the Union army . . . . We, deaf to their cries, dashed madly through and over them, trampling them under our horses' feet, and using our sabres right and left on all within our reach.

Pennoch Huey, *A . . . History of the Charge of . . . the Eighth Pennsylvania Cavalry at Chancellorsville*, Philadelphia, 1883, p. 14.

129. EASTMAN JOHNSON, *The Wounded Drummer Boy*

On Shiloh's dark and bloody ground,
The dead and wounded lay;
Amongst them was a drummer boy,
Who beat the drums that day.
A wounded soldier held him up,
His drum was by his side.
He clasped his hands, then raised his eyes,
And prayed before he died.

William Shakespeare Hays, "The Drummer Boy of Shiloh" (contemporary song).

The Infantry.

"NOTHING IS MORE CONFOUNDING, fragmentary, incomprehensible, than a battle as one sees it. And you see so little, too, unless you are a staff officer and ride about, or perhaps a general."[9] The truth of this is succinctly borne out by the following entry in the diary of a none-too-literate Union soldier, William W. Heath, a private in Company H, 4th Vermont Volunteer Regiment. Heath was present at the battle of Gettysburg, and his entry for the momentous third day of that battle, Friday, July 3rd, reads in its entirety as follows: "On the lines today as scirmyshing today. A hard fight on the right today."[10] Certainly no one will accuse Heath of being prone to exaggerate. While the individual officer or soldier often could get little idea of the overall picture of a large scale battle, the action could not fail to arouse emotions covering the full range of human feeling.

An admiration for the courage of the enemy is encountered frequently in the contemporary journals. A wounded Confederate officer of the Second Louisiana, recalling the charge of Grover's brigade at second Manassas, said, "We stood in these lines. They fell upon us like a thunderbolt. They paid no attention to our volleys. We mowed them down, but they went right through our first line, then through our second, and advanced to the railway enbankment, and there we stopped them. They did it so splendidly that we couldn't help cheering them. It made me feel bad to fire on such brave fellows."[11]

Admiration for bravery was, of course, even more common when it concerned men wearing the same color uniform. "The Twelfth was still rocking back and forth, fluctuating between discipline and impulse, when an officer of Sheridan's staff (a dashing young fellow in embroidered blue shirt, with trousers tucked into his long boots) galloped into our front . . . and pointed to the woods with his drawn saber. It was finer than any scene by Horace Vernet or Wouverman. The whole regiment saw him and rejoiced in him; it flung orders to the winds and leaped out like a runaway horse."[12]

Instances of bravery to the extent of self-sacrifice were not uncommon. Martin Kelley, a private of Company G, the Bucktails Regiment, was one such hero. During the battle of Harrisonburg, it became obvious that the exact position and strength of the Confederates opposed to the Bucktails Regiment was unknown, and the order to advance could only be carried out at a dreadful cost of life. Kelley, with heroic devotion, resolved at the price of his own life to reduce the toll to be

9. John W. De Forest, *A Volunteer's Adventures*, New Haven, 1946, p. 214.

10. Manuscript diary of William W. Heath, Private Company H, 4th Vermont Volunteer Regiment, for January 1 to December 21, 1863, inclusive, in the collection of Marius B. Peladeau, Washington, D. C.

11. Charles C. Coffin, *The Boys of '61*, Boston, 1886, p. 387.

12. De Forest, *op. cit.*, p. 187.

taken of his companions. ". . . As he stepped swiftly from behind a tree, a long line of red flame showed over the crest of the hill, and without flinching, pierced by a volley of balls, Martin Kelley dropped dead."[13]

Undoubtedly the most common sensation during battle was the feeling of fear in some one of its many manifestations. One honest account of the way a soldier felt as he was about to go into battle reads as follows: "Down to this time I had felt nervous, and my knees trembled and legs felt weak. I acknowledge that I was afraid, but being afraid and yielding to fear are two different things. When my mother bade me good by the day my regiment left for Washington, she put her hands upon my head and said: 'My son, never let me hear that you turned your back to the enemy.' The remembrance of that pale face and her command were of themselves enough to make one brave, but I needed no such incentive, for when I saw my comrades falling on either side, fear left me and all my angry passions were aroused. The tears trickled down my cheeks, and I believe I could have fought the whole army."[14]

At the beginning of the War, and for quite some time subsequent to that, the attacking forces were drawn up as on parade and marched forward as a mass of men directly towards the enemy. A description of Pickett's charge by a Confederate infantryman is both vivid and dramatic: "On! men, on! Thirty more yards and the guns are ours; but who can stand such a storm of hissing lead and iron? What a relief if earth, which almost seems to hurl these implements of death in our faces, would open now and afford a secure retreat from threatening death. Every officer is in front, Pickett with his long curls streaming in the fiery breath from the cannons' mouth. Garnett on the right, Kemper in the center and Armistead on the left; Cols., Lieut. Cols., Majors, Captains, all press on and cheer the shattered lines.

"Just here – from right to left the remnants of our braves pour in their long reserved fire; until now no shot had been fired, no shout of triumph had been raised; but as the cloud of smoke rises over the heads of the advancing divisions the well known southern battle cry which marks the victory gained or nearly gained bursts wildly over the blood stained field and *all that line of guns is ours*.

"Shot through both thighs, I fall about 30 yards from the guns. By my side lies Lt. Kehoe, shot through the knee. Here we lie, he in excessive pain, I fearing to bleed to death, and dead and dying all around, while the division sweeps over the Yankee guns. Oh, how I long to know the result, the end of this fearful charge! We seem to have victory in our hands; but what can our poor remnant of a shattered division do if they meet beyond the guns an obstinate resistance?

"There – listen – we hear a new shout, and cheer after cheer rends the air. Are those fresh troops advancing to our support? No! No! That huzza never broke

13. W. H. Rauch, *History of the Bucktails*, Philadelphia, 1906, pp. 154ff.
14. A. R. Small, *The Sixteenth Maine Regiment*, Portland, 1886, p. 75.

Skirmish between L. Brooklyn 14th and 300 Rebel Cavalry.

131. ALFRED R. WAUD, *Hand-to-Hand Fight at Antietam between the Brooklyn 14th and the 3rd Rebel Cavalry*

. . . After moving forward the right received a deadly fire from the woods on the right and a long line of men in butternut and gray rose up from the ground. Simultaneously the hostile battle line opened a terrible fire. Many fell. There was on the part of our men then intense, hysterical excitement, eagerness to go forward, reckless disregard of life, of suffering, of everything but victory.

The Fourteenth Brooklyn Regiment, red-legged Zouaves, came into my line on a run, closing the awful gaps. Now is the pinch. Men and officers of New York and Wisconsin are fused into a common mass in the frantic struggle to shoot fast. Everybody tears cartridges, loads, passes guns or shoots. Men are falling in their places or running back into the corn. The soldier who is shooting is furious in his energy and eagerness to win victory. Many of the recruits who are killed or wounded only left home ten days ago.

The History of the Fighting Fourteenth, New York, 1911, pp. 49f.

from southern lips. Oh God! Virginia's bravest, noblest sons have perished here today and perished all in vain!"[15]

Eventually generals learned by experience that the unnecessary slaughter which such methods inevitably produced was to be avoided unless an absolute necessity. The soldiers soon took advantage of whatever cover was available. They loaded on their backs and fired from a prone position. They learned to make rifle pits or field fortifications or parapets out of fence rails filled with earth and stone.

As a spectacle many of the battles would have been disappointing to the seeker of the grand and picturesque, since so often the enemy was invisible and the only signs of battle were long clouds of smoke of musketry and the graceful masses of smoke from the artillery batteries. Nevertheless, it is hard to imagine anything more stirring and awesome than a typical battle: "Aids and mounted orderlies went dashing hither and thither in hot haste, to the various commands; and generals and their staffs were gathered in groups, anxiously seeing the enemy's movements through the field-glasses. Great clouds of smoke rolled over us like a burning city, and half obscured the columns of men who were marching with quick step in various directions, . . . Bugles blared and drums beat, and high above the awful din arose the shrill cry of some poor soul who had received a mortal wound. I know of no sound so horrible as the fiendish singing of the pieces of bursted shell . . . ."[16]

15. John Dooley, *John Dooley – Confederate Soldier – His War Journal*, ed. Joseph T. Durkin, 1945, pp. 107ff.
16. Small, *op. cit.*, p. 73.

132

The Charge across the Burnside Bridge, Antietam. 1 P.M. Sept 17 1862. O Forbes

133. EDWIN FORBES, *Reforming the Line after the Battle of Antietam*

The Rebels were fast shortening the distance between their line and ours, and we were getting anxious, but finally hear the cautionary command, "Steady, men, wait for the word"; and the Twenty-fifth Regiment stood as steady and silent as if on dress parade. On came the yelling horde until within — it seemed to us — not over twenty-five yards. It was an anxious and critical moment, and it afforded Colonel Pickett an opportunity to see of what stuff his regiment was made. Suddenly came the order: "Twenty-fifth, ready"; and like clockwork every rifle was in position; "Aim," and every eye was glancing along a rifle barrel; "Fire," and that volley, almost like a single shot, sent death and dismay into that Rebel host.

Samuel H. Putnam, *The Story of Company A, Twenty-Fifth Regiment, Mass. Volunteers,* Worcester, 1886, pp. 269f.

◀ 132. EDWIN FORBES, *The Charge across the Burnside Bridge, Antietam, 1 P.M.,*
   September 17, 1862

136

136. JAMES WALKER (after John Badger Bachelder), *The Battle of Gettysburg: Repulse of Longstreet's Assault, July 3, 1863*

A charge is a grand as well as terrible sight, and this one, to my inexperienced eyes, was magnificent. I had often witnessed, with wild delight, the meeting of thunder-clouds in our western storms, the fierce encounter, the blinding lightning, the rolling thunder, the swaying to and fro of the wind-driven and surging masses of angry vapor, the stronger current at length gaining the victory, and sweeping all before it. With an intenser interest and a wilder excitement, did I watch these eight hundred men, as they gathered themselves up for the charge. At the word, every man leaped forward on the full run, yelling as if all the spirits of Tartarus were loosed. In a moment comes the shock, the yells sink into muttered curses, and soon groans are heard, and the bayonet thrusts are quick and bloody. Brute strength and skill often meet, and skill and agility usually win.

William G. Stevenson, *Thirteen Months in the Rebel Army*, New York, 1862, pp. 72f.

134. ALFRED R. WAUD, *Gallant Charge of General Humphrey's Division at Fredericksburg, December 13, 1862*

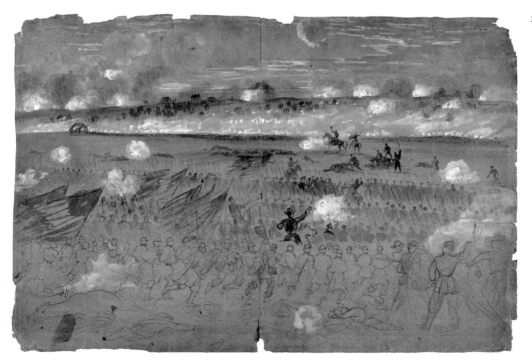

139. WINSLOW HOMER, *A Skirmish in the Wilderness*

There was very heavy firing to the left of the road in a chaparral of brush and scrubby pines and oaks. There the musketry was a steady roar and the cheers and yells of the fighters incessant . . . . I heard the hum of bullets as they passed over the low trees. Then I noticed that small limbs of trees were falling in a feeble shower in advance of me. It was as though an army of squirrel were at work cutting off nut and pine cone-laden branches . . . . I saw a straggling line of men clad in blue . . . taking advantage of cover.

Frank Wilkeson, *Recollections of a Private Soldier in the Army of the Potomac*, New York, 1898, pp. 6of.

141. VICTOR NEHLIG, *Infantry Fighting Hand-to-Hand*

The rebel troops engaged in our immediate front were a part of Talliaferro's, formerly Jackson's. That they fought with their accustomed ferocity, the loss of the First Brigade proved by its list of killed and wounded. Even when the Sixteenth sprang over the works, they showed a brave front, and only after a score or more were bayoneted would they yield to a more determined courage than theirs. Otis Libby, of Company H, crazed with pain from a wound in the head by a clubbed musket, ran two rebels through with his bayonet, and heedless of the fact that his enemies had surrendered, would have continued his ferocious work had not Colonel Farnham pulled him away. Monroe Lyford, of Company E, rushed over the embankment with the fury of a madman, and, running his bayonet through a rebel, yelled, "Curse you, you killed my brother!" which, alas, was too true.

A. R. Small, *The Sixteenth Maine Regiment*, Portland, 1886, p. 69.

142. ADOLF METZNER, *The First Shell – Beginning of the Atlanta Campaign, Crossing Chickamauga Creek, May 10, 1864*

The Corps of Engineers and the Other Corps.

BACKING UP AND SUPPORTING the combat arms were the Engineers, the Quartermaster Corps, the Commissaries, and the Signal Corps. Each of these essentially non-combatant organizations played an important role in the war.

The life of a soldier in the Corps of Engineers differed very little during the Civil War from that of any other enlisted man. In fact there were very few regiments of engineer troops in the service, either Federal or Confederate. As a result, many of the projects which now would be accomplished by engineer troops were carried out by infantry, sometimes under the guidance of engineer officers who were attached to the headquarters staffs.

In the face of obstacles which to many at the time seemed insurmountable, aided by an ingenuity which we like to think is characteristic of Americans in general, deeds of surprising magnitude were accomplished. There was, for example, the famous "bean pole and corn stalk" bridge, so-named by President Lincoln, which crossed Potomac Creek. This amazing structure was rushed up by totally inexpert labor in less than two weeks and was then ready to carry trains across its length. Constructed entirely of wood, this bridge had a height at its greatest point of some 80 feet above water and a length of 500 feet. Another Pharaonic undertaking was General Butler's Dutch Gap Canal, 16 feet deep and 60 feet wide, which was to have connected the shallow arms of a horseshoe bend on the James River. The dam on the Red River, an adventurous and successful engineering project, enabled General Porter's gunboats to avoid capture when the depth of the river fell and his vessels would otherwise have been marooned and at the mercy of the Confederates when the army pulled out of that expedition. The former coal miners of Pennsylvania also accomplished arduous feats in digging a mine under the Confederate fortifications at Petersburg. ". . . the mine was sprung. It was a magnificent spectacle; the mass of earth went up into the air, carrying with it men, guns, carriages and timbers, which spread like an immense cloud, as it reached its altitude. So close were the Union lines that the mass appeared as if it would descend immediately upon the troops waiting to make the charge. This caused them to break and scatter to the rear, and about ten minutes were consumed in reforming for the attack. . . . [As the men advanced they saw] an enormous hole in the ground about thirty feet deep, sixty feet wide, and one hundred and seventy feet long. . . ."[17] Another similar engineering project was carried out on the Mississippi at Vicksburg under equally trying circumstances.

While these achievements were spectacular, the majority of the labors associated with the Engineer Corps were, of course, of a less romantic nature. It would be interesting to know how many miles of corduroy road were actually constructed by Union and Confederate troops; how many miles of field fortifications were

17. Joseph Gould, *The Story of the Forty-Eighth (Penn.)*, Philadelphia, 1903, p. 230.

thrown up; how many fixed timber bridges were constructed across streams; or how many pontoon bridges were stretched from the banks of rivers.

The country to the south of Washington, wherever troops were concentrated, was scarred with innumerable earthwork defenses, built under the supervision of engineer officers. Washington itself was ringed with a series of elaborately constructed earthwork forts. Defenses were often connected by a zig-zag covered way and had bomb proofs and traverses to screen the troops from artillery. Tiresome as the construction work must have been, its completion afforded the men a certain degree of satisfaction, or so it would appear. "The men are so amused with this labor that they hew and shovel in the highest spirits. And we never tire of looking at our fortification; we walk around it and discuss its merits by the hour; we are like little girls with a new baby-house. As you may lack entertainment at home, let me instruct you how to make a fieldwork. Steal all the rails that you can find in a township; then build two parallel fences four feet apart and four and a half feet high; fill in with stones, earth, and green timber, and bank up the front with earth laid at an angle of forty-five degrees; then look across it and wish the enemy would come."[18]

One of the most heroic incidents in the War occurred at Fredericksburg when, in the face of the fire of Confederate sharpshooters posted in buildings on the opposite bank of the river, the engineers threw across a pontoon bridge. "By daylight the work had progressed fairly well, considerable material had been carried to the river, and part of the bridge laid when . . . [a] rebel sentry heard the crackling of the ice as the boats were pushed into the water. . . . Soon a brigade of sharpshooters . . . were firing rapidly at the engineers from behind the rifle pits, fences, walks and from cellars on the other side. They were able to pick off officers, particularly of the engineer corps, engaged in constructing the bridge . . . .[Later] the men of the Seventh Michigan and the Nineteenth Massachusetts took to the boats, twenty in each, and poled across the river under a heavy musketry fire from

18. De Forest, *op. cit.*, p. 168.

---

149. EDWARD LAMSON HENRY, *Westover Mansion*

Sometimes the nerve of the flagman was put to a very severe test, as he stood . . . waving his flag, his situation too like that of Mahomet's coffin, while the Whitworth bolts whistled sociably by him, saying, "Where is he? Where is he?" or, by another interpretation, "Which one? Which one?" Had one of these bolts hit a corner post of the lookout, the chances for the flagman and his lieutenant to reach the earth by a new route would have been favorable, although the engineers who built them claimed that with *three* posts cut away the tower would still stand. But, as a matter of fact, I believe no shot ever seriously injured one of the towers, though tons weight of iron must have been hurled at them. The roof of the Avery House, before Petersburg, was used for a signal station, and the shells of the enemy's guns often tore through below much to the alarm of the signal men above.

John D. Billings, *Hardtack and Coffee*, Boston, 1887, p. 402.

the enemy."[19] It is one thing to face an enemy with a musket ready for action and quite another to work fully exposed with no chance of retaliation while you see your comrades being killed or wounded as they labor beside you.

The Quartermaster General's department supplied uniforms and equipment, provided transportation by land and water, constructed housing for animals and men, and administered all railways and telegraph lines. In addition it distributed the animals and wagons and, indeed, with the commissary department, all the supplies the army needed in the field. While lacking the color, romance and danger of the fighting services, certainly the large trains needed for the supply of the armies in the field made an imposing spectacle both when they were assembled in great parks and, perhaps, more especially, when they were on the move covering miles of road space. "When the Army of the Potomac, numbering 150,000 men, left Brandy Station, Virginia, in May, 1864, it was serviced by more than 4,000 heavy wagons in the campaign. The supply trains carried ten days' rations of the same articles and one day's ration of salt pork. For the remainder of the meat ration, a supply of beef cattle on the hoof, for thirteen days' rations were driven along with the troops, but over separate roads. A general was assigned the responsibility of directing the movements of this great herd of beef cattle by brigades and divisions."[20]

The armies naturally required many thousands of teamsters and wagoners to man the thousands of wagons needed to supply the armies in the field. Many of the teamsters were detailed to this work by their regiments, but even more were hired civilians who were not well disciplined and who committed much pillaging in the army's rear areas. "The waggoners and train rabble and stragglers have committed great outrages in the rear of this army. Some of the generals, particularly Birney and Barlow, have punished pillagers in a way they will not forget."[21] Many teamsters, of course, were men who did their full duty and were detailed to wagon trains because of their experience in civilian life. The principal excitement in which men detailed to the Quartermaster Department were involved was that caused by the necessity of defending the wagon trains and supply depots from the repeated and often successful raids of the opposing cavalry forces. The Union's rich wagon trains filled with a great variety of valuable commodities were much sought after by the Confederates, who needed them to supply their own forces. "Suddenly we . . . caught sight of a party of rebel horsemen approaching the road. We had not time to recover from our astonishment — indeed, I was half-inclined to believe that the strangers were friends, as two of them wore blue overcoats — when they began to fire at us. Watts had his horse's ear slit by the first bullet. We were about getting our carbines into position, when an immense crowd

---

19. Ernest Linden Waitt, *History of the Nineteenth Regiment, Massachusetts Volunteer Infantry*, Salem, 1906, pp. 165ff.
20. *Annual Report of the Secretary of War*, March 1, 1865.
21. George R. Agassiz. *Meade's Headquarters 1863-1865*, Boston, 1922, p. 117.

144. EDWIN FORBES, *The 146th New York Throwing Pontoons across the Rappahanock River near Beverly Ford, August 8, 1863*

145. ALFRED R. WAUD, *Crossing the Pontoon Bridge at Berlin*

Pontoon bridges were a source of great satisfaction to the soldiers. They were perfect marvels of stability and steadiness. No swaying motion was visible. To one passing across with a column of troops or wagons *no* motion was discernible. It seemed as safe and secure as mother earth, and the army walked them with the same serene confidence as if they were. I remember one night while my company was crossing the Appomattox on the bridge laid at Point of Rocks that D. Webster Atkinson, a cannoneer, who stood about six feet and a quarter in boots – dear fellow, he was afterwards mortally wounded at Hatcher's Run – being well-nigh asleep from the fatigue of the all-night march we were undergoing, walked off the bridge. Fortunately for him, he stepped – not into four or five fathoms of water, but – into a pontoon. As can readily be imagined, an unexpected step down of two feet and half was quite an "eye-opener" to him, but, barring a little lameness, he suffered no harm.

John D. Billings, *Hardtack and Coffee*, Boston, 1887, pp. 392f.

of brown-coated cavalry appeared in the woods behind the first party, and swarmed toward us.

"We did not wait to see any more. Our whole party, teamsters and all, commenced a masterly retreat in every direction, every man for himself. The rebels kept up a constant peppering at the fugitives, and shouted to them to surrender. Many of them complied, and were paroled (and robbed) on the spot, to find their way as best they could to Nashville. The victors then cut the mules loose, and set fire to the wagons."[22]

The Signal Corps as such did not come into being until the Civil War. Although small in size, it made a notable contribution. One must bear in mind that at the start of the War telegraphy was not yet twenty years old. The Civil War was the first major conflict to see the large scale use of this quick method of communication. Early in the War both the Confederate and Federal governments assumed nominal control of all telegraph lines. To operate the system extending from Washington to the headquarters in the field, a corps of already trained civilian telegraphers responded to the need for their services and became part of the army. Their devotion to duty under trying circumstances which often involved long hours, while unspectacular, was vitally necessary.

While the telegrapher led a relatively safe existence, the signalman, who dispatched messages by means of signal flags by day and in the night by torches, was more exposed. Since this method of visual communication necessarily required that the signal station be placed on a conspicuous elevated position, the signalman was often an obvious target for sharpshooters and was also in danger of being wounded by shell fragments.

Among the novel techniques which were tried out during the course of the War, the use of balloons for aerial observation had great possibilities. Why this was not carried out on a much larger scale and why it was abandoned after a comparatively brief period of experimentation is hard to understand, since the results were obviously of such great military importance.

Professor Lowe was the principal advocate and practitioner of this technique in the North. In order to overcome the problem of keeping his balloons inflated in the field, especially in areas not adjacent to commercial sources of gas, he designed a mobile field generator which was adapted to an ordinary army escort wagon and which was capable of accompanying troops in the field into almost any reasonable position. The generator was a comparatively simple apparatus consisting of a strong wooden tank five feet high and eleven feet long and the same width as the army escort wagon. The balloon itself contained some twenty-five thousand cubic feet of gas and was constructed of silk. It was controlled from the ground by three manilla guy ropes twelve hundred feet in length.

From a swaying aerial platform it was possible for the military observers to study the enemy lines and encampments and make maps of the terrain showing

22. Fobes, *op. cit.*, pp. 48ff.

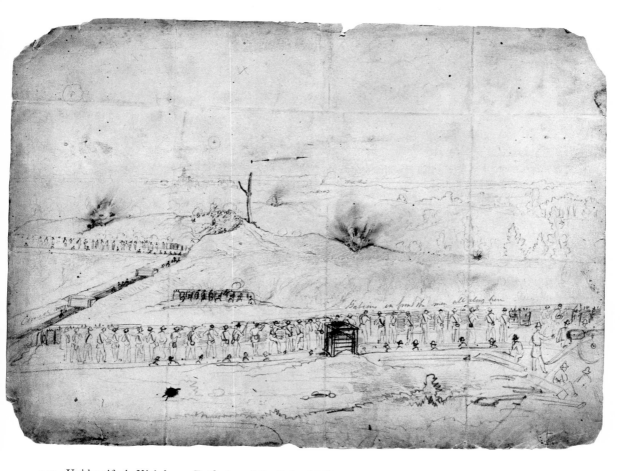

147. Unidentified, *Vicksburg: Explosion of the Federal Mines*

The match was applied at 3:00 p. m. The burst was terrific. For a few seconds, which seemed minutes if not hours to those engaged and to all beholders, the air was filled with dirt, dust, stockades, gabions, timbers, one or two gun carriages, and an immense surging white cloud of smoke which fairly rose to the heavens, and gradually widened out and dissipated. The charge was gallantly made before the debris had entirely fallen, and was as gallantly resisted. The dirt, timber and heavier portions of the works, blown into the air, fell back not far from its original position, only leaving a yawning crater where the mine had been, which was rendered almost impassable by the confused mass. All the Union batteries opened fire at once. The enemy replied vigorously, and the most deafening cannonading of the war to that time ensued for nearly an hour. The Confederates rallied to the reconstruction of their works, timbers were thrown across the breach, dirt banked against these as fast as men could accomplish it, and despite the most heroic attempts we were unable to gain any tenable footing within the rebel works.

Sylvanus Cadwallader, *Three Years with Grant*, ed. Benjamin P. Thomas, New York, 1955, pp. 121f.

their positions. The mapping was done by engineer officers or civilian draftsmen. The balloons were, of course, conspicuous targets and were often subjected to enemy cannon or musketry fire, although fortunately for the occupants no balloon was actually struck.

The Confederates also made some limited use of balloons but the true unsung genius of the Southern side was an anonymous inventor who, according to the following report, was far ahead of his time. "An ingenious but visionary rebel claims to have invented a flying machine, which may be used with terrible effect against an enemy. He calls it the 'Artisavis,' or 'Bird of Art,' and he believes that by the use of a considerable number of them all of the Yankee armies now upon Confederate soil and all their blockading fleets may be driven off or destroyed. To effect this, he proposes to station a thousand of these machines at a distance of five miles from the hostile camp or fleet, and send them thence into the air, each armed with a 50-pound explosive shell, to be dropped from a safe elevation upon the enemy! The Birds are then to return for the purpose of re-loading. The inventor believes that in this manner an army or fleet could be destroyed in a very few hours. The rebel Congress, however, is blind to the merits of his scheme, and, after vainly waiting in the halls of greatness, he appeals to the 'officers, soldiers, and citizens of the Confederate States' for a more enlightened judgment and liberal contributions."[23]

23. *U. S. Army and Navy Journal*, Vol. I. 1863–64, p. 344.

148. JAMES MADISON ALDEN, *Admiral Porter's Gunboats Passing the Red River Dam*

These falls are about a mile in length, filled with rugged rocks, over which, at the present stage of water, it seemed to be impossible to make a channel.

The work was commenced by running out from the left bank of the river, a tree-dam, made of the bodies of very large trees, brush, brick, and stone, cross-tied with other heavy timber, and strengthened in every way which ingenuity could devise. This was run out about three hundred feet into the river; four large coal barges were then filled with brick, and sunk at the end of it. From the right bank of the river, cribs filled with stone were built out to meet the barges. All of which was successfully accomplished, notwithstanding there was a current running of nine miles an hour which threatened to sweep everything before it.

The Lexington succeeded in getting over the upper falls just in time, the water rapidly falling as she was passing over. She then steered directly for the opening in the dam, through which the water was rushing so furiously that it seemed as if nothing but destruction awaited her. Thousands of beating hearts looked on, anxious for the result. The silence was so great, as the Lexington approached the dam, that a pin might almost be heard to fall. She entered the gap with a full head of steam on, pitched down the roaring torrent, made two or three spasmodic rolls, hung for a moment on the rocks below, was then swept into deep water by the current, and rounded-to safely into the bank. Thirty thousand voices rose in one deafening cheer, and universal joy seemed to pervade the face of every man present.

J. T. Headley, *Farragut and our Naval Commanders*, New York, 1867, pp. 369f.

150. UNIDENTIFIED, *Professor Lowe's Balloon Wagon and Gas Generator at White House Landing, Virginia*

"Guess I've got 'em now, jest where I want 'em," said Lowe, with a gratified laugh; "jest keep still as you mind to and squint your eye through my glass, while I make a sketch of the roads and the country. Hold hard there, and anchor fast!" he screamed to the people below. Then he fell imperturbably to work, sweeping the country with his hawkeye, and escaping nothing that could contribute to the completeness of his jotting.

We had been but a few minutes thus poised, when close below, from the edge of a timber stretch, puffed a volume of white smoke. A second afterward, the air quivered with the peal of a cannon. A third, and we heard the splitting shriek of a shell, that passed a little to our left, but in exact range, and burst beyond us in the ploughed field, heaving up the clay as it exploded.

"Ha!" said Lowe, "they have got us foul! Haul in the cables — quick!" he shouted in a fierce tone.

John Truesdale, *The Blue Coats*, Philadelphia, 1867, p. 331.

153. OTTO SOMMER, *Union Drover with Cattle for the Army*

Our beef was driven along with us and slaughtered as it was wanted. As soon as the halt for the night was made the beef was dressed, furnished to quartermasters of regiments, by them to companies and by the company officer to squads, in quantities according to the number of men to be supplied . . . . The amount of meat per man was about a pound per day, and when it is remembered that there were fifteen thousand men in the corps, some estimate may be made of the number of animals necessary to supply the demand for a single day.

William B. Lapham, *My Recollections of the War of The Rebellion*, Augusta, 1892, p. 112.

154. WINSLOW HOMER, *Army Teamsters*

An educated mule-driver was, in his little sphere, as competent a disciplinarian as the colonel of a regiment. Nor did he always secure the prompt and exact obedience above described by applications of the Black Snake alone, or even when accompanied by the sternest objurgations delivered in the mule dialect. He was a terror to his subjects in yet another way; and old soldiers will sustain me in the assertion that the propulsive power of the mule-driver was increased many fold by the almost unlimited stock of profanity with which he greeted the sensitive ears of his muleship when the latter was stubborn. I have seen mules, but now most obdurate, jump into their collars the next moment with the utmost determination to do their whole duty when one of these Gatling guns of curses opened fire upon them. Some reader may prefer to adjudge as a reason for this good behavior the fear of the Black Snake, which was likely to be applied close upon the volley of oaths; but I prefer to assign as a motive the mule's interest in the advancement of good morals.

John D. Billings, *Hardtack and Coffee*, Boston, 1887, pp. 285f.

155. WINSLOW HOMER, *Baggage Guard Defending the Supply Train*

The Seaman's Life.

THE LIFE of a man-of-war's man in the Civil War was compounded of monotony, physical discomfort, rigid discipline, leavened with hope of shore leave and prize money, and enlivened with rare moments of excitement when the enemy was in range. Basically the seaman's life was little changed from that led fifty years before in the War of 1812. Most naval vessels were still, at least partially, under canvas. The need for vessels in order to build up the tiny regular navy quickly to the capacity required to blockade the Atlantic sea coast from Virginia to Texas on the Gulf of Mexico, occasioned the wholesale purchase or charter of a motley assortment of merchant vessels many of which were under sail. True, steam had long before been introduced; side-wheelers and even the latest development, the screw propeller, powered some of the vessels of recent construction. But this little altered the life between decks, although it added a new peril: death or injury from scalding steam when an enemy shell struck a boiler or main steam line.

The days passed with a succession of watches, day and night, in rain, fog, tropical heat or arctic cold. Sails were trimmed, coal was passed into the greedy boilers, food prepared and eaten, sailors' yarns spun between watches, and days passed into weeks and weeks into months.

A midshipman's day just prior to the War is described thus:

"The routine of the ship has commenced in earnest — reveille; dress (and woe betide him who had lost a button or whose shoestring was not properly tied), lash the hammocks, carry them up to the spar deck and stow them neatly in the nettings; breakfast;... drill at the great guns;... infantry drill;... cutlass exercise;... dinner;... boat drill, or loosing, reefing, or furling sail."[1] Then at nine, hammocks were slung and a half-hour later taps were sounded and the day closed.

Life at sea was monotonous. This was especially true on vessels assigned to the blockading squadrons which gradually almost completely closed the Southern ports to shipping; for they often maintained their stations for long months on end. Even though at times in sight of land no one could step ashore to get a drink of clear spring water or chat with the girls. "For weeks this dreary and wearisome blockade was maintained. The lack of exercise and nutritious food was felt by officer and man, and scurvy, that dreaded pest of ship-life in the olden times, was only avoided by the occasional relief which came ... from the steamers bringing

---

1. James Morris Morgan, *Recollections of a Rebel Reefer*, London, 1918, p. 21.

supplies of fresh meats and vegetables."[2] Sometimes the crew of a vessel might not get liberty on shore for as long as eight months at a stretch.

Grumbling and complaints about the way the navy was run were rife among the bluejackets. While they complained that they did not get their fair share of prize money and that when they did the prize brokers swindled them out of twenty-five percent of it, the major growl was over the abolition of the grog ration which had been traditional in the U.S. Navy, for early in the War Congress ordered that the daily issue of grog on naval craft be discontinued and that the men's pay instead be raised five cents a day. Men who had followed the sea for years and to whom their ration of grog was regarded as a portion of their meat and drink were very much affected by this order even to the extent of expressing their opinion in verse:

> "Jack's happy days will soon be past,
> To return again, oh never.
> For they've raised his pay,
>   five cents a day,
> But stopped his grog forever."[3]

One of the inducements to sign on as a jack-tar was the continuation of the practice of awarding prize money to the officers and crew of a man-of-war capturing an enemy vessel. While prizes of consequence were rarely captured by the slower vessels on blockade duty, the swifter vessels and cruisers occasionally had good luck. "... Among the recent prize cases sent by the Navy Department to ... the Treasury for the distribution of the prize money, ... is that of the steamer *Kate Dale*, captured on the 14th of July last, by the U.S. steamship *R. R. Cuyler* ... the amount for distribution was $355,798.12, to be distributed between the United States and the Naval captors. Each seaman ... in this case will receive $711.76; 1st class firemen, each $1,187.93; 2d class firemen, $989.94; coal heavers, each $712.77; landsmen, $475.18, and 1st class boys, each $395.97."[4]

The all-out war which was waged by the Union forces on land and which resulted in the burning of crops, warehouses, and in the destruction of railroads, factories, and anything of potential use to the enemy, had its counterpart on the high seas in the activities of the famed Confederate naval raiders. The passengers and crews on Northern merchant ships anywhere on the seven seas lived in constant fear of attack by those Confederate cruisers which roamed the seas more or less at will. "The panic that ... ensued was dreadful; the screams of women filled the air, and men turned pale [when] they realized the proximity of one of the dreaded Confederate cruisers...." When the vessels of the New Bedford whaling fleet were captured, often "the old whalers, who for ... years had risked their

---

2. W. S. Schley, *Forty-five Years under the Flag*, New York, 1904, p. 31.

3. *U. S. Army and Navy Journal*, Vol. III, 1866, p. 376 states that the song was composed in a ship's squadroom on August 31, 1862.

4. *Ibid.*, Vol. 1, 1863–64, p. 350.

lives in a dangerous calling, stood silent and in tears as they beheld their hard-earned property disappear in a cloud of smoke."[5]

Technologically there were some interesting developments in naval architecture during the War, and of these John Ericsson's new fighting machine, the monitor, "the cheese box on a raft," was the most famous. Fine for fighting in protected waters, as was proved at the engagement between the *Merrimac* and the *Monitor* at Hampton Roads, they were far from safe in blue water. In fact the original monitor foundered with considerable loss of life off the east coast, as did a later version, the U.S.S. *Weehawken:* "Four officers and twenty men were drowned, being below at the time, and unable to reach the deck through the inrush of the water, or, if on deck, unable to keep themselves afloat for the few minutes that intervened before boats were at hand for their rescue. The sailors struggled for life, raising their arms, catching at sticks, planks, and timbers, but help arrived too late. The boats saved only a few of the crew."[6]

The life of a bluejacket aboard a monitor in Southern waters was far from pleasant. The heat below decks coming from the rays of the sun on the steel deck combined with the heat from the steam boilers raised the temperature to 120°, since there was no adequate forced ventilation. Thus, existence in the stuffy and overcrowded confines of the crews' quarters, when "buttoned down" for combat, was an appalling experience.

The use of armor plate was also applied to ocean-going vessels and received its first testing in actual warfare on a large scale. The vessel which clearly demonstrated the worth of this development was the U.S.S. *Kearsarge.* A correct contemporary estimation of the importance of the fight between the *Kearsarge* and the *Alabama* was thus reported: "The remarkable action which has just taken place in the English Channel, off Cherbourg, is not only the first which has been fought between steam war vessels at sea, but also the first that has been fought on the broad ocean since the introduction of horizontal shell-firing, the recent Danish naval fight, perhaps, excepted. As such, it has an extraordinary significance. The relief of the country from the pestilent enemy of all its commerce . . . has been accomplished in this fight. But this is not all. It has given, to a partial extent, an illustration of the comparative merits of the two types of naval architecture and armament of England and America. Our Navy . . . we take to be already the equal of any that floats, in the character of its ordnance, . . . also, in the speed of its vessels . . . .

"The contest off Cherbourg shows to what brief compass of duration naval actions will be brought, when a single shell or two may decide the conflict. The shell which struck the steering apparatus of the *Alabama* decided her fate. This strange and fatal meeting will doubtless be of the deepest significance to the European marine world, as well as to our own. . . . Here, after a circling fight of sixty min-

5. David D. Porter, *The Naval History of the Civil War*, New York, 1886, pp. 638;644.
6. Daniel Ammen, *The Atlantic Coast*, New York, 1883, p. 145.

utes, with an adversary from 900 to 1200 yards distant, the terror of commerce . . . struck, and in twenty minutes more the seas rolled over her . . . ."[7]

There was also a revived interest in both navies in the submarine. However, the technology of the time was not sufficiently advanced to provide the complicated apparatus and controls which would have made them practical engines of war.

For sheer excitement, nothing at sea exceeded the thrill attendant on running the blockade into a Confederate harbor – or out again with a cargo of cotton for the textile mills of England. "Night settled clear, affording an unusually good horizon line. And then the moon sank early . . . [a land breeze brought a mist over the blockade runner]. In half an hour the men could feel on their faces cool, damp air, and then a few drops of moisture. Ahead was as nice a fog as any reasonable blockade-runner could want. Only one light burned on board. It was in the binnacle, carefully covered. Not a word was spoken, and there was not a sound but the throb of the engines and the slight shir-r-r made by the friction of the ship through the water . . . ."[8]

The routine of shipboard life with its succession of watches, drilling at the guns, drilling to repel boarders, tending sail, drilling with practice cutlass, or with the ship's boats, was occasionally interrupted with swift and bloody action, for in naval combat it was usually a case of all or nothing. Only a few well aimed shots were now needed to end an action – to turn a smart, well-armed, well-crewed vessel into a hulk, which soon plummetted to the depths. The following describes the end of the C.S.S. *General Lovell*, sunk by the U.S.S. *Benton* in the engagement at Memphis: "The water pours in . . . the vessel goes down like a lump of lead. Her terror-stricken crew are thrown into the current. It is an appalling sight. A man with his left arm torn, broken, bleeding, and dangling by his side, runs wildly over the deck. There is unspeakable horror in his face. He beckons now to those on shore, and now to his friends on board the boats. He looks imploringly to heaven and calls for help. Unavailing the cry. He disappears in the eddying whirlpool. A hundred human beings are struggling for life, buffeting the current, raising their arms, catching at sticks, straws, planks and timbers. 'Help! Help! Help!' they cry. It is a wild wail of agony, mingled with the cannonade."[9]

The seaman was subject to much more rigid and unremitting discipline than his counterpart in the army. In the army, the gulf between officers and men was real, yet in combat there was little difference in their living conditions; often no one had shelter, food, clothing or money, and it was respect for qualities of leadership, not rank alone, that made discipline work. In the navy, on the other hand, the special limitations of a ship and the tradition of the sea made a never-bridged distinction between officers and men.

---

7. *U.S. Army and Navy Journal*, Vol. I, 1863–64, p. 760.

8. James D. Bulloch, *The Secret Service of the Confederate States in Europe*, New York, 1884, p. 122.

9. "Carlton" (Charles C. Coffin), *My Days and Nights on the Battlefield*, Boston, 1864, p. 305.

156. Xanthus Russell Smith, *Attack on Fort Fisher*

157. Currier and Ives, *The Splendid Naval Triumph on the Mississippi, April 24, 1862*

The enemy was on the look-out, and the vessels had scarcely got under way when signal-lights flashed along the batteries, and then a belt of fire gleamed through the darkness, and the next moment the heavy shot came shrieking along the bosom of the stream. All eyes were now turned on the *Hartford*, as she silently steamed on – the signal "close action" blazing from her rigging. In the mean time the mortar-boats below opened their fire and the hissing shells rose in graceful curves, and, weaving an arch of firey network over the advancing fleet, dropped with a thunderous sound into the forts above. In a few minutes the advanced vessels opened, firing at the flash from the forts. The white smoke rolled and heaved in vast volumes along the shuddering waters, and one of the wildest scenes in the history of war now commenced. The fleet, with full steam on, was soon abreast of the forts, and its rapid broadsides mingling in with the deafening explosions on shore, turned night into fiery day. Louder than redoubled thunders the heavy guns sent their deafening roar through the gloom, not in distinct explosions, but in one long, wild, protracted crash, as though the ribs of nature were breaking in final convulsion. Amid this hell of terrors, a fire-raft, pushed steadily forward by the ram *Manassas*, loomed through the smoke like a phantom from the unseen world.

J. T. Headley, *Farragut and Our Naval Commanders*, New York, 1867, pp. 66f.

184

157

185

Another difference must be mentioned. Our sailors were mostly old hands, not amateurs, and knew their calling from years of prior experience before the mast as seamen, if not as gunners or boarders. Most were old merchantmen or fishermen, and very few were landlubbers. The army, on the contrary, was made up largely of greenhorns possessing no previous martial experience.

There were marked differences in the life of the C.S.N. man and the Union seaman. With the exception of the relatively few C.S.N. raiders who roamed the high seas and the fast blockade runners which were manned usually by foreigners and operated under foreign flags, the Confederate ships had limited range. Not for their men the long hours of monotonous watch at sea in sleet and hail or in the fierce rays of the noonday sun or drenching rain, the scant water and monotonous diet while "on station" for months at a stretch. Confined largely to harbors and river estuaries, the C.S.N. man led no idyllic existence, however; time must have passed very slowly. As the blockade tightened, life became more hazardous, odds more uneven and unfavorable.

158. UNIDENTIFIED, *The* Monitor *and the* Merrimac *at Short Range*

The *Monitor* was a little bit the strangest craft I had ever seen; nothing but a few inches of deck above the water line, her big, round tower in the center and the pilot house at the end. We had confidence in her, though, from the start, for the little ship looked somehow like she meant business, and it didn't take us long to learn the ropes. The crew were exactly sixty strong, with the pilot.

Our first sight of the *Merrimac* was around the Rip Raps. She had been described to us and there was no mistaking her long, slanting, rakish outlines. I guess she took us for some kind of a water tank. You can see surprise in a ship, just as you can see it in a human being, and there was surprise all over the *Merrimac*. She fired a shot across us, but Captain Worden, our commander, said, "Wait till you get close, boys, and then let her have it."

Samuel Lewis (alias Peter Truskitt) in Otto Eisenschiml and Ralph Newman, *The Civil War*, Vol. I, New York, 1947, p. 139.

159. EDWIN HAYES, *Destruction of the Confederate Steamer* Alabama *by the U. S. Ironclad* Kearsarge

. . . Our shell [struck] the enemy's side and fell into the water. We were not aware of the chain armor of the enemy . . . [whose] 11-inch shells . . . [did] severe execution upon our quarter-deck section. Three of them successively entered our 8-inch pivot-gun port: the first swept off the forward part of the gun's crew; the second killed one man and wounded several others; and the third struck the breast of the gun-carriage, and spun around on the deck till one of the men picked it up and threw it overboard. Our decks were now covered with the dead and the wounded, and the ship was careening heavily to starboard from the effects of the shot-holes on her waterline.

John McIntosh Kell, "Cruise and Combats of the *Alabama*" in *Battles and Leaders of the Civil War*, New York, 1887, Vol. 4, pp. 608f.

160. ALEXANDER CHARLES STUART, *The U.S.* Midnight *Hailing the U.S.* Boheo
off Texas

We do not have much to do. We take a short cruise every day to see what we can see, and exercise the men a little to keep their digestion in order; and the rest of the time is passed in sleeping and eating and reading. . . . It gets very monotonous on the blockade, though sometimes the sails appear fairly often, and we keep steam up all the time, and are on a continual chase.

Carroll S. Alden, *George Hamilton Perkins: His Life and Letters*, Boston, 1914, pp. 140f.

163. ALEXANDER SIMPLOT, *Between Decks on a Union Gunboat*

During the entire passage from St. Paul to Sunda Strait the various warlike exercises are daily going on for hours together, an hour or two at "great gun" drill, a shorter time to boarding and repelling boarders, small-arm [infantry] squad or division drill with pistol target-practice [at bottle slung from the fore-topmast-studding-sail boom]. It is an active and at times stirring and exciting drill, particularly in the "boarding rushes," where examples of wonderful activity and quickness may be observed; for Jack takes real interest in his exercises and studies, if we except the handling of small fire-arms. Here no compromise can be effected with Jack. He has a thorough contempt for this sort of a weapon; and you may resign yourself to the stern fact that he will slight and avoid it as far as he dares, to the bitter end. He will never allow you to make him a "soger".

Arthur Sinclair, *Two Years on the* Alabama, Boston, 1896, pp. 178f.

167. David M. Stauffer,
Bucked and Gagged: Triced Up

168. David M. Stauffer,
Punishment for Spitting on the Deck

·BUCKED·AND·GAGED·
·TRICED·UP·

PUNISHMENT·FOR·SPITTING·ON·THE·DECK·
CARRYING·A·SPITTOON·FOR·THE·CREW·

166. CONRAD WISE CHAPMAN, *The Submarine* Hunley

The submarine boat left the wharf at 9:25 AM and disappeared at 9:35. As soon as she sank air bubbles were seen to rise to the surface of the water . . . the hole in the top of the boat by which the men entered was not properly closed. It was impossible . . . to rescue the unfortunate men, as the water was 9 fathoms deep. [Captain H. L. Hunley and 7 men lost their lives.]

Official Records of Union and Confederate Navies, Vol. 15, p. 692.

❧ 7 ❧

Life of a Prisoner of War.

AFTER CAPTURE, a prisoner of war was soon on his way either by foot or by train to a prisoner of war camp. He was a particular object of curiosity to the civilian inhabitants who were anxious to see a real live Yankee or Secesh. Samuel B. Palmer, a Confederate artillerist, on his way to confinement in Camp Douglas near Chicago, wrote: "At Frankfort several beautiful ladies came out to the car and we had a lively conversation as long as the train stopped. One old woman, however, seemed to wish to let us know that not all the ladies of Frankfort were 'secesh', for as the cars passed she exclaimed, 'goody! goody! I'm glad they've got you!' All she got for her pains, was a hearty laugh from 'ye rebels.' "[1]

At the beginning of the War prisoners were comparatively well housed and well fed in prison camps in both the North and South. However, as is all too well-known, conditions deteriorated rather rapidly and not only did the prisons become over-crowded and unsanitary, but, as the supplies of the Confederacy in particular became limited, the rations distributed to the prisoners became of very poor quality and so scant as barely to sustain the spark of life. "Our rations here [Macon, Georgia] were a pint and a half of corn meal and a half pint of sorghum molasses a day, and a scant ration of wood to cook it with. The corn meal was composed of the cob and corn ground together, and before we ate it we sifted it through tin plates punched full of holes. We were hungry all the time on that fare. A few times maggoty bacon was furnished, but that was a great luxury."[2]

Psychologically, the life of the prisoner of war is not different from that of any other type of prisoner held in close confinement. It was a life of great tension caused not only by the fear of becoming sick and dying on foreign soil, but also of anguish for family and friends, concern about one's private business affairs, despondency arising from the fact that one could not see any end to the confinement, and sheer boredom with the monotony and futility of life. "It is an awfully dull life. If I had some books to read I could pass the time away pretty well. I am *tired* and *completely wearied out* with this *hopeless* imprisonment. I say hopeless because it looks as if the entanglement in regard to the exchange will not be settled during the war. Indeed I can't see what compromise can be made. So I suppose we must stay here till the war is over."[3]

---

1. Original manuscript diary of Samuel Bell Palmer in the possession of General and Mrs. John B. Anderson, Washington, pp. 8ff.
2. Sheldon B. Thorpe, *The History of the 15th Connecticut Volunteers*, New Haven, 1893, pp. 191ff.
3. Original manuscript diary of Samuel Bell Palmer in the possession of General and Mrs. John B. Anderson, Washington, pp. 34ff.

172. WINSLOW HOMER, *Prisoners from the Front*

The captured men answered the description we had all so often read of secesh soldiers. Clad in coarse butternut or gray clothing, with the cheapest saddles and military equipments, and with a famished expression of countenance, their appearance told of their poverty, while the avidity with which they seized food and coffee spoke of their long hunger. One told me that his drink of coffee was "worth three dollars, sure, for it is not rye coffee, but *coffee* coffee."

John W. Hanson, *Historical Sketch of the Old Sixth Regiment of Massachusetts Volunteers*, Boston, 1866, p. 187.

Whenever conditions made it even remotely possible, the prisoners attempted to take their minds off their problems by keeping themselves busy: "The mechanical ingenuity exhibited by the captives was manifested in various ways, not only for the purpose of whiling away the tedious hours, but in order to obtain funds with which to purchase some of the necessaries of life. Trinkets of almost every description, finger-rings, breast-pins, ear-drops, watch-chains, and miniature books were carved in the most beautiful style. One of the prisoners made with his pen-knife, in half of a canteen, a clock, which kept good time; while another, with a small coffee-pot for a boiler, made a steam-engine, and had it running on a short track for the amusement of his companions. The Yankees would buy these trinkets, and send them as curiosities to their friends, or to be sold on a speculation."[4]

Very frequently the prisoners banded themselves together into associations and conducted in some cases quite elaborate dramatic programs, studied languages, conducted debates, and in other ways tried to keep their minds occupied. Some even printed their own prison newspapers.

Both governments attempted with some limited success to recruit for their armed forces from among the prisoners. "The bait, which this hand bill represents, was thrown among us one morning by the Federal officers and was immediately swallowed by a few 'snapers'. Impatient of the confinement of the prison, and being also half Union men, they seized this chance of release from prison, even at the price of having to fight against their former comrades. However let them go and peace go with them."[5]

It usually did not take long for the more resolute prisoners to begin to plan to escape. Much ingenuity was used in planning and in digging the tunnels which usually were the only way to pass unobserved from the prison camp. It is surprising how large a number managed to win their freedom, and, with much suffering and difficulties, found their way back to their own lines.

However, for most the hope of exchange was their reliance in the early years of the War. Thousands of prisoners were exchanged. The elation when this occurred was great: "As soon as we passed the rebel lines we ran down the road, cheering and singing . . . One who did not understand the situation would have thought that an insane asylum had been turned loose. We hugged each other, laughed, cried, prayed . . . expressed our joy."[6]

Toward the end of the War, the North, because of a superiority in man power, could always obtain new recruits while the South could not. Therefore, the Union refused to strengthen the Confederacy by prisoner exchange. Thus, as time went on, conditions in the over-crowded and poorly provisioned prisons worsened to such an extent that the mortality on both sides was extremely high.

---

4. John Scott, *Partisan Life with Col. John S. Mosby*, New York, 1867, p. 420.

5. Original manuscript diary of Samuel Bell Palmer in the possession of General and Mrs. John B. Anderson, Washington, pp. 22ff.

6. John G. B. Adams, *Reminiscences of the Nineteenth Massachusetts Regiment*, Boston, 1889, pp. 178f.

173. EDWIN FORBES, *Confederate Prisoners Captured in the Final Charge at the Battle of Gettysburg, July 3, 1863*

Sunday, Sept. 20th 1863. Fifty-one of us were marched out of Knoxville jail with our wardrobes (scanty enough) on our shoulders. We soon knew by the Cavalry escort awaiting us, that we were on our way *north*. Friends and relations gathered around to bid us farewell and our *Union friends* to chuckle over our misfortune. It is a strange thing to be marched, a prisoner of war through streets in which one has passed his life, but such was my experience. Familiar faces looked on us and familiar voices spoke a cheering farewell, bidding us 'Keep a stiff upper lip' . . . .

Samuel Bell Palmer, *Diary*, manuscript owned by General and Mrs. John B. Anderson, Washington, p. 1.

175. DAVID GILMOUR BLYTHE, *Libby Prison*

At last I was taken from this place (Prison No. 2 on Cary Street, Richmond) and sent to Libby Prison, which has often been described; and yet from the description given, no adequate idea of the sufferings endured can be formed. The filth and heat were greater than even the place I had left. With some five hundred others I was crowded into the garret, next the roof, of the prison. The hot sun, beating down upon the roof, made the filthy garret, crowded with men clamoring for standing-room, suffocating in a degree which one cannot well understand who never experienced it. During the day, in the corners of our garret the dead remained among the living, and from these through all the rooms came the pestilent breath of a charnel-house. The vermin swarmed in every crack and crevice; the floors had not been cleaned for years. To consign men to such quarters was like signing their death warrant. Two men were shot by the rebel guard while trying to get breath at the windows.

Warren Lee Goss, *The Soldier's Story of his Captivity at Andersonville, Belle Isle, and Other Rebel Prisons*, Boston, 1869, p. 27.

176. OTTO BOETTICHER, *Libby Prison in 1862*

178. SAMUEL BELL PALMER, *Interior of Prisoner of War Barracks, Camp Douglas, Illinois*

179. ADALBERT JOHN VOLCK, *Interior of a Union Prisoner of War Camp*

Wm. B. McNutt one of the old members of the company, one who was with us at the start, with whom we have been by camp-fire, in bivouac, and on the march, died in the prison Hospital here [Camp Douglas], far away from home and friends. Death seems to get new terrors under such circumstances. Who shall say he did not die as bravely, as nobly for his country as the man who falls by shot or shell? He was a kind comrade and a good soldier. Peace to his ashes!

Samuel Bell Palmer, *Diary*, manuscript owned by General and Mrs. John B. Anderson, Washington, pp. 38f.

181. WILLIAM WAUD, *Released Union Prisoners Dancing on Board the* Star of the South
  at Charleston, South Carolina

And a little later, as we stepped from under the rebel flag which so long had maddened us by
its rebellious folds, to our own steamer, under our own glorious Stars and Stripes, for which
we had fought and were ready to die, what wonder that men were beside themselves for joy,
— that they shouted, danced, wept, even kissed the mute folds of those loved colors! The
kindly beams of the setting sun shed a halo of glory upon the pleasant town as we dropped
down the river, bidding adieu to the rebels until our next meeting upon the deadly
battle-field.

*The Stars and Stripes in Rebeldom — A Series of Papers Written by Federal Prisoners (Privates)
in Richmond, Tuscaloosa, New Orleans, and Salisbury, N. C.*, Boston, 1862, p. 127.

$\circ\mathbf{8}\circ$

Wounds, Disease and Death.

"MY FIRST FEELING after the shock was one of giddiness and blindness, then of partial recovery, then of deathly sickness."[1] Thus did William G. Stevenson describe his sensations when he was struck on the right side by a piece of almost spent shell which came near ending his life.

Weighing the prospects of receiving a maiming wound or a fatal one or similar thoughts were never far from the minds of the soldiers. They dreaded meeting a death such as befell many a helpless wounded soldier in the Wilderness: "The wounded soldiers lay scattered among the trees . . . . The unwounded troops, exhausted with battle, helped their stricken comrades to the rear. The wounded were haunted with the dread of fire . . . the bare prospect of fire running through the woods where they lay helpless, unnerved the most courageous of men, and made them call aloud for help. I saw many wounded soldiers in the Wilderness who hung on to their rifles, and whose intention was clearly stamped on their pallid faces."[2]

A Yankee officer describes the callousness with which men accustomed to sudden death came to regard it: "You would stare to see how little interest is aroused by the fact of a man being shot dead. Half a dozen gather to look at the body and promptly disperse to tell the tale to their comrades, who meanwhile have not left their bunks or their suppers. For a day or so the tragedy is discussed carelessly; . . . then the regiment talks of other things."[3]

The same attitude occurs in a slightly different version in the following incident recounted by Samuel H. Putnam: "At night, as we sat around the bivouac fire talking over the events of the day, our sharpshooters began to come in. We had been talking about them; some had been wounded, and one . . . Brown, was reported killed. . . . This Brown was a happy-go-lucky sort of chap, good-natured, great for foraging; and every one seemed sorry that he was killed.

'He was not so bad a fellow, after all', said one.

'That's so,' said another, 'Good hearted boy,' . . . Just at that moment, who should appear but Brown himself, loaded as usual with plunder, which he threw down at our feet with his cheery 'Hello, fellers.' We were astonished.

---

1. William G. Stevenson, *Thirteen Months in the Rebel Army*, New York, 1862, p. 158.
2. Frank Wilkeson, *Recollections of a Private Soldier in the Army of the Potomac*, New York, 1898, pp. 66ff.
3. John W. De Forest, *A Volunteer's Adventures*, New Haven, 1946, p. 80.

'Well, I'll be blowed,' said one, 'if here ain't that *cussed* Brown.' How soldier-like – praising him when we thought him dead, cursing him when we found he was alive."[4]

Aggressive callousness was also not infrequently displayed, especially when veterans encountered soldiers they considered had been coddled: "Soon the walking wounded came streaming back. These bloody wrecks of soldiers derided the new-comers. Men would tauntingly point to a shattered arm, or a wounded leg, or to bloody wounds on their faces, or to dead men lying in fence corners, and derisively shout: 'That is what you will catch up yonder in the woods!' . . . I saw one group of these wounded men repeatedly cover and uncover with a blanket a dead man whose face was horribly distorted, and show the courage-sapping spectacle to the marching troops . . . ."[5]

The courage and fortitude in the face of pain and suffering which was displayed by the soldiers of both armies is related in countless histories and diaries. Few of us today would be able to equal the nonchalant performance of this blue-belly: "I remember a man seated on a stump who chewed manfully at his hard rations while a comrade tried to dig a buckshot out of his skull with a jackknife.

'God damn it! Can't you start it?' grumbled this unsanctified sufferer. 'Dig in like hell!' "[6]

Equally as admirable as sheer physical courage was the ability, pretty wide-spread, to make a joke under trying circumstances. The following incident occurred during a campaign of the Army of the Potomac that was largely a series of "splendid flank movements" which the enlisted men, as soldiers will, turned into a joke by using the work "flanking" to account for anything from a night march to the capture of a sheep or a pig. One of the correspondents with the Army wrote at this time, "A poor fellow, terribly wounded, yesterday, said he saw the shell coming, 'but hadn't time to flank it.' And he enjoyed his joke with a smile and a chuckle, when his quick eye had sought and found appreciation among the by-standers. The shell had 'flanked' him, by taking off an arm."[7]

It is difficult for us to imagine in this day of anesthetics, pain-deadeners, blood transfusions, sterile equipment, and well-trained and competent surgeons, what passed in the minds of the soldiers in the field, as, with an indomitable courage, they stuck to their regiments in a game in which the cards were stacked against them. It was an exceedingly dense Civil War soldier who did not realize that even a slight flesh wound could easily develop into gangrene, which medical knowledge, even in the large army general hospitals at that time, was unable to combat successfully. The soldier naturally realized that a more serious wound practically guaranteed him death; and the soldier likewise knew that, even if he were not hit

4. Samuel H. Putnam, *The Story of Company A, 25th Regiment of Mass. Volunteers*, Worcester, 1886, p. 149.

5. Wilkeson, *op. cit.*, pp. 84ff.

6. De Forest, *op. cit.*, p. 141.

7. *U.S. Army and Navy Journal*, Vol. I, 1863–64, p. 694.

182. WINSLOW HOMER, *A Trooper Meditating beside a Grave*

Our company buried their dead just before sunset; and when the funeral dirge died away, and the volleys were fired over their graves, many a rugged man, whose heart was steeled by years of hardship and crime, shed tears like a child, for those bound to him by such ties as make all soldiers brothers. One of the worst men in the company excused this seeming weakness to a companion thus: "Tim, I haven't cried this twenty year; but they were all good boys, and my countrymen."

William G. Stevenson, *Thirteen Months in The Rebel Army*, New York, 1862, p. 75.

by an enemy bullet, enemy saber, bayonet, or pike, he was fully as apt to die from fever or one of the contagious diseases which spread like wild-fire through Southern camps. The following was written at Camp Chase, formerly the Lee estate in Virginia across from Washington, by a Connecticut volunteer: "Malaria, like a nightmare settled on the camp, crushing all energy and hope out of the men. Fatal as were the vapors of the Chickahominy swamps, or deadly even as was the fever-stricken air of New Bern, neither there nor in any other place where armies congregated North or South can it be said so much constant destruction to the square foot lurked in the air, as over those accursed Potomac flats."[8]

The quality of medical care by regimental surgeons varied considerably, but was generally pretty haphazard. The surgeons had a regular set routine for dispensing medications at the daily sick call: "The regular prescriptions were numbered six, nine, and eleven, which were blue pill, quinine, and vinum. We soon learned that 'vinum' meant either wine or brandy. I have seen men count from right to left, 'six, nine, eleven,' – 'six, nine, eleven,' and step into ranks just where eleven would strike. It was a sure thing, as the surgeon gave in regular order, as the men filed past him, something as follows: 'Well, what is the matter with you?' 'I don' know, doctor, I've got an awful pain in my bowels; guess I've got the chronic diarrhoea.' 'Let's see your tongue! Give him number six! Next, what is the matter with you?' 'I was took with an awful griping in my bowels – guess I've got the chronic diarrhoea.' 'Give him number nine! Next, what ails you?' 'I've g-g-got an almighty b-b-belly-ache, g-g-guess I've got the chronic diarrhoea.' 'Run out your tongue! Give him number eleven!' "[9] It is amazing that men so treated went back for more, and indeed that they survived it. Many did not.

The burial of the dead had to be adjusted to the situations existing. At times mass graves were dug into which many bodies would be placed, particularly after the biggest and bloodiest battles. If the identity of the body could be determined a crude headboard was placed over an individual grave, but this was not always possible – thus: "Some were marked with name, regiment, etc.; others 'supposed to be' such a one; and several were marked 'unknown.' This, then, was the end – an unknown grave. This is the dark side of a soldier's life – wounds, suffering, death and a nameless grave."[10]

Sometimes the corpse was wrapped only in a blanket before putting it in the grave; in other cases it was possible, particularly in static situations, to have a coffin built. Occasionally a subscription would be raised to send a soldier's body home, but this was often impractical. On many occasions it was not possible to do more than barely cover the bodies with earth, so that animals found them with most unpleasant consequences, and rains would come and expose the bodies or the bones.

8. Sheldon B. Thorpe, *The History of the 15th Connecticut Volunteers*, New Haven, 1893, p. 24.
9. A. R. Small, *The Sixteenth Maine Regiment*, Portland, 1886, pp. 172ff.
10. Putnam, *op. cit.*, p. 94.

When not in the midst of battle, a soldier who died of disease was usually given a full military funeral. A number of men were detailed as a guard, and the coffin was placed on an ambulance. Behind the ambulance a few special comrades followed as mourners. The guards marching in the funeral procession had their arms reversed and were accompanied by the company drummers, whose drums were muffled. These funeral processions were pathetic and moving. The funeral of an officer who died late in the War in a regiment which had been decimated by casualties and disease is described as follows: "His funeral was a pitiable and gloomy spectacle; there were but two officers to follow him, one of them with his arm in a sling; there was but one drummer, and not a single fifer, for the dead march."[11]

11. De Forest, *op. cit.*, p. 153.

183. WINSLOW HOMER, *The Walking Wounded*

July 22d Company A was reduced to its lowest number, and at this time might be said to have ceased to exist as an organization. One sergeant, one corporal, and three privates — five men all told, and not an officer left. For a time roll calls were dispensed with, as there were none to answer. Poor old Company A!

Samuel H. Putnam, *The Story of Company A, Twenty-Fifth Regiment, Mass. Volunteers*, Worcester, 1886, p. 309.

An armistice The battle field ups deep after the conflict. Our men ministering to their Peril

The rebels removing muskets.

184. UNIDENTIFIED, *Tending the Wounded during an Armistice at the Battle of Cedar Mountain*

185. ATTRIBUTED TO ARTHUR LUMLEY, *Fair Oaks Station: Bringing the Wounded to the Cars*

HOSPITAL CARS BETWEEN NEW YORK AND BOSTON. — We have lately examined the new hospital cars, built by the New York and Boston Railway, for the purpose of conveying sick and wounded soldiers between those two cities. Resembling in the outside the ordinary first-class car, the inside is fitted up with nine comfortable stretchers, hanging by rubber bands, that the patients may rest undisturbed by the motion of the car. Twelve easy chairs and several regular passenger seats are provided, and there are attached to the car a complete cooking apparatus, a large medicine chest and a wash-room. The design was to provide all the conveniencies and comforts of an hospital, and it has been very successfully carried out. Two experienced hospital stewards and two nurses have been appointed by the Government to take charge of the patients, and every thing has been provided to secure their safe and easy passage over the road. One of these cars leaves New York and one Boston every evening, the number of sick and disabled passengers from New York averaging twenty a day; a register of their names and complaints is kept by the stewards.

U. S. Army and Navy Journal, Vol. I, 1863–64, p. 261.

187. UNIDENTIFIED, *Dying of Gangrene*

Above 5000 wounded men, demanding instant and constant attendance, made a call too great to be met successfully. A much larger proportion of amputations was performed than would have been necessary if the wounds could have received earlier attention. On account of exposures, many wounds were gangrenous when the patients reached the hospital. In these cases delay was fatal, and an operation almost equally so, as tetanus often followed speedily. Where amputation was performed, eight out of ten died. The deaths in Corinth averaged fifty per day for a week after the battle. While the surgeons, as a body, did their duty nobly, there were some young men, apparently just out of college, who performed difficult operations with the assurance and assumed skill of practiced surgeons, and with little regard for human life or limb. In a few days erysipelas broke out, and numbers died of it. Pneumonia, typhoid fever, and measles followed, and Corinth was one entire hospital.

William G. Stevenson, *Thirteen Months in the Rebel Army*, New York, 1862, pp. 177f.

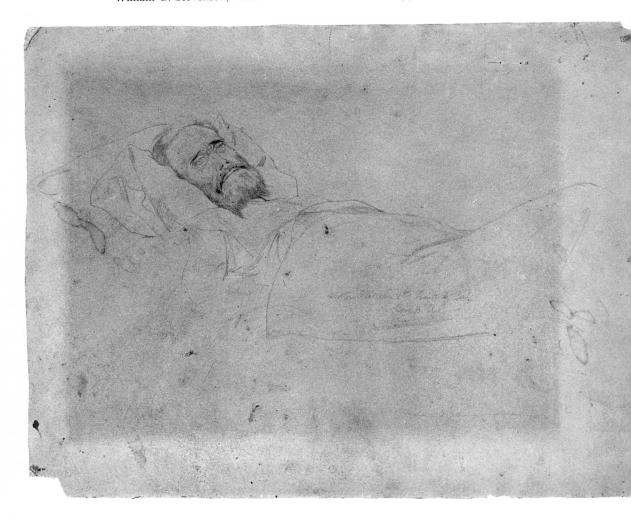

188. ALFRED R. WAUD, *Burying the Dead and Burning the Horses after the Battle of Fair Oaks, June 3, 1862*

It was a horrible sight as we entered the enemy's works – dead and dying men, dead and dying horses, in every conceivable position, some alone, others in little heaps of two or three, all smeared with blood and begrimed with powder and dirt. Many, perhaps most, of the Rebels, were shot in the head. We noticed a dead Rebel soldier, seated on a log, his rifle beside him, and his back supported against a tree. He had been shot in the act of eating a piece of bread; the mouthful bitten off remained between this teeth, ...

Samuel H. Putnam, *The Story of Company A, Twenty-Fifth Regiment, Mass. Volunteers,* Worcester, 1886, p. 110.

194. GEORGE CALEB BINGHAM, *Order No. 11*

On the 25th [of August, 1863] I issued an order requiring all citizens [of four counties in
Missouri] to remove from their present places of residence within 15 days from that date . . .
though this measure may seem too severe [it will be] merciful to the non-combatants I
have ordered the destruction of all grain and hay . . . and have ordered [from our lines
disloyal persons] to prevent the guerillas getting information . . . .

Rebellion Record, ed. Frank Moore, Vol. 7, New York, 1864, p. 517.

॰⑨॰

The Home Front.

Near the Front and under Enemy Occupation.

ONLY BRIEFLY did the foot of the invader stand on Northern soil, but the bitter experience of existing under the martial law of an occupying enemy fell to the lot of the Southerners early in 1861, and as the long years crept by more and more territory was added. To the proud, fiercely independent Rebel, convinced of the vast superiority of the Southern gentlefolk to the Yankee, this was indeed a bitter pill to swallow.

"General Butler was still in the ascendant, putting on all the style of a viceroy and slowly bringing order out of chaos. There were many complaints against his administration, but it must be said that as long as people conformed to the regulations he established they got along well enough.

"People in a conquered city can not dictate terms to the conquerors, and municipal laws must give way to military regulations."[1] Curfews were imposed, the free movement of the individual was restricted, oaths of allegiance were required to obtain free food, troops were quartered in private homes. These were some of the tribulations that had to be endured. Even the freedom of the press was curtailed. "By direction of Major-General Sherman, commanding the Department, the several newspapers published in Memphis are warned that they must cease the publication of reports anonymous or otherwise, of actions or movements of troops within the department. No discussion of the policy or measures of the government will be tolerated, and the editors and publishers of newspapers will be held accountable for the character of extracts published from Northern papers. Neither officers or troops within the command will be the subject of either praise or censure through the newspapers, as neither editors or correspondents have the right or the ability to give praise where deserved, or to withhold it where undeserved. No order of the Major-General commanding department will be published unless accompanied with an order from headquarters of the Department."[2]

For the Union soldiers, on the other hand, occupation duty was a pleasant change from fighting. "We enjoyed now, for a short time, the poetry of soldiering, – comfortable quarters and duty light. It seemed strange to wander about the

---

1. David D. Porter, *Incidents and Anecdotes of the Civil War*, New York, 1886, p. 107.
2. *U.S. Army and Navy Journal*, Vol. I., 1863–64, p. 231.

streets of the captured city; all was new to northern eyes. Most of the houses were abandoned, but some were left with the oldest slaves, while the younger and most valuable ones had been taken away. Streets deserted and silent, save when the stillness was broken by the tramp of the soldier, the citizens – those who remained – keeping inside their houses. Black faces peered at us from all quarters, and pieces of white cloth waved from every corner and Negro shanty. The slaves did not appear to be afraid of the soldiers, although they had been taught to fear us."[3]

Many a well-to-do Southerner saw the efforts of a lifetime, or, indeed, the accumulation of generations melt like ice in a hot sun. There is in the following brief report the element of personal tragedy which was repeated over and over throughout the South: "The United States District Court at Alexandria, Judge Underwood presiding, has ordered decrees of confiscation and sale against the property of thirteen persons, including Captain French Forrest, late of the United States Navy."[4]

The extremes of privation, as always, were felt most severely in the cities and by the poorer class. The wealthy naturally fared better and so did even the poorer whites who lived in the country, as they usually managed to hide away some provisions from the requisitions of the Confederate Commissaries and the succeeding Yankee foraging parties. "Perhaps the most unfortunate natives were those who chanced to live in a house by the roadside in the direct line of march of the army, for, from the time the head of the column struck such a house until the last straggler left it, there was a continuous stream of officers and men thronging into and about the premises, all ambitious to buy or beg or take whatsoever in the line of eatables and drinkables was to be had by either of these methods. The net result of this was to leave such families in a starving condition, and finally begging rations from the army. Those families by whose premises *both* armies marched were in the depths of distress, for Confederate soldiers let little in the way of provisions escape their maws on their line of march, even in Virginia; so that it was not unusual for such families to meet the Union advance with tearful eyes, and relate the losses which they had sustained and the beggary to which they had been reduced by the seizure of their last cow and last ounce of corn-meal. Sometimes, no doubt, they deceived to ward off impending search and seizure from a new quarter, but as a rule the premises showed their statements to be true."[5]

As the blockade tightened, prices skyrocketed and, even with money, little could be bought. Foods which had to be imported simply vanished from the markets, and it was not until the War was over that Southerners could drink a cup of genuine coffee. "...The town is fairly and squarely on the point of starvation. No one denies now that our blockade has been effective.... Unless work is soon found

3. Samuel H. Putnam, *The Story of Company A, Twenty-Fifth Regiment, Mass. Volunteers,* Worcester, 1886, pp. 113ff.

4. *U.S. Army and Navy Journal,* Vol. I, 1863–64, p. 215.

5. John D. Billings, *Hardtack and Coffee,* Boston, 1887, pp. 242ff.

192. UNIDENTIFIED, *Guerillas on the Lookout*

. . . the depredations of guerrillas assume a character that demands the serious consideration of the Government. They destroy the telegraph, rob the stages of mails and horses, plunder the resident population and even the poor laborers on the railroads of their property and money. They fire on steamboats, assume the garb of our soldiers to more perfectly deceive those they desire to destroy, and even carry the national flag to deceive troops sent out against them. They murder their prisoners, even when wounded, and daily butcher citizens suspected of being loyal. General Brown urges that unless severe retaliatory measures are adopted, the district will become depopulated by these fiends, and he recommends that the former associates of these villains, who are held in the military prisons, and who have forfeited their lives by the violation of every law, human and divine, be held as hostages for the future good conduct of these murderers in the brush. He also recommends that the policy of blood for blood, be adopted as the only one to be applied as economy of human life.

U. S. Army and Navy Journal, Vol. I, 1863–64, p. 726.

for these people, I do not see how famine can be averted. Flour ranges from twenty-three to thirty dollars a barrel; Irish potatoes, eight dollars a bushel . . . . Mess beef, which the quartermaster holds at thirteen dollars a barrel, sells in the city at thirty . . . ."[6]

The rebel ladies showed their spirit and patriotism perhaps not the least in accepting without a murmur of protest the extreme shortage of cloth and its by-product, attractive dresses. "There were women in linsey-woolsey, in negro and gunny cloth, in garments made from meal-bags, and men in Confederate gray and butternut brown; a boy with a crimson plush jacket, made from the upholstering of a sofa; men in short jackets, and little boys in long ones; the cast-off clothes of soldiers; the rags which had been picked up in the streets, and exhumed from garrets; boots and shoes down at the heel, open at the instep, and gaping at the toes; old bonnets of every description, some with white and crimson feathers, and ribbons once bright and flaunting; hats of every style worn by both sexes, palm-leaf, felt, straw, old and battered and well ventilated. One without a crown was worn by a man with red hair, suggestive of a chimney on fire, and flaming out at the top! It was the ragman's jubilee for charity."[7]

Pillaging or looting was prevalent under occupation, although the degree to which it was encouraged or frowned upon varied according to the inclinations of individual generals, and even there according to their changing attitudes. "Now all this looting and foraging is a disorder and a shame. Of course it is General Butler who is chiefly in fault for it. He could stop it at once, but he leaves the doors open for it, and the officers understand that he likes to see it. So they use what they want, and pack up the residue to carry away, and believe that they are doing right. It is a very different regime from that of our old general, Phelps, who would not take a private house for himself and fretted over the theft of a sweet potato."[8]

However, not all the pillaging was done by Union soldiers. The Negroes, no longer confined to their slave quarters, roamed the roads "breaking into and plundering the deserted houses, and destroying furniture, books and pictures in mere wantonness."[9]

As a military necessity the Confederate forces themselves inflicted wholesale destruction on the larger cities as they were forced to evacuate. While intended to be limited to military stores, the fires and explosions not infrequently got out of control and private property also suffered. "The torch was applied to Richmond about daylight, the rebel soldiers were coming into the city all the morning . . . . No language can adequately describe . . . the woeful appearances of Richmond as we enter it on this pleasant April morning. All through the latter part of last night after the first crash which occurred near the hour of daylight, about half past four, probably a little earlier, there was an almost incessant series of tremendous ex-

6. John W. De Forest, *A Volunteer's Adventures*, New Haven, 1946, pp. 21ff.
7. Charles C. Coffin, *The Boys of '61*, Boston, 1886, p. 407.
8. De Forest, *op. cit.*, p. 50.
9. *Ibid.*, p. 73.

plosions; their huge flashes lighting up the country for miles around, while the earth quivered and trembled even at great distances."[10]

10. S. Millett Thompson, *Thirteenth Regiment of New Hampshire . . . Infantry*, Boston, 1888, p. 571.

193. EDWIN FORBES, *Coming from the Mill, Rappahannock Station, January 14, 1864*

Since General Augur had taken up a position at Rectortown, his cavalry had foraged almost exclusively on the adjoining country. Every corn-house and corn-field in a large area were visited almost daily, and it was only by secreting small quantities of grain in different places that families were enabled to preserve food for themselves and the little stock they had been able to retain. Among the farms most frequently visited by these foragers was Glen Welby, particularly obnoxious because of the entertainment which Mosby's men was known ever to receive beneath its hospitable roof.

John Scott, *Partisan Life with Col. John S. Mosby*, New York, 1867, p. 329.

195. VOLTAIRE COMBE, *Camp at New Bern, North Carolina*

The night air is as heavy and dank as that of a swamp, and at daybreak the rotten odor of the earth is sickening. It is a land moreover of vermin, at least in this season. The evening resounds with mosquitoes; a tent hums with them like a beehive, audible rods away; as Lieutenant Potter says, they sing like canary birds. When I slip under my mosquito bar they prowl and yell around me with the ferocity of panthers.

Tiny millers and soft green insects get in my eyes, stick to my perspiring face, and perish by scores in the flame of my candle. Various kinds of brilliant bugs drop on my paper, where they are slain and devoured by gangs of large red ants. These ants rummage my whole habitation for rations, crawl inside my clothing and under my blanket at night, and try to eat me alive. I have seen many large "lightning bugs," such as the Cuban ladies sometimes wear in their hair. Also there are black grasshoppers two or three inches in length, with red and yellow trimmings to their jackets, the most dandified fellows of their species that I know of.

John W. De Forest, *A Volunteer's Adventures*, New Haven, 1946, p. 38.

196. James R. Hamilton, *House at Riley's Plantation Used by General Banks as Headquarters*

As I turned in at the gate at the end of the avenue, I beheld a sight that made my heart stand still. A number of horses were tied on the lawn, and in the porch was a group of men. I went straight up to the house, as I came near I saw they were U. S. officers. There they stood in all the glory of their gold lace and epaulettes, but I felt neither awed by their martial appearance, or fascinated by their bravery of apparel. I walked deliberately up the steps until I reached the top one, as I felt that I could be less at a disadvantage in an encounter if on a level with them. When there I stood still and waited for them to speak. One took off his cap and came towards me colouring violently. "Is this Mrs. McDonald," said he. I bowed stiffly, still looking at him.

He handed me a card, "De Forest, U. S. Army." I bowed again and asked if he had any business with me, knowing well that he had, and guessing what it was. Another then came forward as if to relieve him, and said that they had been sent by General Williams to look at the house, with a view to occupying it as headquarters, and asked if I had any objection to permitting them to see the rooms. I told him that I had no objection to them seeing the rooms, but that I had very many objections to having it occupied as headquarters.

Cornelia Peake McDonald, *A Diary with Reminiscences of the War and Refugee Life in the Shenandoah Valley, 1860-1865*, ed. Hunter McDonald, Nashville, 1934, pp. 42f.

Extraordinary Sale of Confiscated Blood Horses at New Orleans - March 3ᵈ 1863 -

197. JAMES R. HAMILTON, *Sale of Confiscated Blood Horses at New Orleans, 1863*

. . . commodities could be purchased very cheaply in the war areas of Louisiana by anyone who had cash, a permit from Butler and the available shipping; and these same commodities could be sold at high prices up North . . . . Later in the year [1862], came the confiscations of rebel property, with frequent sales at auction of valuable commodities . . . .

James Parton, *General Butler in New Orleans*, New York, 1864, p. 411.

198. JAMES R. HAMILTON, *Civilians Applying for Aid to Colonel Thorpe at New Orleans*

These poor people were on the verge of starvation; flour thirty-five dollars a barrel, and no money wherewith to buy it; everything else in proportion. They looked famished and every way miserable; the women in shabby calico skirts clinging around their lean frames; the men without coats, and all as dirty as they were ragged. The large hotel was closed, and nearly all the private houses. We could find no food for sale but a few watermelons, a few stale gingercakes and a dozen loaves of bread. As we bought these, I can't imagine what the people ate next day, unless it might be each other. If the war does not end soon, the South will starve to death.

John W. De Forest, *A Volunteer's Adventures*, New Haven, 1946, p. 34.

201. FRANK VIZETELLY, *Confederate Cotton Burners Surprised by Federal Patrol*

As a natural consequence of her surrender [New Orleans], the forts also gave up, and fair Louisiana with her fertile fields of cane and cotton, her many bayous and dark old forests, lies powerless at the feet of the enemy. Though the Yankees have gained the land, the people are determined they shall not have its wealth, and from every plantation rises the smoke of burning cotton. The order from Beauregard advising the destruction of the cotton met with a ready response from the people, most of them agreeing that it is the only thing to do.
As far as we can see are the ascending wreaths of smoke, and we hear that all the cotton of the Mississippi Valley from Memphis to New Orleans is going up in smoke. We have found it is hard to burn bales of cotton. They will smoulder for days. So the huge bales are cut open before they are lighted and the old cottons burn slowly. It has to be stirred and turned over but the light cotton from the lint room goes like a flash. We should know, for Mamma has $20,000 worth burning on the gin ridge now; it was set on fire yesterday and is still blazing.

Kate Stone, *Brokenburn, the Journal of Kate Stone, 1861–1868*, ed. John Q. Anderson, Baton Rouge, 1955, pp. 100f.

Hearth and Home.

THE SOUTHERN PEOPLE, being closer to the scenes of battle, felt the War more immediately than did the people of the North. Their sufferings and tribulations, although varying in duration and severity, included all the pains and trials suffered by the North, with the added fact or threat of starvation and loss of home and property, directly or indirectly the result of enemy action.

Yet the suffering of the Northern people should not be minimized. While in the early years of the War the Southerners could console themselves for their sacrifices by the encouraging course of the War and the hope of its successful termination, the reverse was true of the North. To the Yankee the progress of the War was for years discouraging, and, to comprehend the emotional drain, one has to interpolate the element of protracted suspense of hopes, continuously raised and dashed, while all the time, an increasing burden of sacrifice was demanded and accorded. The despondency and defeatism prevalent at times among the civilian population, however, did not seem to be paralleled among the troops themselves. "At this time, there was a good deal of despondency at home; and the papers began to intimate that the army was discouraged, and the war was a failure. It was far from that. I wrote at the time in the Boston *Journal:* 'It is true that the enthusiasm with which men are animated on entering the service soon evaporates. It is so always. Who of us does not know that the position, to which we have struggled and aimed for years, when reached is seen in a different light, and that possession is cool where anticipation is ardent? It is also true that there is no little fault-finding and grumbling. Where is this also not true? Men who at home found fault with their dinner and the weather, cannot of course undergo the hardships of camp without indulging in the old habit. The boys feel far better than one might infer from hearing *some* of their talk. For instance, one night one of ours was scolding generally, – running amuck at government, the paymaster, the army, and so on. A good-natured fellow, who perhaps may sometimes have felt just so himself, said: 'suppose you heard a secesh, down town, talking that way, what would you do?' 'Knock him over,' was the quiet response. This anecdote is representative. We find fault; we scold; we grumble; we long to be at home; but, if anybody thinks we are discouraged or demoralized, he is infinitely mistaken. We are here as ready and as efficient as ever we were; and I must believe that is true of our army generally.'"[11]

It was those people who resided in the border states, however, who suffered most appallingly. There, families, towns, counties and states were divided in their loyalties. No let-up was provided by the shifting tides of occupation, first by one side and then the other, since bushwhacking guerrilla bands roamed the states more or less at will – burning, pillaging and killing civilians as well as soldiers. Crops could not be raised, and the direst conditions of starvation and anarchy pre-

11. John W. Hanson, *Historical Sketch of the Old Sixth Regiment of Massachusetts Volunteers,* Boston, 1866, pp. 198ff.

vailed for years. In addition to the small scale bushwhacking in Tennessee, Kentucky and adjacent areas under such leaders as John Hunt Morgan and William Clarke Quantrill, cavalry raids skillfully planned on a large scale kept the inhabitants in sections of Ohio, Kansas, Arkansas and Missouri in a state of terror.

But life behind the lines, removed from danger of invasion and raids, was not to outward appearances much different than before the War. There were the usual concerts, operas and plays – dances and balls even in troubled Richmond late in the War. The absence of young men of military age was more noticeable in the South than in the North. A soldier in the 1st Rhode Island Light Artillery returning home to Providence wrote that he saw "little which indicated the existence of a gigantic Civil War. . . . Familiar faces were met at every corner; the cars were, as usual, bringing and carrying their living freight; the ships at the wharves were loading and unloading with unabated activity; smoke was going up from the numerous factories, foundries, and machine shops, and scarcely noticeable was the depletion in population made by the thousands sent to the front."[12]

Danger was, however, real and constant even far back of the lines of the armies. Northern and Southern seaboard communities both faced the threat of bombardment from the sea. Sabotage, real or fancied, was a threat, and riots caused by a variety of reasons imperiled lives and property. Arsenals and ammunition depots had an unpleasant tendency to explode. Some forty young women making paper cartridges at the Allegheny Arsenal in Pittsburgh were blown up when an iron rimmed wheel of a cart rumbling by their factory ignited a train of spilled black powder. ". . . Of the main building nothing remained but a heap of smoking debris. The ground about was strewn with fragments of charred wood, torn clothing, balls, caps, grape shot, exploded shells, shoes, fragments of dinner baskets belonging to the inmates, steel springs from the girls' hoop skirts, cartridge, paper, sheet iron, melted lead, etc. Two hundred feet from the laboratory was picked up the body of one young girl, terribly mangled; another body was seen to fly in the air and separate into two parts; an arm was thrown over the wall; a foot was picked up near the gate; a piece of skull was found a hundred yards away, and pieces of the intestines were scattered about the grounds. Some fled out of the ruins covered with flame, or blackened and lacerated with the effects of the explosion, and others fell and expired or lingered in agony until removed. . . ."[13]

The ever increasing demands of the armies for essential assistance, not then available through governmental channels, produced a characteristic American response in the fever for holding fairs which swept the North. Every large city had its bazaar to raise money and supplies for the Sanitary Commission, the predecessor of the Red Cross.

As the War progressed, the enthusiasm with which the first contingents leav-

12. John H. Rhodes, *History of Battery "B", 1st Rhode Island Light Artillery*, Providence, 1894, pp. 161ff.

13. *Pittsburgh Daily Post*, Thursday morning, Sept. 18, 1862.

202. THOMAS NAST, *Ladies' Parlor at Willard's Hotel, Washington, March 6, 1861*

March 30th [1861] The great employment of four-fifths of the people at Willard's at present seems to be to hunt senators and congressmen through the lobbies. Every man is heavy with documents – those which he cannot carry in his pockets and hat, occupy his hands, or are thrust under his arms. The whole city is placarded with announcements of facilities for assaulting the powers that be, among which must not be forgotten the claims of the "excelsior card-writer," at Willard's, who prepares names, addresses, styles, and titles in superior penmanship. There are men at Willard's who have come literally thousands of miles to seek for places which can only be theirs for four years, and who with true American facility have abandoned the calling and pursuits of a lifetime for this doubtful canvas; and I was told of one gentleman, who having been informed that he could not get a judgeship, condescended to seek a place in the Post Office, and finally applied to Mr. Chase to be appointed keeper of a "lighthouse," he was not particular where.

William Howard Russell, *My Diary North and South*, New York, 1863, p. 51.

ing for the front were given Godspeed evaporated. Brass bands, collations, flowers and cheering throngs ceased to be the routine accompaniment of troop departures. Units marching to trains became too common a sight to call forth such effort. Draft dodgers went to Canada or abroad for their "health", and young males were seldom seen on the streets except for the maimed and crippled or soldiers home on leave. A visiting Englishman observed: "You meet numbers of Federal officers, invalided and wounded, in New York, on leave of absence. I met a young fellow, only twenty-one years of age, who had been through seventeen general engagements. He had enlisted as a sergeant, and had got a company through his valour and steadiness. He had been wounded, and was on a couple of months' leave. He was enthusiastic in praise of his profession, and was anxious to be on the field once more. There are many brave, gentlemanly fellows like him; but the Northern officers are generally what they are represented in the English papers – coarse and bombastic, not what would be expected from their position and profession. This, no doubt, arises from the fact that many of them have risen from very doubtful origin, and bring some of their obnoxious ways and sayings with them. Of course they chew right and left.

"The men, who often are better born and better educated than their commanders, are of course, as must be expected in conscripts and volunteers so hastily raised, but poorly drilled, and lax in discipline – particularly when compared with the English or French soldiery. They are brave fellows, however, and prove themselves so in many a bloody battle, and deserve a far warmer reception than they usually get on their return to New York."[14]

The principal role of women, both North and South, was to keep their homes operating – the children must still be raised, nursed when sick, and educated. They did, notwithstanding, put in long hours making bandages or sewing for the soldiers. ". . . Every linen garment I possessed, except one change, every garment of cotton fabric, all my table-linen, all my bed-linen, even the chintz covers of furniture, – all were torn into strips and rolled for bandages for the soldiers' wounds."[15] Farm women, with such male help as was at hand, tried to keep the farms going, the stock watered, the crops weeded and harvested. City women went to work in office and factory. Some worked in constant danger and some, indeed, gave their lives.

Mothers and fathers wrote letters to their sons, prayed, scanned the dispatches from the front, read the lists of missing, wounded and dead after each battle, suffered and tried to comfort one another.

In time, living became harder, costs rose, and those with slender or no means, aside from a soldier's allotment, suffered real privation. Conditions varied from section to section in the Union, and this was equally true of the South. But in general the pinch was felt earlier and progressively more severely in the South

14. Horace P. Batcheler, *Jonathan at Home: or, A Stray Shot at the Yankees*, London, 1864, pp. 143ff.
15. Sara Agnes Pryor, *My Day – Reminiscences of a Long Life*, New York, 1909, p. 168.

203. E. D. HAWTHORNE, *Interior of George Hayward's Porter House, New York*

A few words in reference to the imbibing habits of the Americans. It would be impossible to enumerate all their favourite drinks, but here are a few: — gin sling, mint julep, whisky kin, brandy punch, claret cobbler, wine sangaree, claret punch, gin cocktail, sherry cobbler, milk punch, brandy smash, whisky cocktail, apple toddy, brandy pony, Bourbon sour, brandy cocktail, Japanese drink, Tom and Jerry, the bull's milk, and Dan Webster's fixings. New York is unquestionably a city of drinkers; and the first men in it take their refreshers with the dawn, and in fact are at it "from early morn to dewy eve." These drinks are very agreeable to the palate, but have a tendency to render a man, in vulgar parlance, "seedy." Each hotel and restaurant has of course its bar; ice abounds, and is to be had everywhere and at all times. The drinks and ice, spiced with lemon-peel and nutmeg, are poured from one glass into another, and the mixture is imbibed through a straw.

Horace P. Batcheler, *Jonathan at Home: or, A Stray Shot at the Yankees*, London, 1864, pp. 64f.

until in some areas the grim visage of starvation was a constant companion of rich and poor.

Patriotic and self-sacrificing as were the majority, each region had its war-profiteers, its weaklings and its malcontents and opportunists. In the North, war-weariness fostered a strong movement to concede to the South. Ugly riots in Boston and New York were fomented against the Irish. Huge fortunes were made from the sale of shoddy uniforms, blankets, paper-soled shoes. In the South, the principle of States' Rights hampered the movement and use of State troops. Jealousy, self-seeking and incompetence were present in high places.

But North and South, the amazing truth is that both sections – so alike and yet so different – persevered in the face of intermittent corruption, incompetence, economic and financial exhaustion, personal hardship and privation, disheartening defeat, divided council, and this despite the mounting toll of death, until it was obvious to all but the most obdurate that the end had come.

204. LILY MARTIN SPENCER, *The War Spirit at Home – Celebrating the Victory at Vicksburg*

New York always seems full of bustle, excitement, liveliness, and amusement. At present, wherever you turn, you see cripples and worn-out looking soldiers from the war. There are no other signs or tokens of the dreadful struggle going on, excepting the numbers of people to be seen in mourning. I certainly think two-thirds of those whom I beheld wore the trappings of woe. Pretty widows, aged mothers, and pale-faced interesting sisters are to be noticed every hour gliding silently by, bowed down by their weight of grief, but evidently the objects of little pity or remark, however sad their histories may have been.

Horace P. Batcheler, *Jonathan at Home: or, A Stray Shot at the Yankees*, London, 1864, p. 9.

205. ATTRIBUTED TO FRANCIS BICKNELL CARPENTER, *Reception at the White House,*
1863

The Richmond Examiner of November 24th, says: — "Five balls advertised, and flour one
hundred and twenty-five dollars a barrel! Who prates of famine and want? Who is suffering
for the necessaries of life? Does not all go 'merry as a marriage ball?' If the skeleton comes
in, put a ball ticket at five dollars in its bony fingers, a masquerade ball costume upon its
back of bony links, and send the grim guest into the ball room to the sound of
cotillion music."

U. S. Army and Navy Journal, Vol. I, 1863–64, p. 231.

207. SHERMAN ENDERTON, *Quantrill's Raid on Lawrence, August 21, 1863*

The ruffians, when they approached the city, threw a guard around it to prevent any of the men from escaping . . . . [they] shot down [men] while their wives, daughters and mothers were clinging to them and begging that they might be spared . . . . In less than half an hour after the enemy entered the city, it was in a sheet of flame.

Wiley Britton, *Memoirs of the Rebellion on the Border, 1863*, Chicago, 1882, p. 386.

210. WINSLOW HOMER, *The Initials*

Come in the evening,
   Or come in the morning.
Come when you're looked for,
   Or come without warning.
Kisses and welcome
   You'll find here before you
And the oftener you come here
   The more I'll adore you.

              From the lady with the
              "pretty auburn curls."

Manuscript in a private collection, Washington.

211. WILLIAM MORRIS HUNT, *Playing Field Hospital*

. . . "Do you expect your patients to come to you, Nelly?" . . . . "No, I shall go and look for them." . . . "You should have an ambulance and be a branch of the Sanitary Commission" . . . Nelly had often heard the words, but did not quite understand what they meant. So Will told her of that great and never-failing charity, to which thousands owe their lives . . . . When her brother paused, she said earnestly: "Yes I will be a Sanitary. This little cart of mine shall be my amb'lance and I'll never drive too fast, or be rough with my poor passengers, like some of the men you tell about."

Louisa M. Alcott, "Nelly's Hospital" in *Our Young Folks, an Illustrated Magazine for Boys and Girls*, April, 1865.

°10°

The Slaves' Escape to Freedom.

FOR MANY MONTHS after the Civil War started there was great confusion as to what to do about the Negroes in those sections of the South passing under Union control. It was one of many problems which had not been carefully thought out before hostilities began. Soon, however, the mystical word "freedom" spread like wildfire from mouth to mouth by the grapevine which connected the slaves throughout the plantations of the Confederate states. To many a Negro the concept of freedom was the equivalent of paradise on earth, and the realization that freedom in itself did not guarantee all the food one could eat, shelter and clothing, did not enter many minds; nor did the concept that freedom also carried its own obligations. Word from those assisted through the efforts of the "under-ground railroad" had already generated a great enthusiasm for the Utopian life which apparently lay just behind the Union lines. Before long, slaves either singly or in groups made plans to leave their plantations and go North in search of the Union forces. Often at very considerable danger to themselves they set forth, in the dead of night, keeping constantly to the cover of woods and foraging as they went. Slowly they began to pass behind the Union lines and as time went on the flow increased: ". . . thousands of Negroes followed in Sherman's trail, some of them travelling hundreds of miles in the search for freedom. . . . They were pursued by bloodhounds and often shot down like dogs when caught; and sometimes, out of a large number who started from the interior, only a few would reach Savannah, and these in a most forlorn condition."[1]

The arrival of thousands of contrabands became quite a problem for the Union commanders in the field, for the Negroes on their arrival were starving and penniless with only the clothes on their backs. Unprepared for this influx of hungry mouths, Union commanders did what they could to prevent starvation and pestilence. Each regiment shortly had its own little fringe of contrabands, who washed clothes for the men, cooked dinners for the company, or for individual officers' messes. "Among the 'contrabands' in our mess, first and foremost stood the major's boys, Tom Jones, the concentrated essence of Africa; and after him were Clem, John Willis, Lam Babb, and others, whose comicalities helped the mess far more than any other service they rendered, and whose principal effort seemed to be always to be present when they were not wanted, and always absent when

1. Francis H. Buffum, *History of the 14th New Hampshire Volunteers*, Boston, 1882, pp. 325ff.

212. THOMAS MORAN, *Slaves Escaping through the Swamp*

While contemplating the . . . swamp, . . . just imagine yourself in a path, and meeting a
snake at every few rods . . . or a large wild pig or two . . . all around you for many miles a
forest of large trees with tops densely interlacing . . . . [From this swamp we witness the
escape] of bodies of negro refugees. They will appear in the edge of the brush half a mile or
so distant, looking back over their shoulders as if expecting pursuit or capture even there.
. . . Once inside [our lines] away go all fear and caution . . . . They improvise a little jubilee,
jumping up and down and exclaiming: "O bress de Lord-I'se free, I'se free."

S. Millett Thompson, *History of the 13th New Hampshire Infantry*, Boston, 1888, pp. 296ff.

needed."[2] Sometimes they were also employed as nurses and laborers in the hospitals, and the men were frequently put to work, when the situation made it possible, on field fortifications.

The slow process which eventually brought about the emancipation of the Negro started. In April of 1862, General David Hunter declared that all slaves in his military department were "forever free." A week later Lincoln annulled this proclamation. By July 22, 1862, "all national commanders were ordered to employ as many negroes as could be used advantageously for military and naval purposes. . . ."[3] However, it was not until September 22, 1862, that the preliminary emancipation proclamation was issued, and not until January 1, 1863, that the final step was taken.

It was some time before the North came to the conclusion that the enlistment of Negroes into the armed services was desirable, practical, and inevitable. The first units were organized as volunteers in September of 1862. The first regiment of free Negroes was mustered in as the 1st Regiment of Louisiana Native Guards, thus becoming the first group of Negro soldiers mustered as a unit into the United States Army during the War.

The lure of a smart uniform helped enlistments and had the usual effect on the opposite sex. "The colored men . . . choose the arm of service from their fancy for certain colors . . . some the infantry for its blue, the artillery for its red, the cavalry for its yellow. When a young negro . . . returns in full regimentals . . . he struts like a turkey cock. . . .The old men and women throw up their hands with a hundred benedictions . . . the girls languish for a glance of his eye. . . ."[4] However it required quite considerable courage for the colored volunteer to enlist, for not only was he well aware of the hardships that he faced by virtue of having a black skin, but he also knew of the severe treatment he would receive were he to be captured by Confederate forces.

Not many colored regiments saw combat service; many were used for services behind the lines, particularly in connection with what we now call the service of supply. However, the few colored regiments which did see service, such as the 54th Massachusetts Colored Regiment which fought in the assault at Fort Wagner, performed courageously. In the attack on Fort Wagner, the 54th Massachusetts sustained greater losses than any other of the ten Union regiments participating in the attack, and its casualty list of 247 was higher than the total of the Confederate loss.[5]

---

2. John W. Hanson, *Historical Sketch of the Old Sixth Regiment of Massachusetts Volunteers*, Boston, 1866, pp. 153ff.
3. Travis T. Miller, *Photographic History of the Civil War*, Vol. II, New York, 1911, pp. 30ff.
4. S. Millett Thompson, *History of 13th N. H. Infantry*, Boston, 1888, p. 234.
5. Benjamin Quarles, *The Negro in the Civil War*, Boston, 1953, pp. 16ff.

214. EDWIN FORBES, *Contrabands Approaching the Union Lines near Culpeper Court House, November 8, 1863*

From nearly every plantation along the line of march, our column was reinforced by negroes . . . .

"Where are you going?" a soldier asked an old darky, whose hair was as white as wool, and who joined the column at a cross-roads, followed by six or eight children, and something like a score of grandchildren of both sexes.

"Boun' for the Promis' Lan', massa," was the reply.

"Where is the Promised Land, Uncle?"

"Don't know 'zactly, massa; but it's up dar whar Massa Linkum's sojers come from, I reckon."

"Why don't you stay at home?"

"Home, massa? I'se got no home. My ole wife been sold 'way to nudder county. My chil'ren and gran'chil'ren all scattered frew slavery."

"You seem to have quite a number left."

"Dese ain't half, massa. We'se gwyne to de lan' ob freedom and maybe de ress will meet us dar."

"Then you have heard of emancipation?"

"Don't know what dat is, massa."

"Freedom; President Lincoln's proclamation setting the slaves free?"

"Yes, sah; we dun heard ob dat. Bress de Lawd!"

Stanton P. Allen, *Down in Dixie*, Boston, 1888, pp. 372f.

216. FRANK VIZETELLY, *Dead Negro Soldiers at Fort Wagner*

I visited the battery [Fort Wagner] yesterday. The dead and wounded were piled up in a ditch together sometimes fifty in a heap, and they were strewn all over the plain for a distance of three fourths of a mile. They had two (only one, the Fifty-fourth?) negro regiments and they were slaughtered in every direction. One pile of negroes numbered thirty. Numbers of both white and black were killed on top of our breastworks as well as inside. The negroes fought gallantly, and were headed by as brave a colonel as ever lived. He mounted the breastworks waving his sword, and at the head of his regiment, and he and a negro orderly sergeant fell dead over the inner crest of the works. The negroes were as fine-looking a set as I ever saw, – large, strong, muscular fellows.

Letter of Lieut. Iredell Jones, in Luis F. Emilio, *A Brave Black Regiment*, Boston, 1891, p. 95.

217. Thomas Nast, *The 55th Massachusetts Colored Volunteers at Charleston, 1865*

Opposite page:

218. Frank Buchser, *The Volunteer's Return*

Negro volunteers began a new life on discharge from military service. "The increased self-respect of army life fitted them to do the duties of civil life . . . [although some preferred to leave the South because] 'I'se made up my mind dat dese yer Secesh will neber be cibilized in my time'."

T. W. Higginson, *Army Life in a Black Regiment*, Boston, 1870, pp. 265f.

○❚❚○

The Strife Ends:
The Beginning of an
American Legend.

GRADUALLY the unmistakable signs that the Army of Northern Virginia could not continue much longer as an effective fighting force began to multiply. To both armies and to the citizens long anxious for peace, its imminence was hard to grasp after the seemingly endless years of conflict, and when it finally happened, its impact came as a shock. "The evening of the 10th of April I made full notes as follows: After the surrender General Grant shook hands with all present who were not to accompany him, mounted his horse, and started with his staff for Washington without having entered the enemy's lines. Lee set out for Richmond, and it was felt by all that peace had at last dawned upon the land. The charges were now withdrawn from the guns, the campfires were left to smolder in their ashes, the flags were tenderly furled . . . and the Army of the Union and the Army of Northern Virginia turned their backs upon each other for the first time in four long, bloody years."[1] To the veterans of Lee's army who had stuck it out to the bitter end, this was incredible. But the fact had to be accepted. A feeling of relief followed the first numbing shock and with it, the realization that henceforth no new crop of one-legged, one-armed lads would be coming home.

In the North the day of April 10 was passed in the celebration of victory. The populace was delirious with joy. Torchlight processions, transparencies, fireworks and bonfires illuminated the villages, towns and cities. Frenzied crowds roamed the streets singing and shouting. However, for the thousands of parents whose sons were not returning, for the widows whose husbands lay in unmarked graves, for the young woman whose beau would never claim her as a bride, tragedy was not relieved. "[The returning regiment's] arrival . . . was proclaimed by the ringing of church bells . . . [and] blowing of steam whistles. . . . [But all this was] not for a large number of veterans, for there were only two hundred and twenty men in the ranks and marching, with a few, unable to walk, borne in carriages. . . . Many hearts were touched with sadness at seeing an elderly lady, with a bouquet of flowers in her hands to be given to her son, whom she expected to see in the ranks, all unconscious that he had been seriously wounded in a recent battle and was left behind in the hospital. . . ."[2]

---

1. Horace Porter in *Battles and Leaders of the Civil War*, Vol. 4, New York, 1888, p. 746.
2. Alfred S. Roe, *History of the 10th Massachusetts Infantry*, Springfield, 1909, pp. 293ff.

219. ALFRED R. WAUD, *General Lee Leaving Appomattox*

A little before four o'clock General Lee shook hands with General Grant, bowed to the other officers and . . . left the room . . . . Lee signaled to his orderly to bring up his horse, and while the animal was being bridled the general . . . gazed sadly in the direction of the valley beyond, where his army lay – now an army of prisoners. He thrice smote the palm of his left hand slowly with his right fist in an absent sort of way, seemed not to see the group of Union officers in the yard, who rose respectfully at his approach, and appeared unaware of everything about him. [His horse was brought up and General Grant saluted him by raising his hat] . . . Lee raised his hat respectfully, and rode off at a slow trot to break the sad news to the brave fellows whom he had so long commanded.

Horace Porter, *Campaigning with Grant*, New York, 1897, pp. 485f.

220. JAMES F. QUEEN, *General Lee's Surrender*

Headquarters Army of No. Virginia
10th April 1865

General Order
No. 9

After four years of arduous service marked by unsurpassed courage and fortitude the Army of Northern Virginia has been compelled to yield to overwhelming numbers and resources.

I need not tell the brave survivors of so many hard fought battles who have remained steadfast to the last that I have consented to this result from no distrust of them.

But feeling that valor and devotion could accomplish nothing that would compensate for the loss that would have attended the continuance of the contest I determined to avoid the useless sacrifice of those whose past services have endeared them to their countrymen.

By the term of the agreement officers and men can return to their homes and remain until exchanged. You will take with you the satisfaction that proceeds from the consciousness of duty faithfully performed, and I earnestly pray that a merciful God will extend to you His blessing and protection.

With an increasing admiration of your constancy and devotion to your country and a grateful remembrance of your kind and generous consideration for myself, I bid you all an affectionate farewell.

R. E. Lee
Gen.

Brig. Gen. W. H. Stevens
Chief Eng. A.N.Va.

The battles were over. In the North there were the grand reviews and the welcoming home parades of the returning regiments, the final ceremonies of mustering out – and then the beginning of readjustment to civilian life. The Confederate soldier, on the other hand, had to make the long, lonely trek home a-foot, if an infantryman; or if a trooper or artillery man, astride a war-worn horse or mule through a countryside stripped of food by the long years of war and infested with bands of lawless men. And what was there to go home to? Was the house still there – was the wife and family at home or were they refugees in some other section?

There was still tragedy to come. Lincoln was assassinated. Davis was a prisoner of state in close confinement in Fortress Monroe charged with treason. To some, who could not accept the consequences of defeat, there was the alternative of exile in a foreign land. For several years the South existed under martial law. It was not until Christmas Day, 1868, that a general amnesty was promulgated.

For most veterans the War had been the high point of their lives, and it was not long before groups of veterans formed their own associations and commenced to have reunions. The first G. A. R. post was organized April 6, 1866, and grew to become a potent force in local affairs and national politics, with a membership of over 400,000 by 1890. For years after the War, Decoration Day in the North was dominated by the blue clad veterans. Similarly the veterans of the Confederacy commemorated their fallen dead at their own annual gathering on April 26. It was these veteran groups of both sides who, through the recollection of commonly shared experiences during the War as they re-lived them in their joint pilgrimages back to the battlefields, did the most toward healing the bitterness which existed between the two former enemies and toward uniting the nation.

No earlier, and certainly no subsequent war in our history, has had the climacteric effect of the Civil War, not only on those then living, but on posterity. During the Revolution heroic deeds, noble leaders, and vicissitudes of great magnitude were present, yet such was the nature of the war that comparatively small areas and relatively few persons were intimately involved at any one time. Tremendous as were its implications which later were so amply fulfilled, the American Revolutionary War was, after all, when examined in true perspective, of modest scope.

As the Revolution is the birth, so then the Civil War is the country's coming of age. Through it, the adolescent federation, a self-complacent, rather easygoing, self satisfied and loosely bound assortment of states of little import in the course of world affairs, was thrust into manhood. It was a rather awkward and unsure adult, to be sure, but still it was recognized as a country entitled to respect as a significant power.

Where history stops and legend takes over can perhaps not be precisely determined. Yet it can hardly be denied that the one lasting beneficial result of the War has been the gradual evolution of what approximates a myth or a legend – an epic compounded of tragedy not unrelieved by touches of comedy and composed on a truly grandiose scale. This War which split families and divided the nation into

223. THOMAS WATERMAN WOOD, *The Return of the Flags, 1865*

Almost every company of our Regiment possessed a *flag*, but we had no proper "Colors" until in June, 1862, when a beautiful "stand" was presented to the Regiment by Mr. John W. King, our worthy sutler. These colors were made to order, and cost about two hundred dollars. They were carried through the engagements at Bull Run, Frederick City, South Mountain, Antietam, Chickamauga, and Mission Ridge. In the battle of Chickamauga they were so torn that it was with difficulty they could be kept fastened on the staff, but at Mission Ridge they were literally torn to ribbons by shot and shell, and hung in strips about the scarred and splintered staff. They were the first colors planted on the rebel fortifications on the Ridge, and of the three brave men who successively bore them on that day one was instantly killed and two severely wounded.

J. H. Horton and Sol. Teverbaugh, *A History of the Eleventh [Ohio] Regiment*, Dayton, 1866, p. 242.

224. ALFRED R. WAUD, *Mustered Out – Negro Soldiers Arriving Home*

Oh, we're the bully soldiers of the 'First of Arkansas',
We are fighting for the Union, we are fighting for the law,
We can hit a Rebel further than a white man ever saw,
As we go marching on.

We have done with hoeing cotton, we have done with hoeing corn,
We are colored Yankee soldiers, now, as sure as you are born;
When the masters hear us yelling, they'll think it's Gabriel's horn,
As we go marching on.

Capt. Lindley Miller, "Marching Song of the First Arkansas (Negro) Regiment"
(contemporary song).

225. WILLIAM WAUD, *Crowds Filing past Lincoln's Coffin at Cleveland, May 1865*

Coffin that passes through lanes and streets,
Through day and night with the great cloud darkening the land,
With the pomp of the inloop'd flags with the cities draped in black,
With the show of the States themselves as of crape-veil'd women standing,
With processions long and winding and the flambeaus of the night,
With the countless torches lit, with the silent sea of faces and the unbared heads
With the waiting depot, the arriving coffin, and the sombre faces,
With dirges through the night, with the thousand voices rising strong and solemn,
With all the mournful voices of the dirges pour'd around the coffin,
The dim-lit churches and the shuddering organs — where amid these you journey,
With the tolling tolling bells' perpetual clang,
Here, coffin that slowly passes,
I give you my sprig of lilac.

Walt Whitman, "When Lilacs Last in the Dooryard Bloom'd" in
Leaves of Grass, Boston, 1897, p. 256.

247

two opposing camps, which terminated in bitterness, has culminated at the end in the formation of a truly national legend – a glorious legend to which both North and South may claim equal share. This legend is the legacy of the vicissitudes and suffering of soldier and civilian, more poignant because it was fought between friends, between brothers, between sons and fathers, and fought on our own soil – a civil war.

The scale of the conflict was heroic. Scarcely any family was not in some way involved. Almost three million Union soldiers were enlisted – and of those more than a million were not even nineteen years old. The number of Confederate soldiers was proportionately greater in comparison with the white population of the South, although accurate figures do not exist. But we do know that about one person out of every eight was involved in the Civil War, as compared to one individual out of every twenty-seven in World War II. For those of us who are old enough to recall World War II, all that is necessary is to triple in imagination that war's impact to realize how much more severely those living a century ago were affected.

War visited Alabama, Arizona Territory, Arkansas, District of Columbia, Florida, Georgia, Illinois, The Indian Territories, Indiana, Kansas, Kentucky, Louisiana, Maine, Maryland, Mississippi, Missouri, New Mexico, North Carolina, Ohio, Pennsylvania, South Carolina, Tennessee, Texas, Vermont and Virginia. Thus, in twenty-five states out of the thirty-four in the Union at the beginning of the War, shots were fired in anger and in dead earnest. On the high seas there were engagements in the English Channel, the Indian Ocean, the Bering Sea, the Pacific and the Atlantic, the Sea of Japan, the Bay of Biscay. There was even a conflict on the waters of Lake Erie. Thus, geographically, too, the range of the War was of heroic dimensions.

In the vast cauldron of the War, the blood of the descendants of the original immigrants was mixed with that of men of many colors, races and nationalities, most of whom were recently arrived, and some of whom could not speak the language of the country for which they were fighting. Yet they fought as Americans. There was the Hungarian, Major Charles Zagonyi who led a desperate cavalry charge at the head of Frémont's Life Guards at Springfield, Missouri; General Alexander Schimmelfennig, the Prussian, who was wounded at Gettysburg; General Philip Regis Denis de Keredern de Trobriand, poet, duellist and author, one time Colonel of New York's Lafayette Guard, who returned to France to assume the family title after the War.

Of Scots, there were many, and narrowed down to the single patronymic Campbell there are no less than eight of note by that name – including Confederate General Alexander W. Campbell who fought and was wounded at Shiloh and later led a cavalry brigade. Colonel Michael Corcoran, a typical Irishman, was awaiting court martial for refusing to order out the 69th New York in honor of Albert, Prince of Wales, who was visiting New York when war broke out. Private Joseph L. Pierce, of the 14th Connecticut Volunteers, appears in his uniform,

228. EASTMAN JOHNSON, *The Pension Agent*

A total of 500,000 men were wounded during the War. Pension agents in the North functioned as soldiers' representatives in getting pensions. "Invalid Pensions are grants of money to persons who become disabled in the service, either by wounds or other injuries received, or by sickness contracted, in the line of duty, whereby the sufferer is . . . incapable . . . of procuring a livelihood."

George W. Raff, *A Manual of Pensions, Bounty and Pay*, Cincinnati, 1863, p. 1.

still wearing his queue, for, while he had taken an Anglo-Saxon name, he still clung to this vestige of old China. As in all our wars, the descendants of the original inhabitants served willingly, even eagerly, on both sides – one such was Captain Eli Tadpole of the Second Indian Guards. Ortez y Alarid, was a Mexican; and of course there were Poles, such as Vladimir Kryzanowski; Norwegians with names such as Andrew Torkildsen; Swedes, too, J. V. Ahlström; and representatives of every nationality to be found, including many countries such as Saxony, Hanover, and Sardinia which had not long to survive as nations in their own right.

The majestic scale of the War was present also in the greatness of its leaders who were then, as they are now, of inspirational caliber. Great both in spirit and in capacity are Lincoln and Lee, and surrounding them were a host of others only less great by comparison.

Of epic proportion was the suffering endured and the heroism displayed both at home and at the front. The suffering borne by soldiers and civilians, whether it was physical, mental, or a combination, was as great as it was prolonged. Death claimed nearly all the able-bodied men in some villages. Thousands were left homeless, thousands were left penniless, thousands lost arms or legs or were otherwise disfigured. The torture of worry over the safety of son, husband, wife, daughter, fiancé, father and mother distressed the soldiers at the front as well as those at home. An easy heart and mind was far from common in those troubled days. The heroism, too, of South and North was on a noble scale. Whether it was the quiet bravery of a mother parting with an only son, or the mental victory over physical fear of the inexperienced soldier advancing for the first time through enemy fire, heroism was abroad in liberal degree throughout the land.

"And so good-bye to the war. I know not how it may have been, or may be, to others – to me the main interest I found, (and still, on recollection, find,) in the rank and file of the armies, both sides, and in those specimens amid the hospitals, and even the dead on the field. To me the points illustrating the latent personal character and eligibilities of these States, in the two or three millions of American young and middle-aged men, North and South, embodied in those armies – and especially the one-third or one-fourth of their number, stricken by wounds or disease at some time in the course of the contest – were of more significance even than the political interests involved. (As so much of a race depends on how it faces death, and how it stands personal anguish and sickness. As, in the glints of emotions under emergencies, and the indirect traits and asides in Plutarch, we get far profounder clues to the antique world than all its more formal history.)"[3]

---

3. Walt Whitman, "The Real War Will Never Get in the Books", in *Complete Poetry and Prose*, Philadelphia, 1881, p. 80.

229. WINSLOW HOMER, *The Veteran in a New Field*

War had ceased. Two great armies were fraternizing, the victorious feeding the vanquished. The end of the great rebellion in America had come in a day. Our adversaries were told to take new hope, to go back to their dwelling places, rebuild their homes, to dwell in the land with us in peace and Christian unity. By every highway and road the Confederate army melted away never to be reassembled. And the great Northern army, their victorious country-men, without a note of exultation in the presence of the vanquished, lifting on high their victorious ensigns, turned from the front and melted, as an army, from the face of the earth. They surrendered their arms to the keeping of their Government, their flags to memorial halls. Their fame only have they bequeathed to their country, to their offspring, and to the world. What have they been doing since?

Their habit of overcoming obstacles and surmounting difficulties have seized the land. They have been building railroads, opening mines, subduing wild regions, drawing streams of living water down irrigating channels, thus making the wilderness to blossom as the rose. They have girdled the everlasting hills with tracks of iron and steel. They have been extending the blessings of freedom and of free government to wild regions, where the buffalo ranged and the wolf sentineled the passing night, in lands inhabited by no human being save wild and savage tribes.

Horace H. Shaw, *The First Maine Heavy Artillery*, Portland, 1903, p. 205.

Catalogue.

THE WORKS are listed by subject following the sequence of the preceding chapters. All information is that supplied by the lenders: sizes are given in inches, height preceding width – in the case of the oil paintings, stretcher size, and for prints and drawings, sight size. Works in oil are on canvas and drawings and prints on white paper unless otherwise stated. The date of the event depicted is given when known, with the title; the date of the work when given by the artist appears after the size. An asterisk (*) indicates an illustration in the text.

1.
...and the War Came.

1 *The County Election**
GEORGE CALEB BINGHAM, 1811-1879
Oil, 36 x 51. 1851
Lent by The Boatmen's National Bank of St. Louis

2 *Border Ruffians Invading Kansas*
FELIX OCTAVIUS CARR DARLEY, 1822-1888
Wash drawing, 13¼ x 17⁹⁄₁₆
Lent by the Yale University Art Gallery, New Haven, The Mabel Brady Garvan Collection

3 *Railroad Jubilee on Boston Common*
WILLIAM SHARP, active c. 1819-c. 1885
Oil, 39 x 58. 1851
Lent by the Museum of Fine Arts, Boston, M. and M. Karolik Collection

4 *Early Development of Southern Chivalry**
DAVID CLAYPOOLE JOHNSTON, 1799-1865
Water color, 9¼ x 10¾
Lent by Mr. and Mrs. Lawrence A. Fleischman

5 *The Factory of Lazell, Perkins & Co., Bridgewater, Massachusetts*
J. P. NEWELL, active c. 1858-c. 1866
Colored lithograph, 13⅞ x 19¾
Lent by The Corcoran Gallery of Art, Washington

6 *Cotton Plantation**
C. GIROUX, active c. 1850-1865
Oil, 22 x 36
Lent by the Museum of Fine Arts, Boston, M. and M. Karolik Collection

7 *John Brown Led to Execution**
A. BERGHAUS
Pencil, 9½ x 13⅝
Lent by Victor D. Spark

8 *The First Flag of Independence Raised in the South, Savannah, Georgia, 1860**
HENRY CLEENEWERCK
Lithograph, 16 x 20¾. 1860
Lent by the University of Georgia Libraries, Athens

9 *Raising the Flag at Fort Sumter before the Bombardment**
EDWIN WHITE, 1817-1877
Oil, 42 x 62. 1862
Lent by Edward Eberstadt & Sons

10 *The First Gun Fired against Fort Sumter**
WILLIAM WAUD, ? -1878
Pen and wash, 17 x 25½
Lent by The Union League Club, New York

2.
The Call to Arms.

11 *The Drummer Boy**
WILLIAM MORRIS HUNT, 1824-1879
Oil, 36¼ x 26
Lent by Mr. Samuel H. Wolcott

12 *Simultaneous Recruiting for the Confederate and Union Armies, Knoxville, Tennessee, 1861**
SAMUEL BELL PALMER, 1843-1872
Pencil, 6⅝ x 9⅞
Lent by Hermann Warner Williams, Jr.

13 *The Consecration, 1861**
GEORGE COCHRAN LAMBDIN, 1830-1896
Oil, 34 x 18¼. 1865
Lent by the Berry-Hill Galleries

14 *Officers, Vivandière, and Men of the 55th New York (Lafayette Guard)*
ALFRED R. WAUD, 1828-1891
Pencil, 5¼ x 6½
Lent by The Library of Congress, Washington

15 *The Departure of the 7th Regiment New York, April 19, 1861*
GEORGE HAYWARD, active, 1834-1872
Pencil, water color and gouache, 14½ x 20³⁄₁₆
Lent by the Museum of Fine Arts, Boston, M. and M. Karolik Collection

16 *Philadelphia Zouave Corps Passing Independence Hall**
JAMES F. QUEEN, 1824-c. 1877
Lithograph, 16 x 20¼
Lent by Mrs. John Nicholas Brown

17 *The Departure of Union Troops for the Front**
G. GRATO, active, 1860-1865
Oil, 30 x 25. 1864
Lent by N. S. Meyer, Inc.

18 *Federal Troops Entering Alexandria**
Unidentified artist, active, 1860's
Pencil, $5\frac{13}{16}$ x $13\frac{3}{16}$. May 24, 1861
Lent by the Museum of Fine Arts, Boston,
M. and M. Karolik Collection

19 *A Company Street in a Camp near Georgetown*
JAMES WALKER, 1819-1889
Oil, 11 x $15\frac{1}{2}$
Lent by The Seventh Regiment Fund, New York

20 *Night Bivouac of the 7th Regiment New York at Arlington Heights, Virginia**
SANFORD ROBINSON GIFFORD, 1823-1880
Oil, 17 x $29\frac{3}{4}$
Lent by The Seventh Regiment Fund, New York

21 *Troops Drilling in Camp in View of the Capitol**
C. A. HARKER
Pencil on paper with lithographic tints, 8 x $11\frac{3}{16}$
Lent by the Museum of Fine Arts, Boston,
M. and M. Karolik Collection

22 *Torch-light Procession of General Blenker's Division in Honor of the New Commander-in-Chief, General McClellan*
ALFRED WORDSWORTH THOMPSON, 1840-1896
Pencil, gray and blue washes, heightened with white, $9\frac{5}{8}$ x $14\frac{13}{16}$. 1861
Lent by Dr. E. Maurice Bloch

23 *Confederate Camp near Urbana**
ALFRED WORDSWORTH THOMPSON, 1840-1896
Pencil and gray washes touched with blue and white chalk on gray paper, $7\frac{1}{4}$ x $12\frac{3}{4}$
Lent by the Museum of Fine Arts, Boston,
M. and M. Karolik Collection

24 *Terry's Texas Rangers*
CARL G. VON IWONSKI, 1830-1922
Oil, $11\frac{1}{2}$ x 15
Lent by the Witte Memorial Museum,
Muenzenberger Collection, San Antonio

25 *Troops of the 6th Massachusetts Attacked when Marching through Baltimore**
ADALBERT JOHN VOLCK, 1828-1912
Etching on India paper, $4\frac{3}{8}$ x $7\frac{1}{4}$
Lent by the Maryland Historical Society, Baltimore

26 *Reconnoitering the Enemy's Camp*
ALFRED WORDSWORTH THOMPSON, 1840-1896
Pencil and wash on gray paper, $3\frac{3}{8}$ x $12\frac{9}{16}$
Lent by the Museum of Fine Arts, Boston,
M. and M. Karolik Collection

27 *Panic on the Road from Bull Run to Centreville**
Unidentified artist, active, 1860's
Pencil, $9\frac{7}{8}$ x $13\frac{1}{4}$
Lent by the Museum of Fine Arts, Boston,
M. and M. Karolik Collection

28 *The Funeral Procession of General Lander**
ALFRED R. WAUD, 1828-1891
Pencil touched with white on buff paper, $9\frac{5}{8}$ x $12\frac{3}{16}$
Lent by the Museum of Fine Arts, Boston,
M. and M. Karolik Collection

3.
Life in Camp.

FROM REVEILLE TO TAPS

29 *Reveille**
WINSLOW HOMER, 1836-1910
Oil, $13\frac{1}{4}$ x $19\frac{1}{2}$. 1865
Lent by Norman B. Woolworth

30 *Playing Old Soldier**
WINSLOW HOMER, 1836-1910
Oil, 16 x 12
Lent by the Museum of Fine Arts, Boston

31 *Third Kentucky Confederate Infantry at Mess before Corinth, Mississippi, May 11, 1862**
CONRAD WISE CHAPMAN, 1842-1910
Engraving, 14 x 18
Lent by the Boston Athenaeum

32 *Drilling, Battery Bee, Sullivans' Island, Charleston*
CONRAD WISE CHAPMAN, 1842-1910
Oil on composition board, 10 x 12. 1863
Lent by The Valentine Museum, Richmond

33 *Battalion Drill on the Pamunkey River**
WILLIAM MCILVAINE, JR., 1813-1867
Water color, $5\frac{5}{16}$ x $8\frac{3}{8}$
Lent by Mrs. Joseph B. Carson

34 *The Army of the Potomac*
JAMES HOPE, 1818/19-1892
Oil, $17\frac{3}{4}$ x $41\frac{3}{4}$. 1865
Lent by the Museum of Fine Arts, Boston,
M. and M. Karolik Collection

35 *The 12th New York State Militia on Parade**†
JAMES WALKER, 1819-1889
Oil, 25 x 30. 1865
Lent by The Division of Military and Naval Affairs, State of New York
†Now the 1st Missile Battalion, 212th Artillery, N. Y. Army National Guard

36 *Presentation of the Charger "Coquette" to Colonel Mosby by the Men of His Command, December, 1864**
JOHN J. PORTER, active, 1860's
Oil, 14½ x 20¼. 1864.
Lent by Beverly Mosby Coleman

37 *Home Sweet Home**
WINSLOW HOMER, 1836-1910
Oil, 27½ x 16½. 1863
Lent by Mr. and Mrs. Nathan Shaye

38 *Soldiers Around a Camp Fire*
WINSLOW HOMER, 1836-1910
Pencil and wash, 4⅝ x 6¾
Amherst College, Amherst.
(not available for exhibition)

39 *Going into Bivouac at Night*
EDWIN FORBES, 1839-1895
Pencil and Chinese white, 10½ x 14½
Lent by The Library of Congress, Washington

40 *In Front of Yorktown**
WINSLOW HOMER, 1836-1910
Oil, 13½ x 20. 1862
Lent by the Yale University Art Gallery, New Haven

PASSING THE TIME

41 *The Night in the Apple Orchard**
JAMES F. QUEEN, 1824-c. 1877
Water color, 7⅞ x 10¹³⁄₁₆
Lent by Mrs. Joseph B. Carson

42 *Pitching Horseshoes**
WINSLOW HOMER, 1836-1910
Oil, 26¾ x 53¹¹⁄₁₆. 1865
Lent by the Fogg Art Museum, Harvard University, Cambridge

43 *Playing Cards in Camp near Corinth, Mississippi**
CONRAD WISE CHAPMAN, 1842-1910
Oil on cardboard, 5½ x 9½. 1862
Lent by The Valentine Museum, Richmond

44 *A Snowball Battle near Dalton, Georgia, March 22, 1864**
ALFRED R. WAUD, 1828-1891
Pencil and white wash, 8½ x 12
Lent by The Library of Congress, Washington

45 *The Irish Brigade's Horse Race on St. Patrick's Day, 1863*
EDWIN FORBES, 1839-1895
Pencil, 4⅝ x 7⅛. 1863
Lent by The Library of Congress, Washington

46 *The Briarwood Pipe**
WINSLOW HOMER, 1836-1910
Oil, 16⅞ x 14¾. 1864
Lent by The Cleveland Museum of Art, Mr. and Mrs. William H. Marlatt Collection

47 *The Arrival of Newspapers in Camp**
EDWIN FORBES, 1839-1895
Pencil and Chinese white, 10¼ x 14½
Lent by The Library of Congress, Washington

48 *Ball of the 2nd Corps on Washington's Birthday, 1864, in Camp near Brandy Station, Virginia**
EDWIN FORBES, 1839-1895
Pencil, 6⅝ x 9⅞. 1864
Lent by The Library of Congress, Washington

49 *Preaching to the Troops**
SANFORD ROBINSON GIFFORD, 1823-1880
Oil, 16 x 30
Lent by The Union League Club, New York

COFFEE, SALT HORSE AND HARDTACK

50 *The Commissary Department of the 6th Massachusetts**
Unidentified artist, active, 1860's
Pencil, 9⅜ x 13
Lent by the Museum of Fine Arts, Boston, M. and M. Karolik Collection

51 *Drummer Boy Cooling His Coffee**
EDWIN FORBES, 1839-1895
Oil, 12 x 10
Lent by Amherst College, Amherst

52 *The Return of a Foraging Party to Phillipi**
JASPER GREEN, 1829-1910
Pencil, 8¼ x 11¹¹⁄₁₆
Lent by the Museum of Fine Arts, Boston, M. and M. Karolik Collection

53 *Cooks in the Fire Zouave Regiment at Camp Ellsworth near Alexandria*
EMANUEL GOTTLIEB LEUTZE, 1816-1868
Pencil and white wash on tan paper, 9 x 12⅞
Lent by The Corcoran Gallery of Art, Washington

54 *The Last Goose at Yorktown**
WINSLOW HOMER, 1836-1910
Oil, 24 x 30
Lent by Christian A. Zabriskie

55 *The Evening Meal of the 7th Regiment New York in Camp near Frederick, Maryland, 1863**
SANFORD ROBINSON GIFFORD, 1823-1880
Oil, 17 x 29¼
Lent by The Seventh Regiment Fund, New York

56 *"Robbers Row" – Sutlers' Shacks at Hilton Head**
Unidentified artist
Pencil, 6¼ x 9⅝
Lent by The New-York Historical Society,
New York

ANTIDOTE TO LONELINESS

---

57 *Winter Quarters in Virginia – Army of the Potomac,
1864**
GEORGE COCHRAN LAMBDIN, 1830-1896
Oil, 16 x 20. 1866
Lent by the West Point Museum Collections,
United States Military Academy

58 *The Letter Home**
EASTMAN JOHNSON, 1824-1906
Oil on composition board, 23 x 27½. 1867
Lent by the Museum of Fine Arts, Boston,
M. and M. Karolik Collection

59 *News from the Front**
EASTMAN JOHNSON, 1824-1906
Oil, 10 x 15. 1861
Lent by Edward Eberstadt & Sons

60 *Ladies at a Picnic near the Front**
FRANÇOIS FERDINAND D'ORLÉANS,
PRINCE DE JOINVILLE, 1818-1900
Water color, c. 5 x 7. Nov. 10, 1861
Lent by Monseigneur le Comte de Paris

61 *Defiance: Inviting a Shot before Petersburg,
Virginia, 1864**
WINSLOW HOMER, 1836-1910
Oil on panel, 12 x 18. 1864
Lent by the Detroit Institute of Arts

WALKING THE STRAIGHT AND NARROW

---

62 *The Court Martial of Major General Fitz-John
Porter, at Washington, December 1862*
ALFRED R. WAUD, 1828-1891
Pencil, 7¾ x 13¼. 1862
Lent by The Library of Congress, Washington

63 *Punishment for Intoxication**
WINSLOW HOMER, 1836-1910
Oil, 17 x 13. 1863
Lent by the Canajoharie Art Gallery, New York

64 *Riding Morgan's Mule**
SAMUEL BELL PALMER, 1843-1872
Pencil, 6⅝ x 9⅞
Lent by Hermann Warner Williams, Jr.

65 *A Drop too Much**
JAMES WALKER, 1819-1889
Pencil, 10 x 13½
Lent by Kennedy Galleries, Inc., New York

66 *The Fate of a Coward: Drumming out of Camp at
New Bern**
Unidentified artist
Pencil, 6⅜ x 10
Lent by The New-York Historical Society,
New York

67 *Military Execution of James Griffin, alias John
Thomas Barnett, a Private of the 11th Pennsylvania
Cavalry, for Desertion and Highway Robbery at
Portsmouth, Virginia, September 17, 1863**
Unidentified artist
Lithograph, 10¼ x 17
Lent by The Library of Congress, Washington

HURRY UP AND WAIT

---

68 *Mess Boy Sleeping**
EDWIN FORBES, 1839-1895
Oil, 14 x 20¼. 1867
Lent by the Wadsworth Atheneum, Hartford,
The Ella Gallup Sumner and Mary Catlin Sumner
Collection

69 *Escort for a General**
WINSLOW HOMER, 1836-1910
Ink, 9 x 15
Lent by the Collection of Carnegie Institute,
Pittsburgh

70 *Camp of the 59th Virginia Infantry, Wise's Brigade**
CONRAD WISE CHAPMAN, 1842-1910
Engraving, 14 x 18
Lent by the Boston Athenaeum

71 *In Front of Yorktown, 1862**
WINSLOW HOMER, 1836-1910
Ink and crayon, 8 x 14
Lent by the Addison Gallery of American Art,
Andover

72 *Maryland Heights: Siege of Harper's Ferry*
WILLIAM MACLEOD, ? -1892
Oil, 30 x 44. 1863
Lent by The Corcoran Gallery of Art, Washington,
Gift of Mrs. Genevieve Plummer

73 *A Lull in the Fight – Battle of the Wilderness**
EDWIN FORBES, 1839-1895
Oil, 12 x 26
Lent by Hermann Warner Williams, Jr.

ON PICKET, SCOUTING AND SKIRMISHING

74 *Attack on a Union Picket Post**
ALBERT BIERSTADT, 1830-1902
Oil, 15 x 17¾. 1862
Lent by The Century Association, New York

75 *Confederate Picket Post at Diascund Bridge, Virginia*
CONRAD WISE CHAPMAN, 1842-1910
Engraving, 18 x 14
Lent by the Boston Athenaeum

76 *Quarter Guard of the Confederate Forces at Diascund Bridge, Virginia, March 10, 1863**
CONRAD WISE CHAPMAN, 1842-1910
Wash, 6¾ x 4½. 1863
Lent by The Valentine Museum, Richmond

77 *Relief of the Outer Picket**
WINSLOW HOMER, 1836-1910
Pen and ink, 15½ x 21¾
Lent by the Collection of Carnegie Institute,
Pittsburgh

78 *Pickets Firing near Fairfax Court House*
ALFRED WORDSWORTH THOMPSON, 1840-1896
Pencil touched with white on light green paper,
9⅜ x 10¾
Lent by the Museum of Fine Arts, Boston,
M. and M. Karolik Collection

79 *Pickets Trading between the Lines**
EDWIN FORBES, 1839-1895
Pencil and Chinese white, 10¼ x 14¼
Lent by The Library of Congress, Washington

80 *Two Federal Scouts**
WINSLOW HOMER, 1836-1910
Water color, 29 x 23 (w. frame)
Lent by James H. Weekes
(From a letter by Winslow Homer dated Dec. 12, 1887
to the lender's grandfather, James J. Higginson:
"I will state it simply represents the portraits of two
men. Interesting from the fact that they were drawn from
life when in advance of the Army on its last campaign,
March 28, 1865.
P.S. I forgot to say that they are disguised in confederate
uniforms.")

81 *The Scouts' Return**
JOHN ADAMS ELDER, 1833-1895
Oil, 22 x 27
Lent by The Virginia Museum of Fine Arts,
Richmond, Given by Mrs. Hugh L. Macneil
in memory of Mrs. Charles E. Bolling

82 *Dummy Confederate Battery at Harrison's Landing*
ALFRED R. WAUD, 1828-1891

Pencil, 8½ x 12
Lent by The Library of Congress, Washington

83 *The Sharpshooter**
WINSLOW HOMER, 1836-1910
Oil, 13 x 7⅛. 1866
Lent by Wildenstein & Co., Inc.

84 *Feeling the Enemy**
WINSLOW HOMER, 1836-1910
Pencil and ink, 14¼ x 19¼
Lent by The Art Museum, Princeton University

85 *Reconnaissance of the Enemy Position in Front of
Fairfax Court House, October 18, 1861**
ALFRED R. WAUD, 1828-1891
Pencil and white wash, 9 x 14⅝. 1861
Lent by The Library of Congress, Washington

86 *Reconnaissance in Force by General Gorman before
Yorktown, 1862**
WINSLOW HOMER, 1836-1910
Pencil and wash, 8¼ x 13¼
Lent by the Museum of Fine Arts, Boston,
M. and M. Karolik Collection

VOLUNTEERS, DRAFTEES AND REPLACEMENTS

87 *Recruits Wanted**
DAVID GILMOUR BLYTHE, 1815-1865
Oil, 11 x 9
Lent by Mrs. Alexander Nimick

88 *Recruiting of Colonel Sickle's Brigade*
ADALBERT JOHN VOLCK, 1828-1912
Pencil, 5¹³⁄₁₆ x 9½
Lent by the Museum of Fine Arts, Boston,
M. and M. Karolik Collection

89 *The Voluntary Manner in which Some of the
Southern Volunteers Enlist**
THOMAS WORTH, 1834-1917
Lithograph, 10 x 14
Lent by The Library of Congress, Washington

90 *Convalescents from Fortress Monroe Returning to
Duty**
JOHANNES ADAM SIMON OERTEL, 1823-1909
Pencil and neutral wash, 9⁵⁄₁₆ x 11⅜. Oct. 1862
Lent by the Museum of Fine Arts, Boston,
M. and M. Karolik Collection

91 *Exchanged Prisoners of War Rejoining the 31st
New York**
ALFRED R. WAUD, 1828-1891
Pencil on olive paper, 10⅛ x 13¹¹⁄₁₆
Lent by the Museum of Fine Arts, Boston,
M. and M. Karolik Collection

4.
Army on the Move.

BY THE CARS

92 *A Regiment Entraining for the Front**
EDWARD LAMSON HENRY, 1841-1919
Oil, 10¼ x 15¾
Lent by The Seventh Regiment Fund, New York

93 *Confederate Troops Leaving Martinsburg for Harper's Ferry**
ALFRED WORDSWORTH THOMPSON, 1840-1896
Pencil and gray wash, 8⁵⁄₁₆ x 10¾
Lent by the Museum of Fine Arts, Boston,
M. and M. Karolik Collection

BY RIVER AND OCEAN

94 *The U.S.S.* Wabash *Leaving New York for the Seat of War**
EDWARD MORAN, 1829-1901
Oil, 44 x 64
Lent by the United States Naval Academy Museum, Annapolis

95 *Embarkation of Troops at Cairo*
ALEXANDER SIMPLOT, 1837-1914
Pen and ink, 11⅜ x 13¾. 1862
Lent by Mrs. O. G. Simplot

96 *Amphibious Landing of General Butler's Forces at Cape Hatteras, August 1861**
ALFRED R. WAUD, 1828-1891
Wash, 7⅝ x 10⅞
Lent by the Franklin D. Roosevelt Library, Hyde Park

97 *U.S.S.* Sabine *Rescuing Marines from the Foundering Steamer* Governor*
E. T. COTTER, active, 1860's
Pen, india ink and wash, 5⅛ x 8
Lent by the Museum of Fine Arts, Boston,
M. and M. Karolik Collection

BY HORSE AND MULE

98 *Federal Cavalry Camp at Dawn**
PETER MORAN, 1841-1914
Oil on panel, 5 x 20
Lent by Mrs. McCook Knox

99 *Rush's Lancers, the 6th Pennsylvania Cavalry, Embarking at Alexandria**
WINSLOW HOMER, 1836-1910
Pencil and wash, 8⅝ x 15⅞. 1862
Lent by The Cooper Union Museum, New York

100 *The Return of Sheridan's Troopers**
WINSLOW HOMER, 1836-1910
Pencil, 15⅜ x 21⅞
Lent by the Addison Gallery of American Art, Andover

101 *General Pleasonton's Cavalry in a Snow Storm, November 6, 1862*
ARTHUR LUMLEY, c. 1837-1912
Pencil and white wash, 8⅝ x 13⅝
Lent by The Library of Congress, Washington

102 *General Kilpatrick's Raid on Richmond**
EDWIN FORBES, 1839-1895
Pencil, 9 x 22
Lent by The Library of Congress, Washington

103 *Uphill Work**
SAMUEL BELL PALMER, 1843-1872
Water color illustration in *Memories of the War*, 5 x 7⅝
Lent by General and Mrs. John B. Anderson

104 *Heavy Artillery Marching in the Rain in Pursuit of Lee after Gettysburg**
EDWIN FORBES, 1839-1895
Pencil, 3 x 13⅛
Lent by The Library of Congress, Washington

105 *Artillery on a Muddy Road near Spotsylvania Court House, May 12, 1864*
EDWIN FORBES, 1839-1895
Pencil, 9¾ x 13. 1864
Lent by The Library of Congress, Washington

106 *Supply Wagons and Troops Crossing Pontoon Bridges**
EDWIN FORBES, 1839-1895
Pencil and Chinese white, 10½ x 14⅝
Lent by The Library of Congress, Washington

107 *Two Negro Camp Followers**
EDWIN FORBES, 1839-1895
Oil, 19¾ x 30. 1866
Lent by Hermann Warner Williams, Jr.

BY SHANKS' MARE

108 *General Abner Doubleday Watching His Troops Cross the Potomac**
DAVID GILMOUR BLYTHE, 1815-1865

Oil, 31 x 41
Lent by the National Baseball Hall of Fame and
Museum, Inc., Cooperstown, New York

109 *Infantry Column on the March**
WINSLOW HOMER, 1836-1910
Pencil on tracing paper, 20⅛ x 23½. 1862
Lent by The Cooper Union Museum, New York

110 *Washing Day – Column on the March, May 15, 1864**
EDWIN FORBES, 1839-1895
Pencil and ink, 8½ x 11⅝. 1864
Lent by The Library of Congress, Washington

111 *Marching in the Rain after Gettysburg**
EDWIN FORBES, 1839-1895
Oil, 13¹³⁄₁₆ x 29¾
Lent by The Library of Congress, Washington

112 *Troops Marching, New Kent Court House**
JOHN DONAGHY, 1838-1931
Pencil on ruled paper, 3¹¹⁄₁₆ x 12⅛
Lent by the Museum of Fine Arts, Boston,
M. and M. Karolik Collection

113 *General Grover's Forces Marching to the Attack near
Port Hudson**
JAMES R. HAMILTON, active, 1863-1867
Pencil, 9¼ x 14³⁄₁₆. May 24, 1863
Lent by the Museum of Fine Arts, Boston,
M. and M. Karolik Collection

5.
Heat of Battle.

THE ARTILLERY

114 *Battle of Lookout Mountain**
JAMES WALKER, 1819-1889
Oil, 14 x 40. 1863-1864
Lent by the Office of the Chief of Military History,
Department of the Army, Washington

115 *Artillery Battery Firing on Advancing Confederate
Infantry at White Oak Swamp Bridge**
ALFRED R. WAUD, 1828-1891
Black and white wash, 9½ x 14½
Lent by The Library of Congress, Washington

116 *Union Battery Firing at Corinth, Mississippi*
Unidentified artist, active, 1860's
Pencil, 6¹⁵⁄₁₆ x 10¹¹⁄₁₆
Lent by the Museum of Fine Arts, Boston,
M. and M. Karolik Collection

117 *Battle of Gettysburg**
DAVID GILMOUR BLYTHE, 1815-1865
Oil, 26 x 34½
Lent by Maxim Karolik

118 *Captain Ashby's Battery at Petersburg*
ALFRED R. WAUD, 1828-1891
Pencil and Chinese white on gray-green paper,
5⅝ x 10⅞. 1864
Lent by Harvard College Library, Cambridge

119 *The Bombardment of Fort Sumter**
ALBERT BIERSTADT, 1830-1902
Oil, 26 x 68
Lent by The Union League of Philadelphia
(not shown in Boston)

120 *Mortar Boats*
JAMES DAVID SMILLIE, 1833-1909
Pencil and wash on board, 10⁷⁄₁₆ x 6⅞.
April 1862
Lent by the Museum of Fine Arts, Boston,
M. and M. Karolik Collection

121 *Attack on Fort Fisher**
FRANK VIZETELLY, 1830-1883
Water color, 9¾ x 27⅝
Lent by Harvard College Library, Cambridge

THE CAVALRY

122 *The Fight for the Colors**
Unidentified artist, c. 1865
Oil, 26¹¹⁄₁₆ x 21⅝
Lent by the Wadsworth Atheneum, Hartford,
The Ella Gallup Sumner and Mary Catlin Sumner
Collection

123 *A Cavalry Charge**
EDWIN FORBES, 1839-1895
Pencil and Chinese white, 10¼ x 14½
Lent by The Library of Congress, Washington

124 *General Stuart's Raid on the White House, Virginia**
ADALBERT JOHN VOLCK, 1828-1912
Pen over pencil, 5⅜ x 9¹⁵⁄₁₆
Lent by the Museum of Fine Arts, Boston,
M. and M. Karolik Collection

125 *Cavalry Fight near Aldie, Virginia **
EDWIN FORBES, 1839-1895
Pencil, 9½ x 13⅛. 1864
Lent by The Library of Congress, Washington

126 *Charge of the 6th Michigan Cavalry over the Rebel
Earthworks near Falling Waters*
ALFRED R. WAUD, 1828-1891
Pencil, 5½ x 11⅝
Lent by The Library of Congress, Washington

127 *The Fight at Sangster's Station**
VICTOR NEHLIG, 1830-1909
Charcoal with gouache on gray paper, 11⁵⁄₁₆ x 20⅛.
1862
Lent by the George Walter Vincent Smith Art
Museum, Springfield, Massachusetts

128 *Custer's Cavalry Capturing Prisoners near Winchester*
ALFRED R. WAUD, 1828-1891
Pencil, 5¼ x 13¼
Lent by The Library of Congress, Washington

THE INFANTRY

---

129 *The Wounded Drummer Boy**
EASTMAN JOHNSON, 1824-1906
Oil, 49 x 39
Lent by The Union League Club, New York

130 *Battle of Gaines's Mill, Virginia, June 27, 1862*
FRANÇOIS FERDINAND D'ORLÉANS,
PRINCE DE JOINVILLE, 1818-1900
Lithograph, 13⅜ x 29¾. 1862
Lent by Mrs. John Nicholas Brown

131 *Hand-to-Hand Fight at Antietam between the
Brooklyn 14th and the 3rd Rebel Cavalry**
ALFRED R. WAUD, 1828-1891
Pencil, 6⅛ x 9¼
Lent by The Library of Congress, Washington

132 *The Charge across the Burnside Bridge, Antietam,
1 p.m., September 17, 1862**
EDWIN FORBES, 1839-1895
Pencil, 7¾ x 10⅝. 1862
Lent by The Library of Congress, Washington

133 *Reforming the Line after the Battle of Antietam*
EDWIN FORBES, 1839-1895
Pencil and Chinese white, 10 x 14½
Lent by The Library of Congress, Washington

134 *Gallant Charge of General Humphrey's Division at
Fredericksburg, December 13, 1862**
ALFRED R. WAUD, 1828-1891
Pencil and wash, 13⅝ x 20¼. 1862
Lent by The Library of Congress, Washington

135 *Battle of Vicksburg*
Unidentified artist, active, 1860's
Distemper on muslin, 73 x 108
Lent by The Santa Barbara Museum of Art,
California

136 *The Battle of Gettysburg: Repulse of Longstreet's
Assault, July 3, 1863**
JAMES WALKER (after JOHN BADGER BACHELDER)
1819-1889

Oil, 24½ x 59½. 1870
Lent by the New Hampshire Historical Society,
Concord

137 *Battle of Chickamauga, September 19, 1863*
JAMES WALKER, 1819-1889
Oil, 13½ x 40
Lent by the Office of the Chief of Military History,
Department of the Army, Washington

138 *General Hooker among the Pines*
JAMES WALKER, 1819-1889
Oil, 11¾ x 15½
Lent by N. S. Meyer, Inc.

139 *A Skirmish in the Wilderness**
WINSLOW HOMER, 1836-1910
Oil on board, 18 x 26. 1864.
Lent by the New Britain Museum of American
Art, Connecticut

140 *Assault on Fort Gregg, April 2, 1865*
ALFRED R. WAUD, 1828-1891
Pencil and white wash, 5½ x 13⅛. 1865
Lent by The Library of Congress, Washington

141 *Infantry Fighting Hand-to-Hand**
VICTOR NEHLIG, 1830-1909
Pencil, 11⅜ x 16⅜
Lent by the George Walter Vincent Smith Art
Museum, Springfield, Massachusetts

142 *The First Shell – Beginning of the Atlanta Campaign,
Crossing Chickamauga Creek, May 10, 1864**
ADOLF METZNER, 1834?-1917
Tempera, 12½ x 21
Lent by Kennedy Galleries, Inc.

THE CORPS OF ENGINEERS AND THE OTHER CORPS

---

143 *The 5th Vermont Constructing a Bridge near
Lewinsville, Virginia*
ARTHUR LUMLEY, C. 1837-1912
Pencil, 6⅞ x 9½. October 1861
Lent by the Museum of Fine Arts, Boston,
M. and M. Karolik Collection

144 *The 146th New York Throwing Pontoons across the
Rappahannock River near Beverly Ford, August 8,
1863**
EDWIN FORBES, 1839-1895
Pencil, 4⅜ x 7⅛. 1863
Lent by The Library of Congress, Washington

145 *Crossing the Pontoon Bridge at Berlin**
ALFRED R. WAUD, 1828-1891
Pencil touched with white on buff paper, 7¹⁵⁄₁₆ x 12⁹⁄₁₆
Lent by the Museum of Fine Arts, Boston,
M. and M. Karolik Collection

146 *Colonel Pleasants Inspecting the Arrival of Powder in the Mine at Petersburg*
ALFRED R. WAUD, 1828-1891
Pencil, 5 x 5¾
Lent by The Library of Congress, Washington

147 *Vicksburg: Explosion of the Federal Mines**
Unidentified artist, active, 1860's
Pencil, 9½ x 13¼
Lent by The New-York Historical Society, New York

148 *Admiral Porter's Gunboats Passing the Red River Dam**
JAMES MADISON ALDEN, active, 1860's
Water color, 15⅜ x 29¼. 1864
Lent by the Museum of Fine Arts, Boston, M. and M. Karolik Collection

149 *Westover Mansion**
EDWARD LAMSON HENRY, 1841-1919
Oil on panel, 11¼ x 14⅝. 1869
Lent by The Corcoran Gallery of Art, Washington

150 *Professor Lowe's Balloon Wagon and Gas Generator at White House Landing, Virginia**
Unidentified artist, active, 1860's
Oil, 11⅞ x 15$\frac{7}{16}$
Lent by Mrs. Henry P. Kendall

151 *City Point, Virginia: Headquarters of General Grant*
EDWARD LAMSON HENRY, 1841-1919
Oil, 30 x 61
Lent by the Addison Gallery of American Art, Andover

152 *The Army of the Potomac en route to the James River, June 29, 1862*
JOHN BADGER BACHELDER, 1825-1894
Lithograph, 20⅝ x 29½. 1863
Lent by Mrs. John Nicholas Brown

153 *Union Drover with Cattle for the Army**
OTTO SOMMER, active, 1860's
Oil, 30 x 44. 1866
Lent by Victor D. Spark

154 *Army Teamsters**
WINSLOW HOMER, 1836-1910
Oil, 17 x 22. 1866
Lent from The Harold T. Pulsifer Collection at Colby College, Maine

155 *Baggage Guard Defending the Supply Train**
WINSLOW HOMER, 1836-1910
Pen and ink, 9 x 18¼. 1865
Lent by the Collection of Carnegie Institute, Pittsburgh

6. The Seaman's Life.

156 *Attack on Fort Fisher**
XANTHUS RUSSELL SMITH, 1839-1929
Oil, 56 x 123½. 1893
Lent by The Pennsylvania Academy of the Fine Arts, Philadelphia

157 *The Splendid Naval Triumph on the Mississippi, April 24, 1862**
CURRIER AND IVES, 1857-1907
Lithograph, 24 x 28
Lent by the United States Naval Academy Museum, Annapolis

158 *The* Monitor *and the* Merrimac *at Short Range**
Unidentified artist, active, 1860's
Oil on paper, 13¼ x 20. 1862
Lent by the Franklin D. Roosevelt Library, Hyde Park

159 *Destruction of the Confederate Steamer* Alabama *by the U.S. Ironclad* Kearsarge*
EDWIN HAYES, 1820-1904
Oil, 20 x 30⅛. 1864
Lent by the Chicago Historical Society

160 *The U.S.* Midnight *Hailing the U.S.* Boheo *off Texas**
ALEXANDER CHARLES STUART, 1831-1898
Water color, 8¾ x 14¼. 1864(?)
Lent by Hermann Warner Williams, Jr.

161 *Mortar Boats on the Mississippi at the Bombardment of Island No. 10*
WILLIAM TORGERSON, active, 1873-1889
Oil, 33 x 69
Lent by the Chicago Historical Society

162 *Mortar Gun Crew*
JAMES W. MCLAUGHLIN, active, 1860's
Pencil, 5¼ x 8. April 1862
Lent by Ian McLaughlin

163 *Between Decks on a Union Gunboat**
ALEXANDER SIMPLOT, 1837-1914
Pencil, 6½ x 10. 1862
Lent by The State Historical Society of Wisconsin, Madison

164 *Pikemen Away – Repelling Boarders*
ROBERT W. WEIR, JR., 1803-1889
Pencil, 5¾ x 7
Lent by The Mariners Museum, Newport News

165 *Catching the Culprit*
DAVID M. STAUFFER, 1845-1913
Ink, 10⅜ x 7¹⁄₁₆
Lent by Mrs. Joseph B. Carson

166 *The Submarine* Hunley*
CONRAD WISE CHAPMAN, 1842-1910
Engraving, 18 x 14
Lent by the Boston Athenaeum

167 *Bucked and Gagged: Triced Up**
DAVID M. STAUFFER, 1845-1913
Ink, 9½ x 6⅛
Lent by Mrs. Joseph B. Carson

168 *Punishment for Spitting on the Deck**
DAVID M. STAUFFER, 1845-1913
Ink, 9½ x 6½
Lent by Mrs. Joseph B. Carson

169 *Married to the Gunner's Daughter*
DAVID M. STAUFFER, 1845-1913
Ink, 6¾ x 10¼
Lent by Mrs. Joseph B. Carson

170 *Dahlgren Navy Landing Guns in Action on Tranter's Creek*
ANGELO WISER, 1841-?
Pencil, 10 x 14. June 5, 1862
Lent by the Museum of Fine Arts, Boston,
M. and M. Karolik Collection

7.
Life of a Prisoner of War.

171 *Capture of a Rebel Picket at Shroud's Farm*
ALFRED WORDSWORTH THOMPSON, 1840-1896
Pencil and gray wash, touched with white, 5½ x 9⁹⁄₁₆
Lent by the Museum of Fine Arts, Boston,
M. and M. Karolik Collection

172 *Prisoners from the Front**
WINSLOW HOMER, 1836-1910
Oil, 24 x 38. 1866
Lent by The Metropolitan Museum of Art,
New York, Gift of Mrs. Frank B. Porter, 1922

173 *Confederate Prisoners Captured in the Final Charge at the Battle of Gettysburg, July 3, 1863**
EDWIN FORBES, 1839-1895
Pencil, 9½ x 13¼. 1863
Lent by The Library of Congress, Washington

174 *Union Soldiers Attacking Confederate Prisoners in the Streets of Washington*
FRANK VIZETELLY, 1830-1883
Pencil, water color and Chinese white, 6⅞ x 9⅝
Lent by Harvard College Library, Cambridge

175 *Libby Prison**
DAVID GILMOUR BLYTHE, 1815-1865
Oil, 24 x 36
Lent by the Museum of Fine Arts, Boston,
M. and M. Karolik Collection

176 *Libby Prison in 1862**
OTTO BOETTICHER, c. 1816-?
Lithograph, 9¾ x 18¼. 1862
Lent by Mrs. John Nicholas Brown

177 *Playing Baseball at Salisbury Prison*
OTTO BOETTICHER, c. 1816-?
Lithograph, 23½ x 38½. 1862
Lent by Mrs. John Nicholas Brown

178 *Interior of Prisoner of War Barracks, Camp Douglas, Illinois**
SAMUEL BELL PALMER, 1843-1872
Pencil, 6⅝ x 9⅞
Lent by Hermann Warner Williams, Jr.

179 *Interior of a Union Prisoner of War Camp**
ADALBERT JOHN VOLCK, 1828-1912
Ink and pencil, 7¾ x 10¾
Lent by the Maryland Historical Society, Baltimore

180 *Exchanged Union Prisoners on Board the* Eliza Hancox, *November 18, 1864*
WILLIAM WAUD, ?-1878
Pencil, 9 x 13⅝. 1864
Lent by The Library of Congress, Washington

181 *Released Union Prisoners Dancing on Board the* Star of the South *at Charleston, South Carolina**
WILLIAM WAUD, ?-1878
Pencil and wash, 6¼ x 9½
Lent by The Library of Congress, Washington

8.
Wounds, Disease and Death.

182 *A Trooper Meditating beside a Grave**
WINSLOW HOMER, 1836-1910
Oil, 16⅛ x 8
Lent by the Joslyn Art Museum, Omaha,
Gift of Dr. and Mrs. Harold Gifford, 1961

183 *The Walking Wounded**
WINSLOW HOMER, 1836-1910
Pen and ink, 4¹³⁄₁₆ x 7½
Lent by The Cooper Union Museum, New York

184 *Tending the Wounded during an Armistice at the
Battle of Cedar Mountain**
Unidentified artist, active, 1860's
Pencil, 9 x 11⅛. August, 1862
Lent by the Museum of Fine Arts, Boston,
M. and M. Karolik Collection

185 *Fair Oaks Station: Bringing the Wounded to the Cars**
Attributed to ARTHUR LUMLEY, C. 1837-1912
Pencil and white wash, 8 x 13¾. 1862
Lent by The Library of Congress, Washington

186 *The Story of Gettysburg*
JAMES F. QUEEN, 1824-c. 1877
Water color, 14⅛ x 10⅞
Lent by Mrs. Joseph B. Carson

187 *Dying of Gangrene**
Unidentified artist, c. 1863
Pencil, 8 x 10
Lent by the Medical Museum of the Armed Forces
Institute of Pathology, Washington

188 *Burying the Dead and Burning the Horses after the
Battle of Fair Oaks, June 3, 1862**
ALFRED R. WAUD, 1828-1891
Pencil and white wash, 9 x 14¼
Lent by The Library of Congress, Washington

9.
The Home Front.

NEAR THE FRONT
AND
UNDER ENEMY OCCUPATION

189 *Newspaper Correspondent Galloping near the Front
to Scoop His Rivals*
EDWIN FORBES, 1839-1895
Pencil and Chinese white, 10½ x 14½
Lent by The Library of Congress, Washington

190 *Exiles from Tennessee*
FRANK (THOMAS FRANCIS) BEARD, 1842-1905
Pencil and wash, 5¹³⁄₁₆ x 8¹¹⁄₁₆. 1861
Lent by the Museum of Fine Arts, Boston,
M. and M. Karolik Collection

191 *A Virginia Homestead near Madison*
Unidentified artist, active, 1860's
Pencil, 11³⁄₁₆ x 9
Lent by the Museum of Fine Arts, Boston,
M. and M. Karolik Collection

192 *Guerillas on the Lookout**
Unidentified artist, c. 1865
Oil, 25 x 19¾
Lent by Victor D. Spark

193 *Coming from the Mill, Rappahannock Station,
January 14, 1864**
EDWIN FORBES, 1839-1895
Pencil, 6⅜ x 9⅞. 1864 (or '63)
Lent by The Library of Congress, Washington

194 *Order No. 11**
GEORGE CALEB BINGHAM, 1811-1879
Oil, 56 x 79
Lent by the Cincinnati Art Museum

195 *Camp at New Bern, North Carolina**
VOLTAIRE COMBE, active, 1860's
Water color, 11¾ x 21½
Lent by Mrs. John Nicholas Brown

196 *House at Riley's Plantation Used by General Banks
as Headquarters**
JAMES R. HAMILTON, active, 1863-1867
Pencil, 7 x 9⅞
Lent by the Museum of Fine Arts, Boston,
M. and M. Karolik Collection

197 *Sale of Confiscated Blood Horses at New Orleans,
1863**
JAMES R. HAMILTON, active, 1863-1867
Pencil, 9³⁄₁₆ x 14½. March 3, 1863
Lent by the Museum of Fine Arts, Boston,
M. and M. Karolik Collection

198 *Civilians Applying for Aid to Colonel Thorpe at
New Orleans**
JAMES R. HAMILTON, active, 1863-1867
Pencil, 9 x 14¼
Lent by the Museum of Fine Arts, Boston,
M. and M. Karolik Collection

199 *General Benjamin Butler in New Orleans*
ADALBERT JOHN VOLCK, 1828-1912
Ink and pencil, 5¾ x 8¼
Lent by the Maryland Historical Society, Baltimore

200 *Explosion of U. S. Magazine at Mobile*
J. F. YOUNG, active, 1860's
Color lithograph, 10 x 16½
Lent by The Mariners Museum, Newport News

201 *Confederate Cotton Burners Surprised by Federal Patrol**
FRANK VIZETELLY, 1830-1883
Pencil, crayon and Chinese white on light green paper, 9 x 11
Lent by Harvard College Library, Cambridge

HEARTH AND HOME

---

202 *Ladies' Parlor at Willard's Hotel, Washington, March 6, 1861**
THOMAS NAST, 1840-1902
Pencil and wash, 9½ x 14. 1861
Lent by The Library of Congress, Washington

203 *Interior of George Hayward's Porter House, New York**
E. D. HAWTHORNE, active, 1860's
Oil, 33½ x 46. 1863
Lent by The New-York Historical Society, New York (withdrawn from exhibition)

204 *The War Spirit at Home — Celebrating the Victory at Vicksburg**
LILY MARTIN SPENCER, 1822-1902
Oil, 30 x 32¾. 1866
Lent by The Newark Museum

205 *Reception at the White House, 1863**
Attributed to FRANCIS BICKNELL CARPENTER, 1830-1900
Oil, 23¼ x 37
Lent by Winslow Carlton

206 *The Cooper Refreshment Saloon, Philadelphia*
JAMES F. QUEEN, 1824-c. 1877
Lithograph, 16⅜ x 27
Lent by Hermann Warner Williams, Jr.

207 *Quantrill's Raid on Lawrence, August 21, 1863**
SHERMAN ENDERTON, active, 1860's
Pencil, 9½ x 16
Lent by the Kansas State Historical Society, Topeka

208 *The Story of the Battle*
DAVID GILMOUR BLYTHE, 1815-1865
Oil, 20 x 16 (sight size)
Lent by the Duquesne Club, Pittsburgh

209 *Writing to Father*
EASTMAN JOHNSON, 1824-1906
Oil on cardboard, 12 x 9¼
Lent by Maxim Karolik

210 *The Initials**
WINSLOW HOMER, 1836-1910
Oil, 16⅛ x 12⅛. 1864
Lent by Mr. and Mrs. Lawrence A. Fleischman

211 *Playing Field Hospital**
WILLIAM MORRIS HUNT, 1824-1879
Oil on academy board, 11¾ x 8⅝
Lent by Mrs. William N. Bourne

10.
The Slaves' Escape to Freedom.

---

212 *Slaves Escaping through the Swamp**
THOMAS MORAN, 1837-1926
Oil, 32½ x 43. 1863
Lent by the Philbrook Art Center, Tulsa, Laura A. Clubb Collection

213 *Slaves Concealing Their Master*
ADALBERT JOHN VOLCK, 1828-1912
Pen over pencil, 6⅜ x 8¹³⁄₁₆. 1861
Lent by the Museum of Fine Arts, Boston, M. and M. Karolik Collection

214 *Contrabands Approaching the Union Lines near Culpeper Court House, November 8, 1863**
EDWIN FORBES, 1839-1895
Pencil, 9½ x 13⅛. 1863
Lent by The Library of Congress, Washington

215 *Presentation of Colors to the 20th U. S. Colored Regiment at New York, March 5, 1864*
EDWARD LAMSON HENRY, 1841-1919
Oil, 17½ x 27. 1869
Lent by The Union League Club, New York

216 *Dead Negro Soldiers at Fort Wagner**
FRANK VIZETELLY, 1830-1883
Pencil, gray wash and Chinese white, 9 x 10⅞
Lent by Harvard College Library, Cambridge

217 *The 55th Massachusetts Colored Volunteers at Charleston, 1865**
THOMAS NAST, 1840-1902
Pencil, wash and oil, heightened with white on board, 14¼ x 21¼. February 21, 1865
Lent by the Museum of Fine Arts, Boston, M. and M. Karolik Collection

218 *The Volunteer's Return**
FRANK BUCHSER, 1828-1890
Oil, 34½ x 30. 1867
Lent by the Kunstmuseum, Basel

11.
The Strife Ends: The Beginning of an American Legend.

219 *General Lee Leaving Appomattox**
ALFRED R. WAUD, 1828-1891
Pencil, 9½ x 8⅝
Lent by The Library of Congress, Washington

220 *General Lee's Surrender**
JAMES F. QUEEN, 1824-c. 1877
Pencil and wash, 20½ x 26
Lent by Mrs. Joseph B. Carson

221 *Surrender of the Army of Northern Virginia,
April 12, 1865*
JOHN R. CHAPIN, 1823-?
Pencil, 9 x 13½
Lent by The Library of Congress, Washington

222 *Review of the Grand Army of the Potomac, 1865*
JAMES WALKER, 1819-1889
Oil, 25 x 30. 1865
Lent by Mr. and Mrs. Will Hippen, Jr.

223 *The Return of the Flags, 1865**
THOMAS WATERMAN WOOD, 1823-1903
Oil, 37 x 30. 1869
Lent by the West Point Museum Collections,
United States Military Academy

224 *Mustered Out – Negro Soldiers Arriving Home**
ALFRED R. WAUD, 1828-1891
Pencil and white wash, 9¼ x 14⅛
Lent by The Library of Congress, Washington

225 *Crowds Filing past Lincoln's Coffin at Cleveland,
May 1865**
WILLIAM WAUD, ?-1878
Pencil and wash, 9 x 13½
Lent by The Library of Congress, Washington

226 *Jefferson Davis in Prison at Fortress Monroe*
ALFRED R. WAUD, 1828-1891
Pencil and white wash, 4¼ x 6¼
Lent by The Library of Congress, Washington

227 *Harvest Home When the War Was Over*
J. JOHN, active, 1860's
Oil, 54 x 78½. 1867
Lent by The Union League of Philadelphia
(not shown in Boston)

228 *The Pension Agent**
EASTMAN JOHNSON, 1824-1906
Oil, 37½ x 25¼. 1867
Lent by the California Palace of the Legion of Honor,
San Francisco,
The Mildred Anna Williams Collection

229 *The Veteran in a New Field**
WINSLOW HOMER, 1836-1910
Oil, 24 x 38. 1865
Lent by Adelaide Milton de Groot

Sculpture.

230 *"Wounded to the Rear" – One More Shot*
JOHN ROGERS, 1829-1904
Bronze, H. 23½
Lent by The Metropolitan Museum of Art,
New York, Rogers Fund, 1917

231 *Union Refugees*
JOHN ROGERS, 1829-1904
Bronze, H. 22½. 1863
Lent by Amherst College, Amherst

232 *Taking the Oath – Drawing Rations*
JOHN ROGERS, 1829-1904
Bronze, H. 22½
Lent by The Corcoran Gallery of Art, Washington,
Gift of The Honorable Orme Wilson

233 *The Top Sergeant**
Unidentified sculptor, active, 1860's
Wood, H. 63 with 12 base
Lent by the Shelburne Museum, Vermont,
Gift of Mr. and Mrs. Robert Choate

234 *Three Civil War Dioramas*
Unidentified sculptor, active, 1860's
Wood, in 3 units, Unit 1: L. 60; W. 9¾; H. 12
            Units 2 and 3: L. 30; W. 9¾; H. 12
Lent by Stewart E. Gregory

235 *Infantryman of the 14th New York: Whirligig**
Unidentified sculptor, 19th century
Wood, painted red and blue, H. 19
Lent by the Museum of Fine Arts, Boston,
M. and M. Karolik Collection

236 *Negro Mascot of the Union Army*
Unidentified sculptor, active, 1860's
Wood, painted, H. 28¾
Lent by the City Art Museum of St. Louis

Index of Artists.

References are to catalogue number.

235

TYPESET IN MONOTYPE BRUCE OLD STYLE (NO. 31)

WITH THOROWGOOD ITALIC HEADINGS

BY TYPOGRAPHIC HOUSE, INC., BOSTON

PRINTED BY THE MERIDEN GRAVURE CO., MERIDEN, CONN.

ON SN TEXT PAPER 70 LB.

COLOR PLATES BY BRÜDER HARTMANN, WEST BERLIN

BOUND BY ROBERT BURLEN & SON, INC., BOSTON

DESIGNED BY CARL F. ZAHN, MUSEUM OF FINE ARTS, BOSTON